Hitch-hiker's Guide to Europe

How to see Europe by the skin of your teeth

Ken Welsh

Hitch-hiker's Guide to Europe

How to see Europe by the skin of your teeth

revised and up-dated for 1979-80

Pan Original
Pan Books London and Sydney

First published 1971 by Pan Books Ltd,
Cavaye Place, London SW10 9PG
Reprinted 1972
2nd edition published 1973
3rd edition published 1974
4th edition published 1975
Reprinted 1976
5th edition published 1977
This edition published 1979
2nd printing 1979
© Ken Welsh 1971, 1973, 1974, 1975, 1977, 1979
ISBN 0 330 25649 1
Printed and bound in Great Britain by,
Richard Clay (The Chaucer Press) Ltd, Bungay, Suffolk

For Ann, who came too.
And for Ben, who came also.
And for Marcos and Carina.

Contents

Introduction

This book is designed to show you how to get around Europe for about £46 ($92) a week – cheaper if you're tough enough.

Although it's called *Hitch-hiker's Guide* and is aimed at people on a hitch-hiking budget, van and car travellers will also find it useful because it lists facts which someone with their own wheels can use just as well as someone who's moving around on temporarily borrowed wheels.

For every guidebook which is written, three-quarters of its readers can do better than it. That's because they are guidebooks and not at all holy. This book is no exception. And it's certainly not sacred.

Hitch-hiker's Guide gives you a run-down on Europe, Scandinavia, the Middle East, North Africa, and the Communist countries, telling you some of what there is to see and enjoy and giving you an indication of what it would normally cost. But I haven't experienced it *all*. There's lots more and plenty of it will be better than the stuff listed.

I ask those wandering souls who have already covered their first ten thousand miles on the road to skip the section which deals with the practical aspects of hitch-hiking. It certainly wasn't written for them.

Invitation

If you find a deal in eating and sleeping, or a way of saving money in any of the major cities covered in *Hitch-hiker's Guide* you are invited to send your find to me care of the publishers. Your hint and credit will be included in the relevant chapter.

Write to: Ken Welsh,
Hitch-hiker's Guide to Europe,
c/o Pan Books Ltd,
Cavaye Place,
London SW10 9PG

Thanks . . .
. . . to all hitchers who have responded to my invitation and written in with reams of interesting tips. Mail was so heavy during 1977–78 it was impossible to personally answer letters. So thanks to everyone, and thanks again. Keep those letters coming.

Special thanks for assistance in preparing the *Hitcher's Guide* are owed to: Davi Isaacs, Noreen Wells, Isla Stone, Peter Stone, Allen Harbinson, Lynn Kersh and Ginney Ashton – all good truckers.

Hitching Records!
The world record for hitch-hiking (as recorded in the Guinness Book of World Records) is claimed by Devon Smith who, from 1947 to 1971, thumbed 291,000 miles.

Are there aspirants for the title amongst *Hitcher's Guide* readers? If so, write to me (see address above) briefly detailing your travels and enclosing letters from three different people willing to back your claim.

In the next edition I'd like to establish records for:

1 Longest hitch in one vehicle (excluding airplanes and ships).
2 Most miles hitched in any twelve month period.
3 Most miles hitched in any twenty-four hour period.
4 Slowest hitch between two points (include distance, time and brief reason for slowness).

Finally, I'd like to hear from people who've travelled in or on strange vehicles or animals. Who has thumbed the world's craziest lift?
No testimonies needed for these last five categories. Just tell me the facts.
No prizes, either, just brief glory.

'*Hitch-hike*: travel by begging lifts from passing motor vehicles. (Fifteenth century, of obscure origin; partly synonymous with Scots *hotch*, move by jerks.)'
Definition from *The Concise Oxford Dictionary*

'*Hitch-hike*: to travel by getting free automobile rides and sometimes by walking between rides.'
Definition from *The Random House Dictionary of the English Language* (*the Unabridged Edition*)

Hitching? I call it cadging
'When I see so many young people thumbing lifts these days I feel depressed. Have they no pride at all? I can't imagine anything more humiliating than standing at the roadside like a tramp, begging. I always thought that the great thing about young people today was their high principles, independence and determination to make a better job of the world than their predecessors did. But I just can't equate that picture of healthy, intelligent young people, constantly striving for a better life, with the deplorable one of cringing, cadging hitch-hikers swarming the roads in their thousands . . .'

An opinion in the letters column of a women's magazine.

Q: What *are* you rebelling against?
A: Wadda ya got?
attributed to Elvis Presley

The most your pound is worth

at the date of going to press

Algeria	7·86 dinars	Lebanon	5·90 pounds
Austria	27·35 schillings	Morocco	7·80 dirham
Belgium	59·45 francs	Norway	9·99 kronor
Bulgaria	1·72 leva	Poland	62·45 zlotys – Tourist
Cyprus	0·71 pounds	Portugal	89·35 escudos
Czechoslovakia	17·50 korunas – Tourist	Rumania	22·79 lei – Tourist
Denmark	10·43 kronor	Russia	1·31 roubles
Egypt	1·36 pounds – Tourist	Spain	140·90 pesetas
Finland	7·93 marks	Sweden	8·67 kronor
France	8·5 francs	Switzerland	3·14 francs
Greece	71·57 drachmae	Syria	7·77 pounds
Holland	4·09 guilders	Tunisia	0·87 dinars
Hungary	36·33 forints – Tourist	Turkey	48·17 lira
Iran	139·0 rials	USA	1·98 dollars
Italy	1,624·5 lire	West Germany	3·77 Deutschmarks
Jordan	0·58 dinar	Yugoslavia	37·12 dinars

The sterling and dollar equivalents given throughout the book were correct at the date of compilation, but, with the fluctuations of international currencies, they will certainly change during 1979–80.

Warning! Inflation is rampant, currencies in turmoil. Which means big problems for guidebook writers and worse ones for you. Because of printing schedules this book had to be researched months before it went to press. To allow for the inevitable process of inflation between the time I researched the book and the time you will read it, I have automatically upped every price in the book by 25% except in Switzerland, which because of its apparently stable currency, I have raised only 10%. But prices may rise even higher than anticipated. So be prepared . . . an extra £10 in the pocket might make all the difference.

I think your 'what your pound is worth' should be submitted for the 'International Joke of the Year Award'!
Marcel Thomas, Horndean, England

1 On the road

Once upon a time – well it was only eighty years ago – a young man with a romantic head could disappear into the wilderness of his dreams to seek his fortune and become a man of the world.

These days jumbo-jets have made us all men of the world – if we can find the air fare – and the seeking of fortunes starts more often than not in the London School of Economics or in the dollar-shaped halls of learning of American business schools. You don't stake claims any more if you want to make a fortune, you buy shares; and you don't disappear into the wilderness because the wilderness has been turned into real-estate.

Sometimes you can sense all this closing in on you and you know you have to escape. You must get right away and there ain't no more slow boats to China, man, and if there were you'd have to belong to the Seamen's Union before you could get aboard. But you have to get away and the place you can go is on the road, the infinite miles of tarmac and pot-holes which criss-cross the world, the magic ribbon which can lead to a thousand other worlds.

Get on the road and sometimes you get the feeling of what a non-computerized planet must have been like – or rather, what it was like when people *used* machines and didn't *depend* on them. Get on the road and the press-button-something-happens syndrome disappears. The action-reaction principle doesn't apply on the road, unless you count a car not stopping as a reaction to a thumb in the air. On the road you enter the world of pure chance, a world where mathematical equations mean nothing. Because the tenth car doesn't stop doesn't mean that the eleventh will. On the road you are in a world where time passes without the aid of a clock. On the road you even have time to think.

You wake up in the morning – be it in some cheap hotel or in a sleeping-bag beneath a tree in a field – and you get up and have breakfast if you can afford it and then make your way to the road; and the only thing you know for sure is that you *don't* know where you'll be that night. That's a strange feeling the first time it dawns on you.

The thing is that the road takes you. You can't dictate to the road. If you do you might as well be in a train. Hitch-hiking is the art of wondering what will happen to you between your starting point and your destination and taking from everything that *does* happen everything that you can.

And unless you really have to go somewhere, a destination is not all that important. You can set out from London to go to Rome and end up in Lisbon and what the hell? Rome will still be there next time around. And if there isn't any next time? Well, you've seen Lisbon – and it's a nice city.

Hitching is more than anything else an attitude to travel, not just a means of getting from Point A to Point B. If you look upon it purely as a means of getting to where you want to go, you'll probably get very bored very quickly. Hitch-hiking is a cumulative experience, a never-ending happening of unknown factors which contribute, with a little luck, to a memory of what real travelling is all about – not just the chance to say that you've been to a place, but the feeling that at one time, somewhere, even if only for an instant, you felt like you had become a part of the land through which you travelled.

Hitch-hiking involves you. It fufils that need for occasional fast forward movement which seems to be built into the mind of the twentieth-century wanderer – a sense of the looming miles ahead being slashed aside by the roar of a powerful motor – and at the same time it deposits you five, six, seven times a day into the guts of a lonely landscape where the atavistic man who survives in at least some of us can be briefly at home. And by the very nature of the game it is impossible to avoid the citizens of the country through which you are moving. You become, in effect, a mechanized Marco Polo.

That's the bright side of the game, but there's a dark side too, and it comes when you're twenty-seven miles from nowhere in the middle of a black night with rain drenching you and when you have no tent and no cover. It comes when you're sick, it comes when you're tired. Mostly it comes when loneliness hits you like a dart and you've got to be with people and in a light place, a warm place. It comes when it's like that and the cars won't stop and those that do don't seem to be making up the distance between where you are and where you need to be.

It's when the dark side comes that you find out a little about who you are, because the hitch-hiker who moves alone is with himself for a long, long time each day – and not many of us are used to that.

What you do when the dark side comes depends on who you are. Some people invest their remaining money in a train-ticket home and for them, that's the best thing. Other people just wait for something better to happen and it usually does. And some people just keep on moving, which is what it's all about.

The warning, for what it's worth, is given; you pay for what you get and the longer the road the bigger the toll because hitching can be hard travelling.

Mostly, though, it's good travelling, and a hundred miles split between walking, riding pillion on a motor-bike, bouncing on the tray of a huge semi or sitting comfortably in the back of a Mercedes – a hundred miles covered like that on the little-travelled side roads of Morocco or in the hard mountainous terrain of Greece will give you more memories (and bruises) than any sports-jacketed tourist will find as he slumbers in the Relax-Back airplane seat of an air-conditioned bus trying to figure in his travel-fuzzed mind which day it is in his twenty-one countries in twenty-one days super-fantastic luxury tour of the world.

Hitchers' tips and comments
A taster for anyone dubious about undertaking a first hitch trip in Europe: try reading *A Hitch in Time* by Ian Rodger in combination with the *Hitch-hiker's Guide*. Enough to give any prospective traveller itchy feet! (*A Hitch in Time* – recollection of a journey – by Ian Rodger. Published by Hutchinson 1966.)
John Hoad, Eastbourne, England

2 How to hitch

Hitch-hiking is a sport. It's like a motorized version of Snakes and Ladders, except instead of throwing a dice on to the board and automatically moving, you throw a thumb into the air and more often than not don't move.

As with all sports, hitch-hiking has its mythical heroes. You hear stories of guys who can dress like something out of a hippy musical, stand by the side of the road without moving a muscle and take their choice of the cars which screech to a halt in regimental lines on either side of them; cars which not only give them lifts, but which detour thirty, forty or fifty miles out of their way to land the magic men at a stated destination.

And you hear of others who can pick the car they want out of an approaching bunch and always make it stop; and it's always a big Citroën or a Porsche, and its owner always buys them a meal at an expensive restaurant.

It's a fact that if you're a good-looking woman hitching alone you can make this happen. I know a girl who came clear across Germany in one day and never stepped into anything lowlier than a Mercedes. She was also propositioned twice, middle-aged German businessmen being as fast, if not as smooth, as their chariots.

But if you're not a magic man, or if you don't have long blonde hair, you're left with the problem of stopping cars. The only thing on your side when you stand by the road and put up your thumb is that *some* drivers pick up hitchers. Sooner or later one of them will stop – though you shouldn't count on it. You might go the whole day without a ride and then get twelve the next day. What you must do then, is try and raise the odds in your favour and to do that there are some basic things which can be considered.

APPEARANCE. Not many people in Europe have anything against beards, long hair or hip clothes these days, so there are no worries there. But if you think of the problem in terms of how many people will willingly stop and talk to you if you approach them in the street while you're wearing fancy-dress costume and when you haven't bathed for twenty-three days, you get a perspective on how many cars are going to stop for some dingy freak thumbing them from the side of the road. The majority of people who will be picking you up will be ordinary suburban-types. Their own kids wear beards and gear, too, but they are 'nice kids'. Look like a nice kid and you can skid around pretty fast.

LUGGAGE. Carry as little as possible. Try and keep it down to just your frame-pack, or at the most, one hand item as well. I know plenty of people who have hitched carrying a frame-pack, suitcase, camera-bag and portable typewriter, but it's not a good general rule. A lot of cars won't stop because they simply don't have room for your luggage.

ROAD TACTICS. This is the most important thing of all and while plenty of experienced hitchers might argue that you can get away with any sort of appearance because people *want* to pick up freaks for a kick, or that if a driver wants to stop to help you on your way he's not going to worry about extra pieces of luggage, they'll agree unanimously that you have to choose your thumbing position carefully.

First (and most obviously, though it's horrifying how many fools do it), *don't hitch on a bend*. There are three reasons. One, it's deadly. Cars cut through bends and you can get killed. Two, drivers are concentrating too much on the problem of getting through the bend to be worried about anyone trying to stop them from the side of the road. Three, even if the driver was stupid enough to want to stop on a bend, the law forbids him to do so.

Second, *choose your road edge carefully*. Drivers aren't inclined to stop in the middle of the road – it's too dangerous – so you must pick a position, when possible, which has a nice safe edge for them to run off on to, and the more of their car they can get off the road when they stop the more they like it. And the smoother the area the better. Drivers don't like running off the road into mud, or pot-holes, or into a puddle of water when they don't know how deep it is.

Third, *when you're trying for a ride, try properly*. My experience has been that I get rides when I'm standing up and looking like I want to go somewhere. You might get one when you're lying on the ground with your feet up on your pack lazily devouring a bottle of wine, with a daisy stuck behind your ear and nonchalantly waving your free hand up above the grass, but the odds are right against you.

HOW TO CONQUER BOREDOM. Half an hour or more without a ride can leave you feeling a little lost. It's not so bad if you're with a companion – especially one of the opposite sex – but if you're alone you can start suffering from great gobs of boredom. If you're into Zen or Yoga then time is the air around you and you have no problem. If you've got a decent novel, things are OK. Paper and pencil lets you catch up on letters back home or allows you to make paper-aeroplanes complete with military markings. Standard side-of-the-road games, equally suitable for one or more people, include hurling stones at specified targets (hurl at leisure, spin and hurl, five hurls in ten seconds, etc, etc), golf, played with a suitable stick and assorted round stones (across the road on the full counts as a hole in one), tin-can football (hard on the boots), breath-holding, and standing on one foot.

One driver reports pulling up beside two gentlemen of the road who were in the middle of a push-up competition. He offered them a ride but they informed him that the loser was buying dinner and asked if he could wait a moment. The driver – patient type – watched in fascination as the two hitchers battled it out. The loser fell on his nose after the 47th push-up, while the winner did five more just for the hell of it. The hitchers later told him that they held the competition every day.

HOW TO WAVE THE CAR DOWN. My technique depends upon my constitution. Normally I use my thumb – always my right thumb regardless of which side of the road I'm on – but when I'm feeling a little poetic I sometimes change to a regal floating wave of my whole hand which if the driver happens to be feeling in the same mood seems to work wonders. And then, of course, there's the old two-finger wave which, if the car doesn't stop, can be continued in one sweeping movement upwards to tell any rear-vision-mirror observer that you're suggesting up him for the money or sending him on his way with peace. (Once, in Spain, a field worker watched my thumb technique with interest for quite some time. Eventually he inquired if I was trying to stop a car. I said I was, that I was going to Granada. He said I was doing it all wrong and when the next car came, wandered out into the middle of the road waving his hand like a policeman's halt signal. The car stopped and he lined up a ride for me. Not that the driver seemed too impressed with it all.) How *you* do it is your problem, but there's one trick you might try. Always smile, and always latch right on to the driver's eyes as he approaches and don't stop staring or smiling. You can psych some of them into stopping!

COUNTRY IDENTIFICATION. This is purely a matter of choice. I've done one trip with the international AUS for Australia attached to my pack and two cars stopped specifically because the drivers had relatives in Sydney. The question is, how many cars *didn't* stop because of it? Lots of people carry small flags or national emblems and one friend of mine went through Europe like a flash, dressed in a suit and carrying a small suitcase with a notice attached which simply read, 'US Student'. Perhaps you can approach the problem in terms of international political opinion. Try and figure how popular your country is in Europe before you mount a sign.

DESTINATION PLACARDS. These are used by most hitchers purely as last resorts after a rotten day's hitching. You find an old piece of cardboard or paper and print in large letters the name of the city you're heading for. Generally you can't tell how successful the idea is, so it's a matter of choice. I do think a destination placard is worth considering, for instance, on the German autobahns. The only places you're legally allowed to hitch or walk on these, or any other super-highways are at the entrance and exit roads, and because of the ring-road systems a car heading north might only be doing so to get to an exit road to take him south. Which can cause the temporarily north-bound car driver to decide not to stop for what looks like a north-bound hitcher who, in fact, happens to want to go the same way as the soon-to-be south-bound car. (Get it?) German students seem to make a lot of use of placards for that reason.

WHAT RIDES TO TAKE. Providing a driver isn't obviously bombed out of his mind, my rule is to take any car that stops which has its bonnet pointed even vaguely in the direction I want to go. I work on the simple premise that if the ride is only for five kilometres, I'm going to be five kilometres closer to my destination and the next car I want might be sooner or later coming out of a side road we pass during that short drive. Some hitchers prefer to refuse the small rides in the hope that they'll eventually catch the big one. To me, that's a bit like throwing away ten cents in the hope that you'll find twenty-five.

WHEN A CAR STOPS. A lot of drivers who have stopped for you are nevertheless in a hell of a hurry. Most drivers pull up fifty or a hundred yards beyond you. Never risk losing a ride by wandering to them. Run. Grab your bag and move! When you get to the car, just wish the driver a good day in his own language (if possible) and then tell him where you're going. If you can't pronounce the name of the town have a map handy to pull out and point at. From then on, whatever the driver says, just answer *oui*, *si*, *ja* or *yes* as the case may be. It doesn't matter what the driver has said – 'I'm going to Kassel', 'I'm in a hurry', 'It'll be a slow trip' – *yes* is the one word which is the nearest thing to an answer. And keep smiling. Your one object is to get into the car. Once rolling you can work out a way of finding exactly how far the driver is going.

FAST DRIVERS. If you make the mistake of getting in with a fast one who you reckon is taking you both on a one-way ride (and it happens just about every trip), politely indicate that you want out. If he won't stop or doesn't understand what you're trying to say, be a little more obvious and a little less polite and make sounds which suggest you're about to throw-up all over his upholstery. That usually drives the point home. And perhaps saves your life.

FAST DRIVERS (OTHER TYPE). Very occasionally, through no fault of their own, lady hitchers find themselves being attacked by guys who give them a ride. What to do? If it's one man it's not so bad. At least he has to stop the car first, and if he stops it in a suspicious place you've got a lead on what might be about to happen. In that case a simple 'no' (politely offered) will probably work. If it doesn't and he's obviously not a psycho sort of guy, you can try putting on a sick act, telling him you're having your period, that you're pregnant, that you've just had a bad operation or that you've got some dreaded venereal disease. If he *is* a psycho type you've got problems and about all you can do is keep talking until you can see a way out. If there's more than one guy there's not a great deal you can do about it. Screaming will probably get you roughed up pretty bad, fighting back, pulling out the old hat-pin or kneeing somebody in the balls will have the same result. (The knee works OK with one guy, but make sure your aim is good and you get him first try.) Best advice to offer is this: if you are a lady hitcher then travel with a second person. If you must travel alone, just make sure you're on the Pill.

THE LANGUAGE PROBLEM. A lot of timid souls I know tell me that they could never hitch-hike in a foreign country because they just wouldn't know how to handle the language barrier. Well, the excuse is understandable, but it's a pretty sad one. One of the first things any hitch-hiker learns is that lack of language is no barrier to simple friendly communication. English-speaking people who say they don't know one word of a foreign language are either stupid or have no imagination. To start with, *imagination, communication* and most other words which end in *ion* in English are roughly the same in Spanish, French and Italian – they're just pronounced a little differently. And how many people don't know the meaning of *au revoir*, or *vino*, or *grazie*, or *Fräulein*? The point I am trying to make is that anyone who speaks English automatically has a stock of words in other languages he can draw on either because they are the same words, because they have entered the English language through popular usage or because they figure prominently in films and books. Of course he mightn't be able to pronounce them correctly, but at least he has them and it doesn't take too many words to find out someone's name, what they do, where they're going, or if they're married and have kids. And that's the sort of small talk you find yourself indulging in when you're zipping down the highways of Europe and when you don't have a mutual language with the driver.

If you happen to speak a second language you're in business, not just because many Europeans speak at least one other language after their own, but because people who speak two languages, even if they aren't mutual, know enough about word associations to be able to make some sort of conversation.

But many Europeans do speak English and when you get rides with them, that's when hitch-hiking comes into its own. On a good day you might be picked up by half a dozen cars with each of the drivers speaking a little English. Those drivers will usually be a cross-section of their society – young, old, rich, and poor – and from them you can glean a first-hand word picture of their country's attitudes and feelings.

If you don't have a mutual language with your host, don't worry about it. If you try and communicate and he's not interested in playing word games, just practise sitting without talking. If the tension seems to be building (and it often does), break it by offering a cigarette or something to chew – it nearly always works.

As a generalization, I've found that the better educated and/or more affluent my host, the easier it's been for me to talk with him even if he doesn't speak English. I say it as a generalization because I've had some great rides with truckies – particularly Arabs – without exchanging a single word. And it's from rides like those that I learned that communication is not only a matter of utterances, but a willingness to share the pleasures (or discomforts) of a situation. At that basic level, things can get boring but if it's the only level you have you learn to make the most of it.

GETTING IN AND OUT OF A CITY. This is the biggest bug-bear of any hitcher. Towns and small cities aren't so bad because you can walk in or out of them in less than an hour. But try walking out of Paris or London! If your ride has let you off in the suburb of a big city and you want to go to the centre, you can try to hitch, but the odds are right against you. People in a suburban traffic stream usually don't have the chance to stop for you even if they want to. I've managed to hitch in the suburbs of medium-sized cities, but I've never had any luck in the big capitals. If you don't have any money, then obviously you'll have to walk and try to hitch, but the only real answer is to take a train or bus. You'll save yourself a couple of hours of hard work and a lot of energy.

The only way to get out of a really big city, as far as I'm concerned, is to take a train to the nearest small village outside the city limits. This might cost a pound or so, but it's quick and puts you straight on the road you want and away from the traffic-congested areas. And on a long walk out of a city – maybe two or three hours – you usually end up spending 30 or 40p anyway, on drinks and food to keep you going. You can only walk by so many French *pâtisseries* before you break down and step inside!

FINDING A ROOM. European cities and towns are nearly always six or seven centuries old at least, and this rather obvious fact gives the clue as to how to find the cheapest rooms in a strange city. The majority of large towns and cities were built either on rivers or ports for purposes of trade and communication, around a castle which was built for the defence of an area, or around a church which was the religious seat of a parish. The old sections then, and the cheapest, are often around a castle, a cathedral, or on the river, or around the port area.

This doesn't apply so much to very large cities which continually instigate building programmes to clear such areas, but more in the smaller cities. Lisbon is an example of a city with a cheap 'castle area'. Paris used to be an example of a city with a cheap 'river area'. (The Île de la Cité was reputedly the first settled area of Paris. The Marais, supposed to have been the second settled area, is now one of the cheapest places in the city.) Restaurants in these areas are generally very cheap as well.

In villages and towns you can find reasonably priced rooms in private houses. These normally cost about the same as a cheap hotel room except, being part of someone's home, they are usually cleaner and better value for money. If you want one of these and can't spot a 'Room Free' sign, ask at the local bar.

Special note. When you visit a city covered in the *Hitch-hiker's Guide* with a 'Where to Sleep' section, and decide to try one of my recommendations rather than taking pot luck hunting around, you may find it worth investing a few pence in a phone call. Wherever possible I've listed the hostel or hotel phone number beside the address, thus you can check, before you go to the address, that they have a room free, that their prices haven't gone up since this new edition was published and, also, that they are open. Many student hostels close at various times during the year and, because closing dates can vary from year to year, it's hard to make the listings in this book absolutely accurate. A quick phone call could save a lot of trouble (and bus fare money).

TRAVEL ALONE OR IN COMPANY? This is an old argument amongst veteran hitchers. Opinions break down like this: men travel fastest by themselves, but not as fast as a woman by herself. Two women travel faster than two men, but a mixed couple travel faster than any other pair.

Many drivers are wary of picking up more than one person, especially if they're two men. Travelling alone is the ideal, anyway, because when you're by yourself you move at precisely your own speed – you don't have to worry about your partner's fitness or his inclination to go two hundred miles out of his way to catch an exhibition of Russian Ikon art in Geneva.

A lone woman will travel very fast, but it mightn't be pleasant travelling – lots of wolves drive cars. I'm not Moses the Law-giver, but I think girls are crazy to hitch by themselves. Think of all those stalwart gentlemen willing to accompany you, ladies. And if that doesn't appeal, remember that two girls are safer than one and the chances of catching a ride don't drop dramatically. (As *proof* of how fast lone girls can travel, it's worth noting that a recent Warwick University Golden Thumb Hitching race over a 55 mile course was won on the outward leg by Lisa Charalambus (1 hour 45 minutes) and on the return leg (1 hour 40 minutes) by another fast lady, Sarah Pearsall.)

A man and a woman together is the ideal combination if you must travel in company. You don't get lonely on the road or off the road and you still get plenty of rides. Another real advantage of travelling as a couple is that you can share double hotel rooms and cut the cost per head considerably.

To try hitching in the company of *more* than one other person is crazy.

HITCHING AT NIGHT. This is a curly one. Some people swear by night hitching. Others swear about it. Some people say they can always get to where they're going at night. Others say drivers just won't pick them up, and, although occasionally I've had to move at night and done OK, I think of all the times I tried it and didn't get anywhere and agree that it's a slow game. Anyway, you miss the countryside.

If you like the idea of night hitching or find it necessary to make a night-time journey, the following hints are handy: first, try to get under a light (obvious) and try to pick a light which will allow the driver to see that it's safe for him to pull off the side of the road. Second, try for an all-night service station where you can, if necessary, wander over to stopped cars and ask if they can help you on your way. Third, if you are stuck somewhere without light, for God's sake find a straight stretch of road where cars can catch you in their beam from a fair distance; and carry a white handkerchief or a white something to help them spot you. If you've driven a car at night, you'll understand the sense of that.

HITCH-HIKERS AND THE POLICE. If you listen long enough to some of the road-talk around Europe you start getting the idea that cops devote most of their energy to hassling hitch-hikers. But before you finally make up your mind, take a good look at who's doing the talking.

Cops often stop you and ask to see your passport. They blow you up for hitching on an autobahn instead of from the entrance. They tell you to stop eating your lunch on the municipal grass (grass is for looking at, *not* sitting on!). They wake you up and tell you to piss off out of public parks. They ask to see your rail-ticket when they notice you loitering in a lovely warm railway station at three in the morning.

That's usually all they do. Some of those things might be stupid – like so what, you're asleep under the mayor's favourite oak tree – but you have to be pretty up-tight to think a cop is hassling you if he asks you politely (and *most* of them are polite) to abide by some by-law he's being paid to enforce.

Thing is, of course, that a lot of people who consider themselves very cool are so up-tight that their eyeballs are popping. A cop asks them to do something, they start screaming and next thing the cop is frisking them for drugs, asking how much money they've got, wanting to see their return ticket to country of origin and all the rest of it.

Take someone with more authority than you and rub him the wrong way and odds are you'd have trouble on your hands. Cops are no exception. Be nice to the police, ladies and gentlemen, and they'll be nice to you. But when you get way down south and too far east, don't take my word for it.

Mainly, hitching is a matter of persevering. Keep the thumb up. Keep working. You hear of hitchers striking bad luck and moving slowly but you rarely hear of a hitcher who knows his business not getting to where he wants to go.

★**International car identification letters**. It's a good idea to learn a few identification letters. Especially useful when you're hanging around roadside cafés searching out a likely truck to take you on your way. Also interesting to know the nationality of the guy who didn't pick you up as his tail-end disappears in a cloud of dust down the highway.

A Austria	F France	N Norway
AND Andorra	FL Liechtenstein	NL Netherlands
B Belgium	GB Great Britain	P Portugal
BG Bulgaria	GBZ Gibraltar	PL Poland
CH Switzerland	GR Greece	R Rumania
CS Czechoslovakia	H Hungary	S Sweden
DW Germany	I Italy	SF Finland
DK Denmark	IRL Ireland	TR Turkey
E Spain	L Luxembourg	YU Yugoslavia

Hitchers' tips and comments

I note that you think it 'crazy' to hitch in numbers greater than two. I'd
like to inform you that I have just arrived back from a holiday in which
there were three of us – two females, one male. We travelled through
Belgium, Luxembourg, Germany, Austria (Yugoslavia by train), Greece,
Italy and Switzerland. The longest period we had to wait for a lift was 1.5
hours. Our luggage was also far from minimal as we had set out in a car
which broke down in Ashford, Kent!
Christine Wade, Southampton, England

Great book! A 'no wordy crap' tour of Europe!
   Here's some stuff. Re country identification, I reckon I can attribute fifty
per cent of my rides to the Union Jack plastered on to my pack.
   Useful to know that in Europe 'hitching' is known as 'auto-stop'.
   If one is desperate, and in the company of other desperadoes, it's possible
to book a motel room for two and occupy it with, say, six. Works out
pretty cheap!
   A useful end-of-season trick is to go to offices of international car-hire
firms (except Hertz) and see if they need any cars returned to base – for
instance, from Copenhagen to Amsterdam. Sometimes you'll get the job
and you get paid expenses for your effort. Good way of travelling.
   Student cards available for about £2.50 on the Athens black market.
Mike Feeney, Haslow, England

Re your statement that it's crazy to hitch with more than two, I disagree.
I have hitched all over in a threesome (all girls). I even know of a friend
who was out walking with about twelve when they were offered a lift in a
laundry van. Beat that!
Wendy Foulds, Orpington, England
I can't. K.W.

An interesting and useful phenomenon is the USA trailer family migration.
Basically, it moves from Switzerland/Austria in the late spring, making
south and ending in Greece or Morocco in autumn. Very nice and
obliging people.
Clive Gill, Birchington, England

About carrying flags. It's worked for me. I've hitched all year with an
Alaskan flag on my pack and drivers have stopped and picked me up to find
out what country the flag belongs to.
David Fremon, Palatine, USA

I have founded a hitch-hiker's initiative to help hitchers coming to Germany. I am in contact with people in Berlin, Münster and here in Gelsenkirchen. I want to enlarge the initiative and hope soon to have them all over Germany and perhaps in other countries as well.

One thing we're doing is planning an alternative guide to the Ruhr area – you know, the one you call 'the hitch-hiker's hell on earth'. Perhaps with this guide hitchers will find the area a little easier to survive in.

Anyone interested in helping the initiative, giving information about their experiences, or who need information about Germany should write to me: Jurgen Bischoff, Bochumer Strasse 42, Gelsenkirchen, W. Germany.
Jurgen Bischoff

Since I first ran Jurgen's letter in 1975 he's really been working. The hitch-hiker's initiative hasn't gone so well but Jurgen is producing a 16-page booklet called On the Road – Tramper Info. *For the moment the booklet is printed only in German. Jurgen has received letters from hitchers who have picked up his address from these pages and he says he's pleased to answer queries. But please ask him specific questions, not general questions which are impossible to answer briefly. Also help him out by enclosing three International Reply Coupons to cover return postage costs. K.W.*

Here are a few tips: Union Jack attached to my pack got me at least half my rides in France recently – but it should be removable just in case. A torch is an essential item if you're camping or hoping to sleep in churches (which I have done successfully). Definitely agree with you that 'high' packs are more practical than 'wide' packs. Try getting a 'wide' into a 2DC Citroën!
Paul Houghton, Bristol, England

Advise others to travel with someone else and not go off alone. I did and regretted it – I was as lonely as hell!
Walter Stiles Hoyt, Bristol, USA

What's this about W. S. Hoyt getting lonely? Everyone can talk to themselves.
Peter Nash, Chelmsford, England

I've taken to praying to cars on my knees. Works wonders if you're not too proud and can manage a brave smile.
Timmy Mallett, Altrincham, England

Hitching in threes is quite feasible, and fairly easy. One man and two girls can travel as fast as two men. The largest number of people with whom I've hitched and got a lift is 14.
Simon Calder, University of Warwick Golden Thumb Club

For those who can't afford hotels in the big cities, it's worth a few bob to lay the pack up in the left luggage on the main station and see the sights with just a bedroll and washing gear.
Marcel Thomas, Horndean, England

A further comment on the score of women hitch-hiking alone: If there are two or more gentlemen in the car which stops, unless one has very good reasons for thinking otherwise, the answer is obviously 'no'.
Beth Parker, Neunkirchen, West Germany

I bought and learnt to play a small musical instrument i.e. flageolet (glorified tin whistle) and when no vehicles are in sight, I sit down and start tooting away. Passes the time away successfully. Good gimmick for starting conversation with any local too.
Mickey Hohel, Plymouth, England

I've been hitching, mostly in Germany and Austria the last two summer holidays and I found my greatest asset for getting lifts was the wearing of a kilt.
   Some drivers stopped out of curiosity, others were bent double with laughter by the time they stopped, but since they always gave me a lift, this didn't bother me in the slightest.
   So if you've got a Scottish connection, get yourself a kilt!
Andy Deans, Fife, Scotland

Try some yoga. Read a book. Write a letter to ma. Construct paper planes. Throw stones. Play golf with a stick'n stones. Football with a tin can. Hold your breath. Stand on one foot. For godzakes! *What* is that kindergarten stuff? And is *that* what people levitate themselves off their asses and creep'n crawl abroad for?
Pasi Punnonen, Savonlinna, Finland

Hold up a card with PLEASE! written in the local language. You get a smile if nothing else.
Bernard Jennings, Brisbane, Australia

I used a card saying ANYWHERE! Boy, did I hit some wild places.
F. J. Gooding, Birmingham, England

3 What it will cost and how to get it cheaper

The beauty about a hitch-trip is that you can make it on precisely the budget you have. Some people have done it for nothing, working their way everywhere and relying on hand-outs from others.

Basically, though, there are three grades of hitch-hiking, each with its own cost structure, and they are discussed below:

(1) HOLE-IN-THE-WALL HITCHING. This is for the hitcher on the tightest imaginable budget. It's a rough way of travelling, but preferable to not travelling. It involves *always* sleeping out, *always* buying and preparing your own food, *always* visiting museums and galleries on half-price days and *always* sightseeing on foot. It means that you must always walk into and out of cities, that you *must* carry a tent and that you *must* carry some sort of cooking pannikin. The weekly cost structure for this sort of travelling breaks down something like this:

Nil	(Nil)	Bed
£1.25	($2.50)	Main meal with leftovers for breakfast
30p	(60 cents)	Cigarettes and/or coffee
£1.55	($3.10)	a day or £10.85 ($21.70) a week

To make a round figure, add £9.15 ($18.30) a week for fares and sightseeing and for this most basic and foot-weary way of moving it will cost only £20 ($40) *a week*! (And you'll be pretty fit at the end of it all.)

(2) HOSTEL HITCHING. This is the normal way of travelling and for those with an average bank roll. It involves sleeping out whenever the weather is good to save your money, sleeping in hostels, dormitories or dirt cheap hotels when the weather is bad or when you're in the city, eating at hostels or cafeterias, and generally making full use of student and hostel facilities wherever you go. Costs should be approximately:

£1.80	($3.60)	Bed
£2	($4.00)	Main meal
25p	(50 cents)	Breakfast (fruit)
35p	(70 cents)	Cigarettes and/or coffee
£4.40	($8.80)	a day or £30.80 ($61.60) a week

Add, let's say £15 ($30.00) per week for ferry fares, sightseeing, bus or train fares around and out of cities and you have, for what is an average hitch-hiking budget, £45.80 ($91.80) *per week*.

(3) HOTEL HITCHING. This, without a doubt, is the best way to do it if you can afford it. For the money you have the privilege of sleeping in a cheap hotel without the bug of curfews which plague hostel hitchers. You also eat at least one *good* meal a day in a cheap restaurant. Moving this way you're completely your own man, dependent on no one and subject to no rules or regulations. But it costs. Below is a realistic price structure:

£3.50	($7.00)	Bed
£2.50	($5.00)	Main meal
25p	(50 cents)	Breakfast (fruit or inclusive hotel breakfast)
35p	(70 cents)	Cigarettes and/or coffee

£6.60 ($13.20) a day or £46.20 ($92.40) a week

Add, let's say £20 ($40.00) per week for ferry fares and a general good time, and for the most luxurious and enjoyable way of hitching it costs you an even £66.20 ($132.40) *a week*.

How to get it cheaper
When you're travelling on a hitcher's budget every cent counts. You have a certain amount of money and that money must get you around your route. Tricks to make your roll last as long as possible are important. Here are a few:

INTERNATIONAL STUDENT IDENTITY CARDS. These things are invaluable. In many countries they will get you into museums, galleries, monuments and theatres at half-price – and that can save you a *hell* of a lot of money. In Paris, for instance, some central cinemas were offering 25 per cent reductions to holders of student cards as we go to press.

In some countries card holders were offered reduced air fares between international cities. (But no one these days pays the full air fare anywhere. To give an example: as we go to press, a scheduled return air fare London–Malaga–London costs about £125. But if you're willing to stand the minor inconvenience of travelling on a certain day of the week and returning on that same weekday within seven weeks you can find the same trip for around £50. Check travel pages of local papers for full details.)

Elsewhere you get discounts on everything from jewellery to

tape-recorders. The company of Lillywhite Frowd, for instance, at 18–29 Mora Street, London EC1, offers holders of student cards up to 20 per cent discount on all sports and camping equipment, while H. J. Cooper & Co, 19–21 Hatton Garden, London EC1, offers wholesale prices on items like watches and typewriters. That can mean a saving of around 30 per cent.

Obtain these cards, or the information on how to buy one, from your college or university. For Britons, or foreign students in Britain, who require an International Student Identity Card, contact:

The London Student Travel Bureau,
117 Euston Road
London NW1 (Tel: 01-388 7051).

If you're not eligible for one of these magic money-savers, it's worth mentioning that there is a very healthy black market in them throughout most university cities in Europe. The cards aren't hard to pick up and aren't very expensive. Last price I heard was £5.00 ($9.00) (in Brussels).

It's also worth mentioning – just in case you couldn't guess – that faked student cards are just as highly illegal as faked anything-elses.

YOUTH HOSTELS. There are three main disadvantages about youth hostels. First, they are often so far out of town it takes you an hour or two to locate and get to them; second, they have curfews which are usually strictly enforced, and third, they have a completely institutional flavour about them (though in fairness it must be added that some of the new hostels are superbly designed and extremely well administered). The advantages of hostels are equally obvious. They guarantee you a clean bed for a very reasonable fee and they supply (in some countries) excellent meals for a fraction of what they would cost outside. And married couples will be pleased to know that if there is plenty of free space in the hostels (usually only during, or towards the off-season) the staff will do their best to put you in a room together. In fact, off-season hostelling (when you can find them open) is great fun. You end up getting hotel conditions for a half of the price you'd pay in a hotel.

There are over 4,000 hostels in 44 countries throughout the world and a large number of them are in Europe. There is no maximum age limit for hostellers except in Bavaria in Southern Germany (27). However, priority will always be given to members under the age of thirty if beds are filling up fast.

The *average* cost of a youth hostel bed in Europe is £1.80 ($3.60). The *average* cost of a meal is £2.00 ($4.00) – and a good meal, at that. Cooking facilities are available in many hostels if you wish to cut costs even further by preparing your own food.

Full information on the location of all International Youth Hostels can be found in two volumes of the *IYH Handbook*. Volume I deals with youth hostels in Europe and the Mediterranean area, Volume II with hostels outside Europe and the Mediterranean. They cost about £1 ($2.00) each and can be obtained through any national youth hostel association.

The cost of joining the Youth Hostels Association is extremely cheap in view of what you gain by membership.

Addresses to contact regarding membership of YHA are:

ENGLAND AND WALES
14 Southampton Street, London WC2E 7HY.
8 St Stephen's Hill, St Albans, Herts.

SCOTLAND
7 Glebe Crescent, Stirling.

NORTHERN IRELAND
93 Dublin Road, Belfast.

REPUBLIC OF IRELAND
39 Mountjoy Square, Dublin 1.

UNITED STATES
National Campus, Delaplane, Virginia.

CANADA
333 River Road, Vanier City, Ottawa Kil 859, Ontario.

AUSTRALIA
184 Sussex Street, Sydney, NSW 2000.

NEW ZEALAND
PO Box 436, Christchurch, C1.

SOUTH AFRICA
PO 4402, Cape Town.

You can cut basic living costs by better than a half if you're a member of the YHA. So, if you think you can put up with the disadvantages mentioned, join!

Warning! Guard your stuff well in the hostels. There's a lot being ripped off. Leave valuables at the desk (if they have facilities) or take them with you. Careful of your watch when you take it off to shower!

FREE MAPS AND LITERATURE. These days there is no need to buy maps of European countries. Most national tourist agencies will supply them for free if you ask. Failing that, many service stations in many countries offer free maps. These maps aren't as good as Michelin or Hallwag, but then they don't cost a pound apiece. They're certainly good enough to help you find your way between the major cities and points of interest.

Don't be afraid to ask for literature, either. Tourist offices have tons of it and it's there for only one reason – to give away. City maps, descriptions of the sights, just about any information you can imagine. But tourist offices are funny. They rarely give until they're asked. So ask. Nicely.

WHAT TO BUY WHERE. You can save the odd pound or dollar by being aware of which countries sell which items cheaper than other countries and stocking up before you cross borders.

For instance, buy cigarettes on ferry-boats crossing international waters (where they are duty-free) or in Belgium, Luxembourg or Spain which are the three cheapest countries in Europe for tobacco. Even if you don't smoke you should always buy your quota for re-sale. If, for example, you carry 10 packets of cigarettes from Spain where 20 filter-tips cost 15p (30 cents), into Denmark where 20 filters cost around £1.70 ($3.40), you can reasonably expect to sell them for around £1.40 ($2.80) a pack and thus make a profit of about £3.00 ($6.00) – enough to keep you on the road for an extra day. The same goes for bottles of spirits. Always buy your quota if you think you can sell it across the border at a profit.

Anyone thinking of camping out would do well to stock up with instant coffee in England before crossing to the Continent where, in many countries, it is more than twice as expensive. And the same goes for tea drinkers.

Hitchers with worn-out boots can buy the cheapest boots in Europe in Spain. Those with worn-out clothes can find the best bargains in new clothes at sales in Germany or England. Those who want second-hand boots or clothes should head for the flea markets in any of the big cities. Amsterdam, Paris, Madrid, London, Rome all have big open-air markets where you can buy anything cheap if you haggle long enough.

SOMETIMES CHEAPER TO BUY A TICKET. If you're in a big hurry to go somewhere for a specific reason, remember that it's sometimes cheaper to buy a bus or train ticket than to hitch. For instance, you can get a third-class rail ticket right through the length of Spain for about £18 ($36.00). That works out roughly the same as hitching it. In Turkey, if you're in a hurry, buses are much cheaper than hitching. Sometimes it's even cheaper to *fly* than to hitch if you join up with a charter flight.

A big thing these days – especially in holiday resort areas on the Continent – is to buy the remaining half of someone's charter holiday ticket after they decide they don't want to go home. It means you might go, for example, from Corfu, Greece, to Luton airport, north of London, for only £30 or so. It's a great way of flitting around, but it's illegal, because tickets are not transferable. You've been warned! But usually if you can get by the baggage check and passport control of the airport you are departing from you'll be OK. There's not much they can do when you arrive at the other end. If someone nabs you, you just plead ignorance.

As there's always a chance you'll be turned back from the airport you are trying to leave from it's not a bad idea to make some arrangement with the person from whom you're buying the ticket that if you miss out you get a refund.

BLACK MARKETS. There aren't many black markets in money left in Europe these days, but you'll find them in the Communist countries, in the Middle East and also in Morocco, though that one's not worth worrying about.

Basic rules to follow when making a black-market deal are (1) know the bank rate of exchange on the currencies you are trying to trade, (2) always try and choose your own ground on which to make the bargain so that you make it harder for any would-be informer to arrange for the police to see the transaction, (3) try never to make a black-market transaction alone, but always in the company of a friend who can keep discreet watch for you, (4) haggle like hell because the first rate you'll be offered will probably be too low, (5) never exchange traveller's cheques on the black market because if there is any police crack-down and your man is picked up they may be able to trace you.

If those rules sound too James Bondish, just remember that when you play the black market, you are breaking the law. Any black-market dealing is risky. If you're caught – and there are people who make a living by passing information to the police – you'll either be thrown out of the country (if you're lucky) or thrown into jail. Make sure the market is worth it before you play it. To get an idea if the market really *is* worth playing check through foreign exchange listings in magazines like *Newsweek*. *Newsweek*'s list has three columns: name of country, what the dollar is worth in that country (based on foreign currency selling rates in Zurich), and what the official rate is in that country. As we go to press on this edition I note that, for example, in France the dollar is worth 4.75 francs and that the official rate is 4.80 francs, so obviously there won't be a very healthy market there. But on the other hand, in Algeria the dollar is worth 8.30 dinar and the official rate is only 3.87 dinar. So, in Algeria you have the chance of making your money last longer . . . as long as you don't make a stupid mistake. Consider well!

TRAVELLERS' CHEQUES. When you set out on your hitch-trip you'll probably have a fair wad of money. The safest way to carry it is in travellers' cheques which can be cashed just about anywhere in the world. The cheques cost a small amount to buy and you must pay a small commission when you cash them, but if you happen to lose your wallet or it gets stolen, you can make arrangements to cancel those cheques by going straight to a bank. It's a good idea, though, to keep a few dollars or pounds sterling in the pocket just in case you do want to play around on a black market.

RESTAURANTS. Only go into restaurants (or bars) where you can check the price-list first. If you go into a place without a price-list and have an absolutely disgusting meal and they ask $8 for it, you're obliged to pay (if they can catch you). *Always* check!

HOTELS. When you ask the price of a room and you are told, do not accept immediately. Try the downcast-face act and ask gently if there isn't a somewhat cheaper room in the house, for instance, on the fifth floor. It's surprising the number of times, especially in France, when you'll be offered something a fraction cheaper.

There are dozens of little ways of saving on your expenses. Always be on the lookout for them – youth hostels are where you hear of many – and when you discover them pass the word around. Help others travel cheaper, too!

Warning! If you want to buy a camera, radio, cassette recorder, etc it's best to wait until you get to Switzerland or Germany where such things are cheaper. Better yet, wait until you reach a duty-free port or airport. But this is the warning . . . some so-called duty-free ports and airports offer very bad deals on some items. For instance, I have seen cameras at London's Heathrow airport with higher price-tags than you can find in a good discount store right in the centre of town. Don't be fooled by the words 'tax-free' or 'duty-free'. Check out prices.

★For van vagabonds only: An easy way to save money is to know petrol prices in countries you plan to drive through. 4-star petrol in Belgium, for instance, may be cheaper than in neighbouring France, so by simply filling up in Belgium before crossing the border into France you can save quite a lot of money. In a van with a 10 gallon tank capacity it could be as much as £1.50 which stays in your pocket. For a current list of petrol prices around Europe write to The Royal Automobile Club (Foreign Touring Department), 83–85 Pall Mall, London SW1.

★Drivers should also know that in some countries (Italy, Czechoslovakia, Poland and Greece, for instance) tourists can buy petrol coupons which offer discounts as high as 40 per cent on petrol bought in those countries.

★Remember, also, to nurse ailing vehicles into cheaper countries where workers' wages are considerably less than in the north and where motor repairs can be a lot cheaper.

Hitchers' tips and comments
On my last two trips to the Continent I discovered that the only places which would change money and travellers' cheques on Saturday nights, Sundays or public holidays were Bureaux at railway stations, airports or hotels. Also, it's worth noting that most places will only exchange travellers' cheques from the most prominent world banks or travel agents. Anyone carrying cheques from minor banks can have trouble.
Sue Pyle, Geelong, Australia
True enough, especially in outback areas. Perhaps best to stick to big names like Cook's and American Express. Also, I've noticed that trying to get rid of lesser known currencies – like Australian dollars! – is like trying to give away rocks . . . no one is interested. K.W.

My student ID card helped me get reductions all over France, for instance free entrance in Versailles and in the Ste Chapelle in Paris, a reduction in the Bayeux Tapestry museum and even on the Pointe de Grave ferry near Bordeaux. All in all it saved me a lot of money.
Jurgen Bischoff (again)

4 What to take

The only sure thing that's going to happen on a hitch-hike trip is that you will get sick of lugging your pack around. It's an unavoidable millstone which is always too heavy.

Some hitchers are very aware of this and it's not unusual to see people wandering around Europe with a hold-all which has scarcely the capacity of an airline bag. When you figure it, all you basically need, apart from the clothes on your back, is a toothbrush, a change of socks and underwear, and a spare shirt. But that's pretty rough travelling and, for myself, if I'm hitting the road for anything longer than a couple of weeks, I like to carry enough stuff to keep me comfortable and reasonably clean throughout any situation I'm likely to encounter.

Any list of what to take on a trip – as with any other suggestion in this book – can only be a guideline to a plan you might finally adopt for yourself. The two lists which follow soon are based on what my wife and I carry when we set out.

The first thing you need, of course, is a pack. The only type worth considering, in my opinion, is a frame-pack with some sort of adjustable system which allows you to vary the tension strap, which sits just above your buttocks, so that a load, no matter what its weight, can be kept from digging into your spine. The shoulder-straps, also, should be adjustable so that you can find the most comfortable carrying position and they should be made of leather, rather than the cheaper webbing material, because the latter tends to crease and become very uncomfortable.

Examine the shoulder-straps well before buying because, if you're carrying any sort of load, it's your shoulders which will take the bashing for the first few days until you get fit. Some more expensive packs have canvas-encased sponge-rubber strips sewn to the inside of the strap. These are great. You can fit them on to a cheaper pack yourself.

Another important point to consider when buying is that there are 'wide packs' and 'high packs', meaning that the volume of the pack, when filled to capacity, comes either from the width or from the height. I favour the high pack because it's easier to carry through crowded streets without slaughtering people and, more important, it's less trouble to get through the door of a small car.

If you can't afford a frame-pack consider an army or navy duffel bag. You can usually rig them up fairly comfortably.

If your budget doesn't run to sleeping in cheap hotels, you'll need a sleeping-bag. (Even if you're sleeping in hostels, which charge a small fee for the use of bedding, you can save money by having your own bag.) The bag you should buy is the best you can afford for the conditions you expect to meet. If you've any sense you won't be considering sleeping out in anything much less than freezing and therefore you *do not* need something like Hillary took to Everest. Any good camping shop should be able to give you a run-down on what is available. The minimum requirements are that the bag will keep you comfortable at freezing point, that it is reasonably water-resistant and that it is light.

If you take a sleeping-bag, then you need something to lay it on – a ground-sheet of some kind. Don't buy a regular ground-sheet because they cost money and weigh a couple of pounds. The best thing – and for free if you look around – is a six feet by four feet sheet of heavy-duty plastic (like factories encase new mattresses in) which is light, disposable and easily replaceable, and which doubles perfectly as a poncho if you're caught in the rain.

If you're a hole-in-the-wall hitcher (which means that to make your money last you have to sleep out every night and always prepare your own meals) then it might be worth investing in a lightweight inflatable air-mattress. You'll curse the extra weight by day, but bless the comfort it offers you by night. (Remember to take a puncture repair outfit along with the mattress!) If you reckon your shoulders can stand it you might consider taking the midget stove that the Gaz people put out. You can buy refills in just about every European country. (Spain is the cheapest country I've found for refills.) It's cheaper to make fires, but also more hassle, especially if you're just thinking you'd like a quick cup of coffee.

Suggested men's list
Passport and money
Good pair of light boots
  (you'll be walking quite a few miles a day)
Sandals for city wear when you're resting up
2 pairs of trousers
2 shirts (drip-dry)
1 good jacket with plenty of pockets
2 changes underwear
2 pairs of socks

3 handkerchiefs
Sweater
Toilet bag containing:
Toothbrush and paste
Small bar of soap – use other people's where possible
Toilet paper (most toilets on the Continent seem to be without it – stolen
  by hitch-hikers, no doubt)
Nail scissors and file
Sticking plaster (for blistered feet – very handy during first week)
½ dozen aspirin tablets
Dozen anti-diarrhoea tablets
Needle and cotton
Pocket knife (doubles as eating knife and fork)
Spoon
Plastic cup
Combination bottle-opener, corkscrew and can-opener
  (simplest type possible or it won't work)
Notebook, pen and envelopes
Reading matter
Spare box of matches
Maps of areas to be travelled through

Suggested women's list
Passport and money
Good pair of tough shoes or light boots
Sandals for city wear
2 pairs of slacks or jeans
3 blouses (drip-dry)
1 light crush-proof, drip-dry dress
3 changes underwear
3 pairs of socks
3 handkerchiefs
Sweater
Toilet bag containing:
Toothbrush and paste
Small bar of soap
Toilet paper
Small pair of scissors and nailfile
Sticking plaster
½ dozen aspirin tablets
Dozen anti-diarrhoea tablets

Couple of sanitary towels – which can be hard to find if you're stuck in small Southern European and North African villages. Same goes for the Pill. Take them with you.
Needle and cotton
Pocket knife (doubles as eating knife and fork)
Spoon; plastic cup
Combination bottle-opener, corkscrew and can-opener
Notebook, pen and envelopes
Reading matter
Spare box of matches
Maps of areas to be travelled through

Those lists, depending on your sense of proportion, will seem impossibly long and stupid or the exact opposite. If the latter, you can only be warned that every extra pound you carry in your pack will be like lugging around dumb-bells. Don't be tempted to put in too much else. If you are, try and dispense with some other item. For instance, if you see the necessity for an extra shirt, try and *not* see the necessity for the sandals.

Reading matter is something I was trapped into taking on my first hitch-trip. I figured I'd have plenty of time to catch up on some stuff I wanted to read and took six paperbacks. Well, I had plenty of time all right – on some Portuguese back-roads – but I never got around to reading three of the titles because I'd given them away after the first day. Plus I was wishing to God I'd left half my clothes home and had managed to subdue my camera-bug to the extent where I was carrying a Kodak Instamatic instead of the heavy SLR I use.

(One item I *do* carry, mainly because it dispenses with several others, is a Swiss army knife. They are advertised as pocket workshops and it is an accurate description. The one I have has two blades, a screwdriver, a bottle-opener, a tin-opener, a corkscrew, a punch, a pair of scissors and a miniature wood saw which is strong and sharp enough to cut small branches for campfire kindling. I've lost count of the number of things I've managed to do with it when I've been on the road. There's a super *de luxe* version, incidentally, which even has a pair of tweezers and a plastic toothpick.)

Best rule is to pack only what you absolutely need and then get ruthless and dispense with 20 per cent of it. Remember that you'll probably pick up odd bits and pieces to take home and you'll need room in the pack for them – and the strength to carry them.

The tougher you are before you set out, the more you're going to like yourself when you're slap bang in the middle of what you just know is going to be a rideless day. One of those days when the only place you're about to go is where you get around to walking to!

Hitchers' tips and comments

If your budget stretches to it try 'Sportsman's blankets' (sometimes called 'Space blankets'). Indestructible, lightweight, plastic-backed foil sheets that reflect body heat and have many uses; blanket, poncho, windbreak, ground sheet. Around £5 and worth it! Also, when on long stretches in the backwoods, a water bottle is worth its weight in gold.
Kelley and Gail, Muswell Hill, London

I travelled with a friend five months and spent only $550. Big money saver was our two-man tent. Weighs only 3½ pounds and worth the effort of carrying. We spent most nights kipped down free and were worried only once.
Chris Klehm, Allison Park, Pa, USA

A few things I think a traveller should carry, but which you don't mention: International Driver's Licence, so you can help out drivers on long hauls; mini-radio, which can help conquer boredom on the road; clothes-washing materials, like a small ball of plastic string and a couple of pegs.
Daniel Kidren, Henzligger, Israel

For cheap, comfortable sleeping, try a hammock. A light nylon job costs about £6. Do it in style, lads!
B. J. Brock, East St Kilda, Victoria, Australia

Useful addition to the *Guide*'s list might be: A light plastic water bottle; one pair of woollen gloves – it gets damn cold in Switzerland even in September – a luxury well worth including; large felt pen marker for quick easy destination placards; assorted tupperware food containers (tops double as plates); plus if you live in the UK as much cheap food as you can carry – it will save pounds in the first week on the Continent.
John Hoad, Eastbourne, England

5 How to survive

FOOD. If you're down and out for food, remember that the cheapest buys are always in the markets. In-season fruit will never cost you more than 5p (10 cents) apiece and if you're that broke you can find bruised pieces which the stall-holders will probably give you. Also check the floors where you can often find edible wastage. Just cut out the bad sections and give what's left a wash under running water and you're all right.

Chinese restaurants – and just about every city in Europe has them – always serve plain boiled rice. Not the tastiest of dishes, but at 20–25p (40–50 cents) a bowl it's cheap, and if you splatter it liberally with the free soy sauce you can get it down.

Every country in Europe knows about potato chips. A big plate of these – and make it obvious that you need them! – won't cost more than 25p (50 cents) and they'll hold you together until you can figure something out.

Salvation Army and other religious organizations often have free soup kitchens. To locate them ask fellow hitchers or, in an emergency, ask the police. Don't free-load on them! Only use them if you have no alternative.

Bananas, apart from being nutritious, are about the most filling item weight-for-weight that you can buy. Two bananas and a small loaf of bread will keep you going all day. Cost? Around 25p (50 cents).

In country areas, try the old tramp trick. Approach farmers or house-owners, explain the problem as best you can and offer to do an hour's work for a good feed. You'll get a lot of knock-backs, but there are enough good people around to agree to such a simple bargain.

When you're a long way from home and the money's getting low you nearly always have to start cooking for yourself. This is not so bad if you balance your diet – though the whole deal tends to get a little boring after a while. I find that in such emergencies it's possible to eat fairly well for 60p ($1.20) a day, by eating only one meal and watching what I buy. The following list is an example of the type of hot, nutritious meal you can prepare:

Couple of potatoes (bake them in the campfire ashes)
Couple of eggs (boil them in a tin can)
One or two sausages (barbecue them on the end of a stick or piece of wire)

Loaf of bread (toast it)
Couple of pieces of fruit
 (try stewed apple or mashed banana on toast)
Coffee (boil water in tin can)

The two basic condiments you need to make a meal worth eating are sugar and salt. Salt is cheap anywhere, sugar not so cheap. Don't be afraid to go into a shop and ask for only 100 grammes of sugar. It's enough to last half a dozen cups of coffee.

Fire-making isn't hard. The 'pyramid' type fire is the easiest. You put small sticks and any old paper you can find in the middle and then build larger sticks in a pyramid shape over them, making sure you leave plenty of room for the fire to breathe. Try and put a low wall of large rocks on the down-wind side of the fire – it reflects heat back into the fire and it's something of a safety measure. Always, of course, cover the fireplace with dirt and trample on it before you leave.

SLEEPING. If you're a hole-in-the-wall or hostel hitcher you'll have a sleeping bag with you. You must have one to sleep out in Europe. The nights can get chilly even in summer.

Sleeping out on good nights is no problem. You just sack down. Rainy nights are when you're in trouble and want to head for the nearest hotel or hostel. But if you have no money, what do you do?

In the country
If you're carrying a tent you can hole up in that, but if you haven't you must start improvising. Plastic wrapping material is the stuff – if you can find enough of it. You need enough to cover your sleeping-bag completely and it has to be broad enough so that with the aid of a stick you can erect a miniature tent over your head.

You can sleep in the rain just with a ground-sheet and sleeping bag, but even waterproof bags (unless they are very expensive models) tend to forget their maker's claims and sog up. Two nights of rain spells the ruin of most bags unless you have the chance to dry them out properly.

If you don't have a tent, then your choice of action is limited. Bridges and culverts are good bets. Animal shelters in the fields are OK if you can get one to yourself without the company of a cow. Failing that, approach a farmer for permission to sleep in one of his out-buildings. Some will let you, some won't. (Southern Ireland is the place for that. I know many hitchers who have not only been given permission to sleep in the hayloft, but have been supplied with blankets *plus* breakfast the next morning!)

In the city

In towns and cities you have more chance of finding a dry place to sleep. There are railway stations, which are nearly always impossible to sleep in, but which at least are warm and where also, more often than not, you meet other people to talk to. (Of course, if you haven't got a ticket for a train departing the next day you stand a good chance of being booted right back into the cold, cold night, but with luck you'll get by.) There are churches (particularly in France) which are sometimes left open. There are sites with half-constructed buildings which offer superb shelter (and the occasional watch-dog to keep you on your toes). There are street foyers to large office buildings where you can at least find a corner in which to squat out of the wind. There are Salvation Army type relief places, the addresses of which you can get from fellow hitchers or from the police. And finally, particularly in smaller towns or city suburbs where the police are more easy going, you can always beg the loan of a cell for the night. It's been done before, though for me that'd be the absolute last resort!

Warning! Sleeping out alone in cities is getting dangerous. (See Hugh Darlington's and Clive Gill's letters at the end of this chapter.) There are too many stories like this in the pipeline for it to be a joke. It's happening all the time. And it's not just things getting stolen. There's often violence involved and I've met more than one girl who has either been raped or just managed to fight her way out.

Sometimes, because of the money problem, you just have to sleep out, so what to do?

Ideally get with a group of people so that thieves will think twice about trying to sneak up to the camp. If you have to sleep alone, conceal yourself as well as you can (you should, anyway, to avoid visits from police, park guards and night-watchmen). Always keep your passport, papers, money and travellers' cheques on your person, or at least in your sleeping-bag. Finally, if you're by yourself, keep a dirty great stick handy by your sleeping-bag.

If you're ever attacked – be it at night, as the result of a ride you've hitched, in a bar, anywhere – remember that the surest way of saving your skin is to run like hell and forget all about being a hero.

If you're cornered and you have to fight, fight dirty. Anyone who is attacking you will presumably have no hesitation in laying you out and you have to fight on those terms. Unless you're a trained boxer or at least a brown belt judo man, forget all about fancy holds and upper-cuts. Only experts can defend themselves scientifically. Fight like an animal and *get out* of the vicinity.

If you are attacked by several opponents and can't escape you've got big problems on your hands. Safest thing is to give them everything you've got. That way you *might* save yourself a beating up. If you're convinced they're going to bash you even if you hand over your stuff, or if you decide to give it a go, the odds of you winning are slim. But with considerable luck you might be able to break through them and get room to run (and if you've got your money and passport on your person the loss of your pack isn't so important).

If you go down and you know there's no way you can get up again all that's left is to save yourself from as much damage as you can. Lie on your belly to protect your crutch and get your arms up to protect your head. That leaves your kidneys and back exposed, but there's nothing else you can do; except play dead.

And, of course, during the brawl – whether you're fighting one man or five – scream at the top of your voice for help. You *might* get some.

MEDICAL. The worst thing that can happen on the road is that you might get ill. If you're moving with someone, it isn't so bad – you've got moral support. But just one day alone on the road when you're physically ill can be hell. You feel like you're never going to make your destination.

The only thing you can do is keep moving and if it's some ordinary little thing which any doctor can fix, stop off at the nearest village, search around and find someone who can speak your language (bars and cafés or the police station) and enlist their aid to help you out. If you find you can't pay the doctor, all you can do is give him your name and address and promise him that you'll send him the money when you have some. If he won't buy that you might have to give him something as collateral. Give him anything except your passport! Most doctors, though, like most people, aren't going to strike a rotten bargain if they see you can't pay.

APPENDICITIS is one of the most dangerous things that can hit you while you're on the road. If it should happen when you're in a city, present yourself to the nearest tourist information office and convince them to take it over from there. (Play it sicker than you are if you have to, because they'll be able to get you to a decent hospital faster than you can yourself.) If you're out in the country, get yourself to the nearest town or village and let the police take over. Wherever you are, the best rule for something as serious as appendicitis is to somehow put yourself into the hands of a person or organization that has the facilities to act for you while you rest. If you can get straight to a hospital, well and good, but they usually take some time to locate and it is important that you should move as little as possible. The effort you'll put into flagging down a ride, if you're on the road, is going to take all the strength you can afford.

A SPRAINED ANKLE is something which can quite easily happen to you on the road. What you must do is bind it tightly and keep off it as much as possible. It may mean holing up in a hostel or somewhere for a few days. While resting you can bathe it in hot water. If you even vaguely suspect it might be more than a sprain, hobble along to the nearest chemist and let him take a look. That way you get a qualified opinion for nothing. If he thinks it is something more serious, *then* you can spend money at the doctor.

Remember that whatever you think you might have, providing it's not obviously serious, a chemist can give you an opinion and prescribe simple drugs and medicines much cheaper than a doctor will.

DIARRHOEA is something which will get just about every hitcher if he stays on the road long enough or does enough trips. For that reason I always carry a couple of dozen tablets which a doctor friend once prescribed for me. They are the sort of tablet you take *after* you get the attack. There are other prescriptions you can take to fortify your intestines *before* you go into an area (like Morocco or Turkey) where you might pick up a bug. Talk to a chemist before you start on your trip. Take something with you – it's worth the effort.

If, however, you are on the road and are suddenly stricken there's nothing you can do but wait it out. Eat as little as possible – dry biscuits and black tea without sugar seem OK – and rest.

(A friend of mine once got an attack in Algeria. He was in the middle of nowhere and he reckons he was in a bad way. He had no paper except one book which he hadn't read. He tells of sitting on the side of the road, frantically reading page after page so he'd have a back-log of paper to see him through his next attack. The book? Richard Aldington's *Death of a Hero*.)

If you're convinced your stomach will give out when you hit the wilder regions there are a couple of things you can do to lessen the chances of complete tragedy . . . Don't drink tap water but stick to bottled drinks like local mineral water, beer or Coca-Cola. Don't eat uncooked vegetables and only eat fruit which you peel, like oranges and bananas. (Human dung is used as fertilizer in some Arab and Eastern countries.) Eat only meat which is well-cooked. (Long cooking won't save you if the meat is bad before it's cooked, but at least it'll destroy any lurking kitchen germs.)

TOOTHACHE, of all the things you can get on the road, is probably the least dangerous and yet the hardest to put up with. The methods of holding the pain down while you get yourself to a dentist are legion. My favourite is to get a bottle of whisky or cognac and to hold mouthfuls of the stuff over the offending tooth. Each mouthful usually holds the pain down for five minutes or more. It's a nice way of handling the problem if you can afford the luxury, and after a couple of hours you're so pissed you don't give a damn about anything anyway. Mouthfuls of cold water held over the tooth sometimes help for very brief periods of time. The only cure is to get the tooth removed or filled as soon as possible. All you can do is stay sane until you reach a dentist.

SELLING BLOOD. Blood is one thing that everyone has and which plenty of people need and in several areas in Europe it is possible to sell it at rates which vary from £1.50–£4.80 ($3.00–$9.60) a half-litre (about a pint). The biggest markets are, at the moment, in Greece, Turkey and Spain. Whether they will remain the markets is another question. Information on which countries and which hospitals in those countries are buying can always be picked up on the road from other hitchers and in youth hostels. The facts are continually changing so I am not listing any places here.

The idea of selling rather than giving blood may be repugnant to plenty of people and I agree, but this chapter is to do with survival, and selling your blood is a more honourable way of making a dollar than some others I can think of.

If you decide you have to hawk your blood, keep a very close watch on what is happening to you, particularly if you're in some out-of-the-way type country and some backwoods hospital. Check, for instance, that the needle is clean and make sure they don't take more than half a litre from you. When you leave the hospital go and sit in a café or bar and have a coffee and something to eat and generally relax for half an hour. *And don't, under any circumstances, give blood more than once a month!*

SELLING AND PAWNING OTHER THINGS. It's remarkable the number of people you meet on the road who will moan, 'Christ, man, I'm stoney broke.' And sitting on their wrist is a £25 watch. It reminds you of the motorist who dies of thirst in the desert because he forgets to moisten his lips from the water in his car radiator.

Most big cities have pawn shops and even if you can't find one there are plenty of other shops which will buy your gear. Sleeping-bags, tents, cameras, watches, wallets, rings, even haversacks (bundle your stuff into something else) are all items which are easy to sell, although you'll only get a fraction of what you paid for them. Youth hostels are great places to unload tents and sleeping-bags to people looking for a bargain. You'll also get a better price there than you will from a shop or outdoor market.

(At outdoor markets set up your own pavement stall – but be ready to scoot when the inspector comes and make sure you don't set up on a local's pitch.)

In effect, you're never really down and out until you're down to the clothes on your back and your boots. And a good pair of boots are worth a few dollars to anyone!

Survival is purely a matter of common-sense and imagination. Use both and there's no great problem.

★**Money belts:** When you're on the road you can afford to lose everything except your passport, money and any return tickets you've got. You should always keep those three items on your person wherever you go. Good way to do this is to buy one of those old-fashioned money-belts, or make one from light canvas or suede. A cheaper alternative is to sew a deep pocket onto the *inside* of your trousers. If you do that just make sure you don't move too far away from your trousers.

Hitchers' tips and comments

Re your invitation to offer information . . . The buy of my life has been a small gas burner for £2 ($4.00) in Paris. They're light, compact and fool-proof. Refills are cheap and give you a good week's cooking. A pan and a plate and you're set for a feed anywhere. If you can take the weight, a kilo of spuds and onions doesn't go astray either.

· Here's a good recipe. Vegetable stew. Use a packet soup for a base, boil up spuds, onions, carrots, salami – anything that looks a fair thing – and eat with plenty of bread. It's not the best eating in the world but it's a lot better than starving to death and I've had some nights that have changed my life sitting around that burner in cheap pensions with a bit of good company. (Find a freak with another burner and you're getting into a two-course feed!)
Frank Scahill, Punchbowl, Australia

Dear Sir: Stuff the *Hitch-hiker's Guide to Europe*. I've had three copies ripped off in hostels in as many months!
Peter Lane, London

Don't leave cameras, radios, etc, in hostel rooms. My mini-radio was lifted in Rome. Check them in at desk.
Mike Feeney, Haslow, England

It's worth a mention that people who wear glasses should always carry a spare pair with them.

Also, the cheapest boots anywhere are to be found in Czechoslovakia and Yugoslavia.

Dave Williams, Birmingham, England
It's probably worth carrying your optician's prescription with you, too. K.W.

You have plenty of instructions on how to keep dry – plastic bags, etc, but have made no mention about protection from the sun. Sunburn can be one of the most distressing and painful afflictions to affect the hitcher. So how about a hat and sun glasses and a light, plastic tube of barrier cream?

And how about a packet of vitamin pills to keep the pecker up when food is scarce?

Dr Ivy Garnham, Salisbury, Rhodesia

Lomotil pills are the best cure for diarrhoea.

Unsigned, South Kensington, London

Watch out for National Holidays all over Europe. You can get stuck without bread because you can't cash your travellers' cheques nor pawn things. You can change money at the big hotels, but the rates are a bloody rip-off.

Last summer I took along a tube of Steratabs, which are water sterilizing tablets. They come 200 for 50p and also seem to have a gut reinforcing effect after a couple of weeks' use. (Very handy in North Africa.)

Definitely forget about dossing out in a big Spanish town. I got a truncheon in the ribs one night. Stations, subways, everything is patrolled. If you sleep sitting upright on a park bench you're OK (preferably with your eyes open!) Watch out for the 5 a.m. high-pressure street hosing all over Europe.

Clive Gill, Birchington, England

If you need food really bad, pick a big and busy self-service place. Join the line and just buy a cup of coffee. When you pass the cash register pick a table where three or four people have just left after a big meal, sit down and get stuck into their left-overs.

Paul Rush, San Francisco, USA

I write as a fellow traveller who has found the *Hitch-hiker's Guide* most useful. I did, however, come unstuck and will give you a brief account of my fortune and misfortune.

I left England with the intention of hitching to Istanbul and then taking the overland route through the East to Australia. My second lift landed me in Paris for two days and then I made a château near Orleans where I stayed for a further seventeen days. I hitched in Spain for a couple of weeks and then back to Marseilles and asked at the dock about a boat for Italy and was immediately put in touch with a guy delivering a brand new yacht to Genoa – three days on the Med with all expenses paid!

I finally ended up in Rome (after Venice), having spent six fantastic weeks travelling on a minimum budget, having met the kindest and most generous people imaginable. I then referred to your book and headed for the Borghese Gardens where I crashed out in my sleeping bag for free. I woke at four in the morning to find my pack had been stolen. It contained my entire kit, including my addresses, diary, maps, books and all the hints I had collected from people *en route*. Also my contact lenses and worst of all . . . my *trousers*! Fortunately I had my wallet and travellers' cheques in my sleeping bag and my passport and papers in a bag around my neck.

I met a Belgian a couple of days later who, in the same park, had been forced to hand over his pack to a bunch of thugs on the threat of his life.

I ask you to suggest that people don't crash out alone in Italian parks!
Hugh Darlington, Oxford, England
PS My copy of the *Hitcher's Guide* was in the bag. Got a spare one?

You can sell blood at an average $12 for half a litre at the Blood Research Centre, 32 Ioulianou Street, Athens (Tel: 821 575). Open Monday to Saturday, 8 a.m. to 8 p.m.

If you need to sell anything go to American Express on Constitution Square. Lots of people there.

If you cross by ferry from Italy to Greece, buy American cigarettes to sell when you arrive. You can make a profit.
Molly Bounds, Decatur, USA

Check out coin return slots. Telephones are an obvious place, but also in the endless banks of automatic lockers in airline terminals. Best place to panhandle is at an International Airport. Hit US tourists returning home for the odd foreign coins they got stuck with and couldn't change back into dollars.
Len Tower, Bay Shore, New York

Great places for sleeping rough are football stadiums and sports grounds. They are usually easy to enter and it's not necessary to be up and away too early in the morning. I've also had good kips in grounds beside open-air swimming pools. For late autumn and winter when nights are freezing try underground car parks (easy once you slip by the attendant) and under the stairs in foyers of office and apartment blocks.
Danny Long, Saffron Walden, Essex, England

I sold some blood in Spain (for 1,000 pesetas), but if you have any North African stamps in your passport it's no deal.

I always buy plenty of packet soup before leaving on a big hitch. Mixed with macaroni or rice it really sticks to the ribs. Follow that with bread and cheese and coffee and you can tackle Mt Everest!
Dennis Chubb, Bletchley, England

If you're stuck in coastal towns on the Continent and can't find the price of a hotel, try the Missions to Seamen. These are really for seamen, but most of the padres in charge are kind-hearted blokes and many let you kip on a couch in the TV lounge.
J. P. Ridley, Falkirk, Scotland

If you are crashing out (roughing it) take something (cream ointment?) for the mosquito bites – 'cause whatever you do these crazy goddam creatures'll get you.
Capt'n Clem, Bristol, England

In cold weather try the old tramp trick of keeping warm by putting two thicknesses of old newspaper between your shirt and jumper.
C. J. Major, Cambridge, England

Easy money: Collect empty coke bottles from dirt bins or especially along beaches and claim the deposit. I know someone who kept himself for six weeks in Torremolinos, Spain, this way.
Lesley Kountaff, South Africa

One of the most useful items I packed was some fishing tackle. Just some line, a few hooks and float, nice way of passing time on any coastline, lake or river in Europe. Camping rough it provides food or even passes an afternoon's pleasure waiting for a ferry ride somewhere.

For those who get their *Hitcher's Guide* ripped off – try a plain paper cover!
Marcel Thomas, Horndean, England

Selling blood in Greece, you've got to be over 21 – they check your passport for all particulars.
Dave Martill, Leicester, England

Spain is still good for selling blood, but you must weigh over 55 kg otherwise they won't take it.
Unsigned

A few lines to all would-be travellers going camping or hiking abroad. To

cover you for medical care write to your local Social Security for an E111.
This is an exemption form for medical costs abroad.
Miss E. Reed, Peterborough, England
*I understand that Britons carrying this form in EEC countries don't have to
pay for medical services. Brits should check at their Social Security
Office. K.W.*

One thing you don't seem to mention is travel insurance. Luggage, money,
medical and personal accident can all be covered with a good company
very cheaply.
S. Derrick, Southampton, England

Appearance: I try to save a clean shirt (at least) for the journey home and
keep my face, hands and nails clean if I'm broke. Then I *look* OK even if I
stink.
Bernard Jennings, Brisbane, Australia

For toothache: Even better than booze is a packet of dried cloves available
from most chemists or health food shops. Just let them dissolve over the
offending tooth and the ache vanishes. Warning: don't chew them or
have more than two at a time, unless you want a hole burnt in your throat.
Simon Barry, Isle of Man, GB

What I've often resorted to (e.g. hitched from Athens to Luxembourg City
with *no* negotiable money) is going into bakeries in the morning and asking
for yesterday's leftovers. Often got a fresh loaf; often got yesterday's
pastries. Was rarely refused totally.
Roger Brown, author of Travellers Survival Kit Europe (Published by
Vacation-Work, Oxford)
Roger: Great book! K.W.

Stay clear of Persian drivers if possible – we crashed outside Munich after
several heart attacks. They are far worse than the Belgians.
Jonah, Neath, South Wales, GB

I had all my luggage ripped off from a *locked* left-luggage locker in Gare
du Nord, Paris – on the last day luckily. Fortunately it was insured and
I've been able to replace it all with better stuff – except the photos which
are the only thing I regret losing.
Dave, Southampton, England

Your advice about knocking on farm doors for food works. I did that in
Germany, after being dropped off on an autobahn, and even though they

didn't speak English and I don't speak German, I got food and blankets for the night.

Alan Smith, Sunderland, England

If you do this, remember to offer to do an hour or so's work the next day. It keeps the image up. K.W.

If you need tomato sauce or mustard for home cooking visit self-service restaurants with a plastic bag.

Thrifty, Israel

Plainclothes cops dressed like freaks mix in cafés, bars and discos all over Europe whenever city fathers decide to do a 'clean-up'. They're after smokers and other 'undesirables'. Watch it!

J.D., Notting Hill, London

6 The British Isles and Ireland

Most Australians and North Americans use England as the base for their European trip for one of two reasons – one sound and the other unfashionable. The sound one is that if you can get the correct papers (see chapter on *Working in Europe*) you have more chance of working in England than in any other European country. The second reason, the unfashionable one, is that England remains in a manner of speaking the object of an Oedipus complex. It's the Motherland and even if most of her sons have long since left, via means of secession, revolution and diplomacy or have just wandered off disinterested, she still offers the solution to the most puzzling question of all: where did our families come from?

Plenty of people find the answer a little disappointing. The tiny island crammed with over 55,000,000 people is hardly the green field of yesteryear which grandmothers and grandfathers back in the old ex-colonies talk about so fondly. England can present a mean face. Many of her people rarely see whatever green fields are left because they can't afford the train fare. Her gasping cities are grimed and blackened by industry. Too many Britons are literally fighting for survival midst over-population. It's not unusual to find city children who have never seen a cow, much less the cow in its green field. And that sad observation is, of course, as true of New York as it is of London.

But have no fears. London is a great city and a load of fun, even if it never did swing with quite the momentum *Time Magazine* would have liked to believe, or if Antonioni's *Blow-Up* turned out to be as much a blueprint for London to fashion itself by as London ever was a set for a movie. But it's all fun if you can enter into London's idea of fun which, along with its discotheques and cinema clubs and thousand life-styles is also the place where you try and convince yourself that your 10×10, dirty-floored bed-sit is the next best thing to a palace (in London it is, unless Daddy is supplying you with a nice fat allowance each week); and that the solid wall of bus, lorry, car and train fumes which you breathe is as healthy as the next cubic mile of poison. And not to mention the noise. Take a walk in Hyde Park one day, around midday. Stroll a hundred yards in from Park Lane and stop amongst the green silence and listen to the dragon of sound flowing around beyond you.

But when you finally leave the big city, there *are* places you can go on that

1. N.W. Highlands
2. Grampians
3. Southern Uplands
4. Cheviots
5. Pennines
6. Cambrian Mountains
7. Cotswolds
8. Dartmoor
9. Mourne Mountains
10. Wicklow Mountains

John O'Groats
Thurso
Ullapool
Gairloch
L. Maree
SCOTLAND
Inverness
Loch Ness
ATLANTIC
OCEAN
Balmoral
Fort William
Braemar
Mallaig
Ben Nevis
NORTH
SEA
Glen Coe
Dundee
Loch Lomond
Crieff
Glasgow
Stirling
Clyde
Edinburgh
Abbotsford
Ayr
Melrose
Alloway
Selkirk
Jedburgh
Dumfries
Carter Bar
Hadrians Wall
Londonderry
Stranraer
Carlisle
Donegal
Carrick Fergus
Larne
Keswick
N. IRELAND
Belfast
Lake Windermere
Sligo
Haworth
IRISH
SEA
Blackpool
Manchester
Grimsby
Galway
Liffey
Dublin
Conway
Liverpool
EIRE
Caernarvon
Bangor
Chester
Humber
Limerick
Kilkenny
Harlech
Nottingham
Adare
Cashel
Birmingham
ENGLAND
Tralee
Clonmel
WALES
Kenilworth
Warwick
Killarney
Aberystwyth
Stratford-upon-Avon
Blarney
Cork
Cardigan
Abergavenny
Severn
Stow-on-the-Wold
St. David's
Oxford
Thames
London
Carmarthen
Monmouth
Windsor
Cardiff
Bristol
Westerham
Canterbury
Bath
Amesbury
Dover
Stonehenge
Winchester
Battle
Salisbury
Hastings
Chichester
Brighton
Portsmouth
Lands End
CHANNEL ISLANDS
FRANCE

0   50   100 Miles
0   50   100 km

tiny island. One of them is northern Scotland, way up in the damp
Highlands where you can walk for hours and never see a person and
where the only noise is that of continually falling rain – clean rain – and
where the smell is of pure air and not of nearly pure carbon-monoxide.

And then, just a little way across the water is Ireland, especially
southern Ireland where the people are just a fraction wild and where the
landscape is a fraction wilder, and nearly as beautiful as the people.
Southern Ireland, like northern Scotland, is a place you can absorb, which
you can let run over and into you – not like the North in England
where even though you may be living it up and enjoying yourself you have
to keep it all at arms' distance in case it kills you with an overdose of
claustrophobia.

But don't get me wrong. Dirty, cancerous, black-faced London is one of
the most exciting and one of the greatest cities in the world and you may
find that the diminishing green countryside of which it is capital harbours
more than a handful of memories for you.

England

Population	46,000,000
Size	50,332 square miles
Capital	London, population 7,212,000
Government	Constitutional Monarchy
Religion	Protestant Episcopal
Language	English, with very little of anything else spoken or understood

England is stacked with sights to see. But where to start ? From London, a
trip into the South and South-East is a great introduction to Britain. Some
twenty miles south of the capital is the town of **Westerham** and near it is
Chartwell, the country home of the late Sir Winston Churchill (open March
to October) where you can see a collection of the statesman's paintings, the
study where he wrote many of his books, and amongst many other things,
the famous wall which he built with his own hands and which looks exactly
like a wall.

Heading farther south is the village of **Battle**, one of the crucial
landmarks of English history, for it was here that in 1066 the Battle of
Hastings was fought. An Abbey was built on the site by William the
Conqueror after the conflict.

Canterbury, on the A2 if you're heading to Dover on your way to the

Continent, is worth a stopover for its Cathedral. It's a classic and famous as the scene of Thomas à Becket's assassination in 1170. The city's worth a look, too.

Heading west along the coast through **Rye, Winchelsea** and **Hastings,** and then along the South Downs through **Brighton** (one of England's most popular seaside resorts), you eventually come to the old walled cathedral city of **Chichester.** Next is **Portsmouth** where, in the naval dockyards, you can see Nelson's flagship the *Victory* in dry-dock. You can board the 180-year-old ship and look over all its decks. Also in Portsmouth is the house in which Charles Dickens was born.

A little to the north is **Winchester,** ancient capital of Saxon England and famed for its superb Norman Cathedral.

Salisbury is yet another city with an outstanding Cathedral. It and the Close which sit on the River Avon make for one of the most often painted and photographed scenes in all the British Isles. By following the pretty road through Woodford, along the Avon, you join the A303 at **Amesbury** and you're within a couple of miles of **Stonehenge,** the mysterious stone circle possibly connected with the Druids of Ancient Britain. Also in this area (if you have spare cash for the admission fee) is **Longleat,** home of the Marquess of Bath, yet another titled gent of England who has to make ends meet by turning his family seat into a profit machine. The Marquess does it by having lions and other wild animals roaming in his grounds.

Hitching farther west from here takes you into Devon and Cornwall, two of England's most beautiful counties. Devon is renowned for its rolling countryside (Dartmoor and Exmoor), sunken lanes, tiny fields, red soil, and its quaint sea ports on both north and south coasts. Cornwall has an even grander coastline on the north, stormswept by the Atlantic, and a more peaceful but equally lovely sub-tropical south coast.

Whilst in the West Country, do not miss **Bristol,** England's greatest medieval port, with its wealth of history and interest. And see **Bath,** with its Georgian architecture and Roman baths, a city renowned for its spa where you can take the piping hot natural waters.

Starting from London again, you can head out to **Windsor** with its huge castle which is still used by the British Royal Family (you can wander in the grounds and the castle when the Royal Family are not in residence) and nearby **Eton** – where there is a school on whose playing-fields (some people would like to believe!) the battle of Waterloo was won.

Fifty miles north on the A10 you reach **Cambridge** – named from a bridge which crossed the River Cam in ancient days – and since the 13th century one of England's great seats of learning. Peterhouse College was founded in 1284. Prominent Britons who were educated at Cambridge included Newton, Darwin, Macauley, Milton and Byron. See Kings College Chapel and, just beyond, a classic English scene, green slopes leading down to the River Cam where punters drift in peaceful waters.

About 85 miles south-west sits another of England's great educational institutions and Cambridge's famous rival, **Oxford**, which has been a student centre since the twelfth century. Have a look at Magdalen College and Merton College (founded in 1264), walk down the High Street (so *very* English), see Christ Church which was founded by Cardinal Wolsey and try and get in to see the very important Bodleian Library which contains 3,000,000 volumes and 50,000 manuscripts.

Continuing north on the A34 you are skirting the **Cotswolds**. Short detours will take you through quaint villages with such outlandish names as **Stow-on-the-Wold, Chipping Norton,** and **Shipton-under-Wychwood,** until you finally reach **Stratford-upon-Avon** – Shakespeare country.

In the town (if you can fight your way through the busloads of tourists) you can see Shakespeare's birthplace, Anne Hathaway's Cottage (she was the playwright's wife), Hall's Croft where Shakespeare's daughter lived, and three miles out of town is Mary Arden's House – she having been his mother. All of these places are worth seeing if you're at all interested in Shakespeare or Elizabethan architecture. Two other places to visit are Holy Trinity Church where the man was baptized and where he is buried and the Royal Shakespeare Theatre where from March to November performances of his plays are held. Booking is usually well in advance if any well-known actor like Paul Scofield is playing. To be thoroughly English in Stratford, try hiring a punt and poling yourself around the river for an hour or two.

Just eight miles north of Stratford is **Warwick** with the huge Warwick Castle which, though expensive, is in my opinion well worth the visit. And five miles farther north is **Kenilworth** with the ruins of the castle which Sir Walter Scott wrote about. The jousting grounds outside the walls make a nice camping area if you're at all romantically inclined.

From Kenilworth you are on the way to **Worcester** and **Hereford** and the remote and unspoiled Welsh Border country.

But you may prefer cities and their associations, in which case from Kenilworth you move on through **Coventry** by way of the A447 to **Nottingham,** the city around which the legendary Robin Hood is said to have operated. There's scarcely anything left of Sherwood Forest these days, but if you care to travel out to **Edwinstowe** you can see the church where they say Robin married the Maid Marian. Nottingham Castle, from where the Sheriff hatched his plans against Robin, is now a museum and art gallery. Two of England's oldest public inns are in Nottingham – the Trip to Jerusalem (twelfth century) and the Salutation Inn (thirteenth century). Those interested in theatre should have a look at what is becoming one of England's best, the Nottingham Playhouse.

Liverpool, of course, is the home of the Beatles and it's also the home of close on a million other Liverpudlians. Have a look at the Royal Liver Building, the newly completed Anglican Cathedral, the fantastic futuristic Roman Catholic Cathedral and the Walker Art Gallery.

South of Liverpool is Chester, a great town for a whiff of the Middle Ages. Two miles of walls enclose the city and its streets are riddled with architectural leftovers from medieval times. The city was known to the Romans as Deva and in the Grosvenor Museum is an excellent collection of Roman artifacts. The Chester Zoo is famous for its pachyderms.

North of Liverpool is Blackpool which is the English working-man's idea of a Good Time. It's full of holidaying Mums and Dads and associated brats and in its own neon-lit, garish way is quite fascinating.

From Chester via Manchester, you reach the Yorkshire Dales, and Haworth, near Keighley, on the edge of the moors, where the extraordinary Misses Brontë lived and wrote *Jane Eyre* and *Wuthering Heights*.

To the east lies York, which embraces nearly twenty centuries of history, and remains England's most medieval looking city. Four gates still open through the three miles of Roman walls which girdle the city. Visit the incredible York Minster which took 250 years to build and still dominates the city. Don't miss the 2,500 square feet of stained glass which comprise the Great East Window. Photographers will love the lurching buildings in streets with names like Whip-ma-Whop-ma-Gate, the Shambles and Goodramgate. See also the Castle Folk Museum, housed in an old prison which features reconstructions of York streets, and The National Railway Museum where you can board The City of Truro, the first 100 mph train in England.

North West again and you're in the English Lake District, a spectacular and beautiful area, very easy to take after the smog and bustle of the great industrial cities of the Midlands. Here there is a lot to see in a small space and if you are an English literature fan a trip along the A591 will take you by Lake Windermere and along to the tiny village of Grasmere. It was here that William Wordsworth lived for many years in Dove Cottage which is now the Wordsworth Museum. The poet is buried in the Grasmere

churchyard. After Wordsworth moved out of Dove Cottage, Thomas
de Quincey (*Confessions of an Opium-eater*) – perhaps the first turned-on
Englishman – set up house there for twenty years. **Keswick,** just a dozen
miles further on, is a town in which Lamb, Keats, Shelley, Scott, Carlyle,
Tennyson and Ruskin all stayed at one time or another.

Carlisle, a city of 71,000, boasts an eleventh-century cathedral, a
museum featuring Roman remains, and a castle in which Mary, Queen of
Scots was imprisoned in 1568. From here also, you can find your way out to
Hadrian's Wall – although a better place to see it is near the village of **Wall**
just north of **Hexham** which is on the A69.

North of the Roman Wall and you've made Scotland.

★**Annual events and customs** England is a great country for celebrating
its own history and customs. It seems that just about every village and town
has some celebration some time in the year. For full details of what's
happening where and when, you'll have to check at tourist offices, but
here's a sample of the type of thing to look for: *Pancake Day Race* at **Olney,**
Buckinghamshire, on Shrove Tuesday (February). *Cheese Rolling* at
Cheltenham, Gloucestershire, in June. *Brick Throwing and Rolling-pin
Throwing Contest* at Stroud, Gloucestershire, in July (this is an international
event amongst Strouds from England, Australia, Canada, and the USA).
Shakespeare Birthday Celebrations in April and *Shakespeare Season of
Plays* at Stratford-upon-Avon, Warwickshire, from March to January.
Bottle Kicking and Hare Pie Scrambling at Hallaton, Leicestershire, at
Easter. *Manchester to Blackpool Veteran and Vintage Car Run*, in June.
Southport Music Festival at Southport, Merseyside, in September and
October. *Wassailing the Apple Trees* at Carhampton, Somerset, in January.
The Hot Penny Ceremony at Honiton, Devon, in July. *Annual Carnival and
Rolling of the Tar Barrels* in November, at Ottery St Mary, Devon. *East
Kent Morris Men Hop Hoodening Tour of Kent* in September. *Isle of Thanet
Ploughing Match* at Margate, Kent, in October. *Bonfire Celebrations* at
Lewes, East Sussex, in October. *The Appleby Horse Fair* at Appleby,
Cumbria, in June, which is a gathering of gypsies for a horse fair. *Guy
Fawkes Celebrations* all over the country in November. *Oxford v Cambridge
University Boat Race* from Putney to Mortlake every March.

★**Cigarettes** Tobacco and alcohol are tremendously expensive in England,
so if you're a smoker and you're entering the country, don't forget to
pick up your maximum quota of everything from duty-free shops on ships
or at airports. These shops will have lists posted telling how much you are
allowed to import free of tax.

★**Hitching in England** Hitching is OK except around the tremendously congested and built-up areas. It's best to clear those by bus or train – but one tip, when in big cities (and this applies all over Europe), is to go to the central markets very early in the morning, say 4 or 5 a.m., and try to pick up a ride from the scores of lorry drivers who have delivered produce. They'll be heading home in every direction. You can pick up some long, long lifts. Hitching is fast on the big highways. It's much, much slower on the small roads – and considerably more pleasant, too.

★**The Islands of the British Isles** For information write to the following addresses:

Isle of Wight Tourist Board at 21 High Street, Newport.

Orkney Islands Tourist Association Information Centre, Kirkwall.

Isle of Skye Tourist Association at Meall House, Portree, Isle of Skye.

Jersey Tourist Information Bureau, Weighbridge, St Helier.

Guernsey Information Bureau, PO Box 23, St Peter Port.

Isle of Man Tourist Board at 13 Victoria Street, Douglas.

★**Money savers** If you anticipate doing a lot of sightseeing around the British Isles it's well worth buying special passes which are available. One allows you to visit all sites administered by the Government including 'musts' like the Tower of London and Stonehenge. Another, more expensive, gains you entry to all of those plus many of the National Trust properties around the country. The Open-to-View ticket is available from the London Tourist Board at Victoria Station (near platform 15), and from the British Tourist Authority, it costs £6 and lasts one month. For full information, write to the British Tourist Office in your country.

★**Van vagabonds** If you feel like hiring some wheels for a week or two on the road, the cheapest way you can do it is by hiring a Dormobile. In fact, if you can get together with, say, four other people you can probably drive cheaper than you can hitch! You can hire a Dormobile in the low season (October to May) for around £80 per week, plus insurance and a £50 returnable deposit. Add in, say, £6 a day for petrol and you're still only up to about £125 for the week – or £25 a head. Considering that four bodies can sleep in the van (take it in turns to sleep in the annex tent) and that you can cook on the premises, it works out pretty cheap. (Of course, if you're planning on van vagabonding for more than two weeks you're better off buying a beat-up heap so you can sell it when you've finished with it and recover some of the money.) The only problem with Dormobiles is that the minimum age for insurance cover is 25, 'unless people are able to transfer their own vehicle policy to the satisfaction of the Hire Operator'. (Whatever that means.)

London: where to sleep

The great majority of hitchers, at one time or another, make their base in London. Canadians, Australians, New Zealanders, and other Commonwealth citizens will probably have ideas of working there and Americans might be considering chasing a work permit as well. For anyone staying in London for a fortnight or more the only answer is to hook up with another person and find a room in bed-sit land. (You can find singles, but doubles usually work out much cheaper per head.) Two good central areas to do this are in Notting Hill and Earl's Court – although both areas are getting more and more expensive. These areas have two advantages. One, they are within 20 minutes of just about everything and, two, they are crawling with students, travellers, and kindred souls.

Single bed-sits cost from around £10–£12 per week. Doubles start from around £14. The advantage of taking one, even for a short period of time, is that you can save a small fortune by doing your own cooking on the two-ring burners which come with the room. If you only intend staying two or three weeks, best you don't tell the landlord that. He's looking for long-term tenants. Mutter something under your breath about being in London for three or four months, or that you're studying. Work it out from there. You'll be expected to pay a week in advance and may have to put down a returnable deposit against your key and against possible damage of furniture and fittings in the room. (Seventy-five per cent of London landlords seem to think that anyone under age thirty is automatically going to destroy the entire building or, failing that, hold wild orgies and opium parties on alternate nights. They're not always wrong.)

There are two basic ways of finding a room. The cheapest is to check the notice-boards around the Earl's Court or Notting Hill Underground stations (ask anyone to tell you where the boards are located) and to note from the pinned-up cards what is being offered. Make a note of the telephone numbers and ring up to make an appointment to see the room. This costs phone money but saves a lot of time and shoe leather because many of the rooms are gone within minutes of the notice being put on the board and the void notice will stay there for days.

The second method is to go to an accommodation agency and pay them a fee to locate a room for you. The agencies advertise in newspapers or on the same notice-boards as the landlords. It'll take you longer to find the room by yourself – especially in autumn and winter because of the influx of university students – but it'll work out a few pounds cheaper. Beware of some agencies who are rip-off artists! *Time Out* magazine often runs exposés on these people.

For serious room hunting and particularly if you're going to be staying in London for any length of time, it's worth buying a copy of *The Atlas of London* published by Geographia and selling for around 90p. This 250-page book is indispensable for finding your way around the 27,000-odd streets of London and its environs. The free Underground map supplied at Tube stations is the weapon needed to tackle the more than 250 Underground stops.

The London Tourist Board at Victoria Station (near Platform 15) will supply information about hotel and student accommodation. They place bookings in student hostels, hotels, dormitories and, in the summer, in schools at prices as low as £1.75. Visit the centre in person on the day accommodation is required, or write well in advance to the London Tourist Board.

For casual beds in Youth Hostel Association hostels (you must be a member) prices are from £2.00–£2.75, with meals from 70p to £1.00. (For addresses of individual hostels, Tel: 839 1722.) Lower priced hotels are from around £4.00 per night, these prices sometimes including breakfast. A selection follows:

Holland House Youth Hostel at Holland House, Holland Park, Kensington, London W8 (Tel: 937 0748).

Youth Hostel at 38 Bolton Gardens, Earl's Court, London SW5 (Tel: 373 7083).

Youth Hostel at 86 Highgate West Hill, London N6 (Tel: 340 1831).

Youth Hostel at 36 Carlton Lane, London EC4 (Tel: 236 4965).

Salvation Army Red Shield Club for men at 66 Buckingham Gate, London SW1 (Tel: 222 1164).

Salvation Army Red Shield Club for women (and married couples) at Cambria House, 37 Hunter Street, London WC1 (Tel: 837 1654).

The Salvation Army also runs four dormitories for men only. They are very basic and very cheap, costing about £2.00 a night, and are cheaper if you stay by the week. Addresses are:

122 Spa Road, London SE16 (Tel: 237 1107).
116 Middlesex Street, London E1 (Tel: 247 1914).
18 Great Peter Street, London SW1 (Tel: 222 1546).
259 Waterloo Road, London SE1 (Tel: 928 4591).

Hopetown Dormitory at Hopetown Street, London E1 (Tel: 247 2693). This place is run by the Salvation Army. I spoke to one of the women who works there and she said that lots of readers of *Hitch-hiker's Guide* had rung up during the last two years. She turned a lot of people down – not because she didn't want to give them beds, but because a lot of her clientele are down-and-outs in pretty bad shape. But, if you still want to give it a try, the dormitory costs 80p and a private cubicle about 90p.

Youth Travel Bureau dormitories at 34 Cranley Gardens, London SW7 (Tel: 370 2842). Men only (16–26) £13 per week in dormitory (including breakfast).

Hood's House at 358 Finchley Road, London NW3 (Tel: 435 6147).

Gayfere Hostel at 8 Gayfere Street, Westminster, London SW1 (Tel: 222 6894). Students only at 222 1402. Dormitory.

Sane Guruji Hostel at 18a Holland Villas Road, London W14 (Tel: 603 3704). Dormitory. Book in advance if possible. £11 per week. No meals but cooking facilities.

YWCA and YMCA. For complete information write to YWCA, National Offices, 2 Weymouth Street, London W1N 4AX (Tel: 636 9722/6), or to YMCA, Metropolitan Region, 31 Craven Terrace, Lancaster Gate, London W2 3EL (Tel: 723 0071).
There are YWCA hostels at:
Central Club, 22 Great Russell Street, and 12–14 Endsleigh Gardens, WC1 (Tel: 636 7512).
Elizabeth House, 118 Warwick Way, SW1 (Tel: 834 0313).
Hyde House, 9 Bulstrode Street, W1M 5FS (Tel: 935 7887).
There are YMCA Hostels at:
YMCA, 112 Great Russell Street, WC1 (Tel: 637 1333).
The Barbican YMCA, Fann Street, London EC2 (Tel: 628 0697).
The German YMCA, Lancaster Hall Hotel, Craven Terrace, London W2 (Tel: 723 9276).
The Indian Student YMCA, 41 Fitzroy Square, London W1 (Tel: 387 0411).

London Central YMCA, Amalgamated Hostels, 83 Endell Street, London WC2 (Tel: 836 3201).
King George's House YMCA, Stockwell Road, London SW9 (Tel: 274 7861).

Hotel Melita at 76 Fordwych Road, NW2 (Tel: 452 1583).

Lancaster Hall Hotel at 35 Craven Terrace, W2 (Tel: 723 9276).

Deaconess Guest House at 90 Holland Road, W14 (Tel: 603 3773). Women only. It's run by Lutheran sisters, but is open to anyone of any religion. Good bargain at around £3, but big disadvantage is that it locks up at 11.30 p.m.

Howard Hotel at 64 Princes Square, W2 (Tel: 727 6062).

Mrs Garnet's Hostel at 23 Estelle Road, NW3 (Tel: 485 3734). Cheap, very nice. But also very small. Absolutely essential you ring first.

Alliance Club at Newington Green, N16 (Tel: 226 6085). Men only. Special rates by the week.

Concord House at 49–51 Leinster Square, W2 (Tel: 229 7388). Long term ladies only.

Princes Square Hotel at 23–25 Princes Square, W2 (Tel: 229 9876).

(With most of these listings costing £3.75 or over, they might seem like budget-breakers. But remember that in England most hotels give you bed *and breakfast* – which makes the pain a little easier to bear.)

The Greater London Council has a chain of about a dozen hostels for men and women. Prices are reasonable. For full information write to Director of Housing, County Hall, SE1 (Tel: 928 5000, extension 7736). Write to the International Students House, at 229 Great Portland Street, W1 (Tel: 636 9472) who have rooms at their residences in Great Portland Street and 10 York Terrace East, NW1 for around £4.00 a night.

Try Hackney Camping, Tent City, who run a camp site in the summer at very reasonable prices. For full information contact Barnaby Martin at 11 Chesmere Road, East Twickenham, Middlesex TW1 2DJ (Tel: (01) 892 3570).

For sleeping rough, there are plenty of hide-away spots in Hyde Park or Kensington Gardens. The police make checks, but these are very big parks. Also, the city is dotted with greens and churchyards (as are most big cities)

where you can kip down if you're quick enough getting out of sight
and quiet enough after you do.

London: where to eat

A good filling meal in London usually comes out at around £1.50. You get
this deal by choosing carefully at the chain restaurants. Names to look out
for are *Wimpy*, *McDonalds*, *ABC*, *Pizzaland*, *The Golden Egg*, and the lesser
known *Dino's*. But Indian restaurants – and there are plenty of them – are
without a doubt the cheapest places to eat, and they aren't plastic like
the chains. (The Indian Embassy, Bush House, Aldwych, WC2, serves rice
and curry lunches for about 90p.) An Indian meal will rarely cost you more
than £2 and that's for as much as you can eat. If you're on the cheap,
remember that you can buy plain rice dishes for 35p and you can liberally
sprinkle the rice with the free, nutritious soy sauce you usually find
on the tables.

An invaluable little book is *Fuel Food: Eating Out in London for
£2.00 and Under* (Wildwood; £1.25) by Mike Bygrave and Joan Goodman.

Following are some places which serve decent meals around £1.20
(but remember that the cost of food is rocketing every month):

The Stockpots. There are four of these around London and they offer very
good food at a very good price. Addresses are:
40 Panton Street, SW1
6 Basil Street, SW3
5a Hogarth Place, SW5
23 Lancashire Court, W1
98 King's Road, SW3 (This one is known as the Chelsea Kitchen, but is
run by the same people.)

Bedford Café, 43 Bedford Street (off Strand), WC2. Good hot meals
around £1.50.

In all big cities, wherever you find a big concentration of offices and
office workers, you find a proliferation of cheap eating spots. In London,
in these areas, you can eat as cheaply as anywhere in Europe. Examples:

F. Bennett's Fresh-Cut Sandwiches at 14 New Row, WC2. A take-away
sandwich bar.

The Market Snack Bar at 15 New Row, WC2.

Apollo Restaurant at 19 New Row, WC2, gives excellent value for money.
Right opposite is **The Regency**, a very small place and a favourite with

theatre types from the nearby New Theatre. It's a trifle more expensive, but good value.

Ye Olde Round Table in St Martin's Court (just across from New Row) and at the side of Wyndham's Theatre. Try their pub lunch.

Summit Sandwich Bar in Lisle Street, WC2 (in Soho and off Wardour Street). It's unnumbered, but beside the Falcon Pub.
At 25 Lisle Street is **Chan May Mai**. Very popular with the local Chinese. A few doors up is the **Mirama Chinese Restaurant,** also very popular with the locals.

Nelson Restaurant in Whitcomb Street, WC2, has a top-value daily special every lunchtime. The place has no number and is up on the first floor.

Restaurant Casali at 6 Maiden Lane, WC2, gives you a really good feed at a decent price.

Avery's Salad House in Hind Court (off Fleet Street, EC4) on the way up to Doctor Johnson's House.

Ludgate Sandwich Bar at 31 Pilgrim Street – just off New Bridge Street at Ludgate Circus, EC4, and on your left.

Mick's Café at 148 Fleet Street, EC4 (Open day and night). Rough and ready and *very* cheap. Opposite is

Lieto's Café at 39/40 Whitefriars Street. Simple British food so good that even the journalists use it!

On the corner of Apothecary Street and Blackfriars Lane (just off New Bridge Street) health buffs will find the **Food for Health Restaurant**. A good meal costs around £1.50 but I reckon it's worth it. The owners are authors of a book, *The Home Book of Vegetarian Cooking* (Faber and Faber), and they claim that they want to prove that vegetarian meals need not be a drag. They have a health food counter where you can buy things like live yoghurt and pure sugars, and they have another restaurant at 85 London Wall, EC2.

Other vegetarian restaurants are **Sage** at 7 Riding House Street, W1, **Cranks Salad Table** at 8 Marshall Street, W1 and **Sharuna** at 107 Great Russell Street, WC1 (which specializes in Indian-style vegetarian cooking).

The India Tea Centre on the corner of Woodstock and Oxford Streets sends you on the Big Tea Trip. Fantastic range: Darjeeling, Assam, Nilgri, Lemon, Orange, Black Cherry, Redcurrant, spiced and iced. But it's 35p a glass!

Most of the workers' tiny cafés, for instance around the side streets between Ladbroke Grove and Portobello Road, or around the Petticoat Lane area, in short, any of the poorer areas, serve reasonable meals for around £1.10. A feed of take-away fish 'n chips can be had nearly anywhere in London for 90p.

There are thousands of pubs in London and a fair proportion of them sell food of one kind or another. Some might only offer snacks like sandwiches or sausages, others put on proper hot meals. The point is that pub food offers one of the best deals to be had in London. Check with people in your area for the pubs which offer the best value for money.

If you take a bed-sit and decide to do your own cooking, one of the cheapest places to buy supplies is at any of the *Tesco* branches. They buy in bulk and sell under their own brand-name and don't advertise so heavily. Consequently, many items are a little cheaper than anywhere else.

London: what to see and do

TOWER OF LONDON at Tower Hill. Entrance charge. Great if you're a history fan. Ten centuries of England staring you right in the face. See the Crown Jewels (extra charge), the Armoury, the rooms where Raleigh was imprisoned, site of the old chopping block, and lots more.

THE MONUMENT in Monument Street. Cheapest way to get a good view of London. The column, which is 202 feet high and was erected the same number of feet from where the Great Fire of London started in Pudding Lane in 1666, was designed by Wren. You can climb to the top for a small fee.

ST PAUL'S CATHEDRAL on Ludgate Hill. Free to enter, but it costs to go into the upper galleries. Worth paying, though, because from the Golden Ball on the top (only one person can enter the Ball at a time) you get a great view. You can also look straight down through a glass panel a couple of hundred feet to the cathedral floor. All sorts of people buried in the crypt.

WESTMINSTER ABBEY in Parliament Square. Beautiful building founded in 1042 and serving as a burial ground for some of England's greatest. Poetry fans should look over Poets' Corner.

SPEAKER'S CORNER at Hyde Park, Marble Arch. Free. Any fine Sunday from around 2 p.m. Great place to let off steam, meet people, hear some really crazy people sounding off and (occasionally) to hear some clever speeches. Heckling is the order of the day.

BRITISH MUSEUM in Great Russell Street. A complete display of just about anything you're interested in. This must be the most complete summing up of the human race in existence.

VICTORIA AND ALBERT MUSEUM in South Kensington. A complex of museums. Art, architecture, furniture, clothes. If it's not at the British Museum it'll be here. If it isn't at either, it probably doesn't exist.

NATIONAL GALLERY in Trafalgar Square. Great collection. Just about everyone is represented. Fantastic collection of Rembrandt. Monet's 'Water-lilies', too.

TATE GALLERY on Millbank. Modern stuff, mostly. Superb collection of Turners and Blakes. Good retrospective exhibitions every now and again (which usually cost, but which are worth it).

MADAME TUSSAUD'S in Marylebone Road. Costs to get in. Huge display of waxwork figures, historical and contemporary, goodies and baddies. Some of the politicians seem more businesslike in wax than they act in real life. Downstairs is the Chamber of Horrors. The waxworks were started when Madame Tussaud arrived in London in 1802 with models of the heads of guillotined victims of the French Revolution.

LONDON PLANETARIUM next door to Tussaud's in Marylebone Road. Admission charge. If you're an Arthur C. Clarke fan, it's great stuff.

HOUSES OF PARLIAMENT by Westminster Bridge. Admission free. Good building to wander in. Royal thrones, etc. Check from officials as to when the public is permitted to sit in on debates at the House of Commons. If you are doubtful about the efficiency of the English political system, you should try and listen to at least one debate.

WESTMINSTER HALL in Parliament Square. Part of the original complex which was once the Palace of Westminster. Apart from being a superb example of architecture of its type, it was here that Sir Thomas More (*A Man for All Seasons*) and later Charles I heard their death sentences pronounced. Admission free.

THE CENTRAL CRIMINAL COURT (known as the Old Bailey) in Newgate Street, on the site of the famous Old Newgate Prison. Free entry to the public galleries to hear court in session. Best to arrive around 10 in the morning.

LONDON STOCK EXCHANGE in Old Broad Street. Visitors' gallery open weekdays from around 10 a.m. Free. Watch the immaculate men throw their money around. (Make sure your jeans are pressed.)

BUCKINGHAM PALACE The Mall. Not open to the public. Official London Home of Her Majesty the Queen. (She has several other homes, as well.) See the Changing of the Guard at 11.30 a.m.

FREE BAND CONCERTS by Charing Cross Station. Around 12.30 in summer. They've never heard of an electric guitar, but they try hard. For full details of a variety of free or nearly free outdoor entertainment, including occasional Shakespeare productions in Regent's Park, buy the booklet *Open Air Entertainment*. For free rock concerts in London check *Time Out*, or ring the London Tourist Board (Tel: 730 0791).

TRAFALGAR SQUARE Good place to rest in. Usually plenty of people around in like circumstances wanting to exchange information. Opposite the Square is ST MARTIN IN THE FIELDS, a church. In the Crypt, some nights, a charity organization gives free soup to those who need it. If you're really stropped for a meal, they'd probably help out in return for half an hour's work. But avoid troubling them if possible. Their time is taken up with alco's and mainliners.

PICCADILLY CIRCUS Around the statue of Eros in the centre there are nearly always people who can give you information on stuff you aren't going to find in guidebooks. But they're strange people. Ignore the tourist shops and restaurants because this is an enormously expensive area.

MARKETS: PORTOBELLO ROAD (go to Notting Hill Gate and ask from there). Fruit and vegetables one end, then antiques beyond that. Most people stop there. Keep walking. The junk section beyond is where you find the bargains. Good place to pick up second-hand clothes and shoes if you need them. Don't take the first price. Never buy in a shop, even in the 'gear' shops. It's cheaper on the street. Best day, Saturday, or Friday morning if you just want to check the junk section. PETTICOAT LANE, Middlesex Street, E1: huge outdoor market every Sunday morning. OK and worth seeing but packed with tourists. For a better market continue up Bishopsgate to the animal market. Nearby are endless streets and alleys packed with junk of every description. Sundays only. Closes at 1 p.m. Up in this area you'll be pleased to know you're in Jack the Ripper land. Check London Transport for free guides to London's markets.

SOHO is, more or less, the area bounded by Charing Cross Road, Oxford Street, Wardour Street and Shaftesbury Avenue. It's London's square mile of sin and great to wander through. Fun parlours, strip joints, blue movies, porn shops, prostitutes ('Slinky black model. First Floor').

THEATRES Sit up in the gods (the gallery) and you can have a ticket for as little as £1. The National, the Aldwych and the Royal Court are three which consistently present good plays with good actors. Also, there's a big boom in lunchtime and fringe theatre, and they're cheap. Check *Time Out* for details.

PUBS Plenty worth visiting, especially in the evening (5.30 p.m.–11.00 p.m. Mondays to Saturdays, 7.00 p.m.–10.30 p.m. Sundays). Try the *City Barge* at 27 Strand-on-the-Green, Chiswick, W4. *King's Head* at 48 Gerrard Street, W1. *Prospect of Whitby* at Wapping Steps, E1. *Sun in Splendour* at the top of Portobello Road, W11. *The Hansom Cab* at 84 Earl's Court Road, W8, and *The Swan* at Lancaster Gate, W2. *Dirty Dick's* near Petticoat Lane, on the corner of Middlesex Street and Bishopsgate. *The Ship* in Wardour Street, W1. *George Inn* at 77 Borough High Street, SE1 (near London Bridge). Absolute musts are *Ye Olde Cheshire Cheese* and *Ye Olde Cock Tavern* in Fleet Street.

NIGHTCLUBS cost money, of course, but great for special occasions. *The Troubadour* at 265 Old Brompton Road, Earl's Court, SW5, is England's oldest folk club. Membership not required. Admission about £1.00. *Marquee Club* at 90 Wardour Street, W1. Membership about £1.00. Entrance 80p–£3.00. *Ronnie Scott's Club* at 47 Frith Street, W1. Strictly a dress-up place, and, with about £5 entrance fee a pocket buster. Drinks *extremely* expensive, but the best names in British and American jazz lay a tune in Ronnie's. Free membership if you have a Student ID Card.

DISCOTHEQUES Various admission prices and popularity varies from month to month. Try *Samantha's* at 3 New Burlington Street, W1, *Blaise's* at 121 Queen's Gate, SW7, *The Cromwellian* at 3 Cromwell Road, SW7, *Le Kilt* at 60 Greek Street, W1 or *Edelweiss Club* at 19 Oxford Street, W1.

CINEMAS Unlimited choice of programme. Particularly try the *Electric Cinema* in Portobello Road and the *Paris Pullman* in Drayton Gardens, SW7. Best for double bills and limited distribution movies are *Phoenix* at East Finchley and the *Screen on Islington Green* (at guess where). West End prices are out of this world, £2.50–£3.00 for a decent seat. But most shows go out of the West End and into the suburbs within a month or so of release.

RIVER TRIP A nice way of moving through London is by river launch. For instance, if you're in the centre of town and want to go to the Tower of London you can pick up a boat from Charing Cross Pier and get off at Tower Hill. Costs around 75p, but it's more interesting than going by bus.

LONDON ZOO A great collection and well worth the visit – if you can afford it. One interesting feature is the Moonlight Hall where night and day are reversed so that you can see nocturnal animals and birds alert and awake in the middle of the day. For an extra charge you can see the excellent London Zoo Aquarium complete with man-eating sharks, stingrays and what-have-you's. At Regent's Park, NW1.

Meetings, discussions, ins and outs of what's happening, etc

Several publications tell you all you need to know. The best single magazine for a complete run-down of everything happening in London in just about every field of interest is *Time Out*. Art, music, cinema (including every film on in London that week), demonstrations – you name it, *Time Out* has got it. Indispensable, especially if you're only in town a short time.

Other publications which really give value for money are Nicholson's *Students' London*, *Alternative London* and *Visitors London Guide Book*. *Students' London* includes city maps, Underground maps, bus routes, cheap eating, cheap sleeping, info on studying in London and lots more. *Alternative London*, by Nicholas Saunders, is far and away the best book ever written on how to live in London. Saunders examines every aspect of living in the big city, starting with getting somewhere to live and hints on how to furnish it cheaply, moving on through food cults, London markets, the mystical scene, sex, drugs, and on and on for a couple of hundred pages. If you can't cut your living costs by a third after studying this book you can count yourself stupid.

Project London was a drop-out booklet distributed free in 1969. It was banned because of some of the frankly silly and dangerous crap it contained. It remains, though, one of the most fascinating documents ever written on how to survive in a big city for practically nothing. Richard Neville's book, *Playpower* (Paladin), reprints a lot of the booklet.

Free newspapers: just pick them up out of the rubbish bins at any Underground station or in the central city streets. Latest editions. Wide range available.

Robinson and Watkins Bookshop at 19 Cecil Court (off Charing Cross Road) for an amazing collection of tomes on mysticism and the occult.

Problems

If you strike hard times in London there are several organizations which will help you out. Two of the best are BIT who have vast amounts of information on the alternative society and RELEASE who are backed up by lawyers and doctors and who specialize in civil rights, what to do when you're busted for drugs, etc. Refer to BIT for general information,

RELEASE for the heavy stuff. Don't bother either of them without good reason – they're busy. They both give information and help free and don't ask for money, but if you could spare something after they've helped you it would help them. Check any of the underground publications for phone numbers and addresses.

Transport in London

There are two ways of moving around London by public transport. Bus or Underground. Both are expensive. Prices depend on how far you want to go, of course, but an average (say, six-stop) trip on the Underground will cost about 50p. If you expect to be in town for only a short time and want to see as much as possible check with the London Tourist Board or at London Transport inquiry desks in main stations for details of special tickets available to visitors. (For example, a 'go as you please' ticket for about £9 allows you unlimited travel on city buses and trains for four days, while a Red Bus Rover ticket for £1.50 allows a day's unlimited travel on the red buses.)

Bicycles can be hired for around £15 per week (with a £15 returnable deposit) from several addresses, including Savile's, 99 Battersea Rise, London SW11 (Tel: 228 4279), and Lester Ward, 25 Bedford Hill, London SW12 (Tel: 673 2753). Rent-A-Scooter at 7 Broadwell Parade, Broadhurst Gardens, London NW6 (Tel: 328 4060) will rent you a moped for £4 per day or £25 per week with a returnable deposit (around £25 if you're over 23, more if you're not), or, if you want to be more fancy, a Lambretta scooter for double that price.

Student discounts

There is a tremendous amount to be gained from student discounts all over Great Britain and Ireland. Museums, galleries, concerts, cinemas, restaurants, bars, dry-cleaning, cameras, tape-recorders, typewriters, watches and clothing are just some of the places and items you can enter at a reduced rate, or buy at a discount, if you belong to the magic club. For details:

NATIONAL UNION OF STUDENTS
302 Pentonville Road, N1 (Tel: 278 3291).

Addresses

Main Post Office (for Poste Restante) at King Edward Street, London EC1.

American Express at 6 Haymarket, London SW1 (Tel: 930 4411).

London Student Travel Bureau at 117 Euston Road, NW1 (Tel: 388 7051).

British Tourist Authority at 64 St James' Street, Piccadilly, London SW1 (Tel: 629 9191).

London Tourist Board Information Centres at 26 Grosvenor Gardens, London SW1 (Tel: 730 0791); Victoria Station, London SW1 (near Platform 15); Selfridges store (in Oxford Street), ground floor; and Harrods store (Knightsbridge), fourth floor.

US Embassy at 24 Grosvenor Square, London W1 (Tel: 499 9000).

Hitchers' tips and comments

Here's some tips I'd like to pass on to fellow hitchers. For sleeping rough in London, a good place (if you can put up with drunks) is on the embankment near Westminster Bridge. The police move you on about 6 a.m., but it's still OK. Also, in the same area there are plenty of cheap cafés where you can eat well. Wimpy's ask a service charge on all meals, so if you don't have much bread, miss them. For other cheap meals try cafés around London docks. A tip for really cheap eating – mix Oxo cubes with hot water. You get six cubes for 20p.
E. J. Major, Gunhild Close, London

Sleeping rough in London: in Hyde Park you usually get moved on by police who sometimes have dogs. But you get away with it some nights. Don't go deep into the park because of muggers. Stay opposite the Playboy and Hilton where it's lighter.
  Check *Exchange and Mart* (in England) under 'travel' for things like ultra-cheap coach trips. Sometimes cheaper than hitching.
Dennis Chubb, Bletchley, England

British pub meals are value for money but the rolls and sandwiches are not. Better to go to Woolworths or Littlewoods cafés.
  Heading north from London up the M1 most hitchers take the tube to Hendon Central, but there are often 40 or more hitchers at this point. Alternative route: get tube to Watford Junction then take A412 and A405 to M1.
Dave Martill, Leicester, England

Wales

Population	2,700,000
Size	8,000 square miles
Capital	Cardiff, population 260,000
Government	Principality
Religion	Protestant
Language	Welsh and English

Best way into Wales is across the tremendous **Severn Bridge** just outside Bristol. Then, within a couple of miles, is Wales' first big tourist attraction, the beautiful ruins of **Tintern Abbey**.

If you continue on to **Monmouth** and then turn west along the A40 to **Abergavenny** where you meet up with the A465, you can travel through some of the strangest country in the British Isles. Luxurious green valleys, scarred by black cuts of coal-mines – villages which from the distance seem to be gentle and fairytale-like turn out to be places of cold brick coated with the black dust of the mines.

Cardiff, down on the coast, is the capital of the country. Sights to see include the National Museum of Wales, the Welsh Folk Museum (this is at St Fagan's, four miles out of town) where typically Welsh buildings have been reconstructed to give the visitor an idea of the rural architecture of the country, and Cardiff Castle. Cardiff Castle is just one of more than 150 in Wales and that fact may bear out the Welsh Tourist Office claim that their country has more castles per square mile than any other country in Europe.

Dylan Thomas fans will want to drop in on the village of **Laugharne** which is on a side road off the A49 just outside **Carmarthen**. The poet lived a good deal of his life in the village and is buried there.

St David's, on the A487, has the dubious distinction of being the smallest city in the British Isles. Its population of 1,650 supports a cathedral and the ruins of a bishop's palace.

On the **River Teifi,** which reaches the sea at **Cardigan**, you might be lucky enough to spot a fisherman in a coracle. These wicker-basket boats are the earliest form of water-transport known to man except for the log.

Heading north along the coast you reach **Aberystwyth,** an important university town, while farther north again is **Harlech** with its famous castle. North again, takes you to another castle town, this time **Caernarvon**, traditional site of the investiture of the Prince of Wales. It happened to Prince Charles in the summer of 1969 with due pomp and ceremony.

Certain strata of the Welsh population – those interested in breaking ties with England – were not impressed. Hitchers wanting more information on that subject can probably find it amongst the students at Aberystwyth.

Just outside **Bangor,** which has a Museum of Welsh Antiquities, is a village with only one claim to fame. It's called:

Llanfairpwllgwyngyllgogerychwyrndrobwllllantysiliogogogoch.

The main street isn't as long as the name. For wanderers new to Wales, the word is a fair introduction to the Welsh language.

Heading back towards England along the A55, there's at least one more worthwhile stop and that's at **Conway** which is a pleasant enough town with yet another famous castle.

Scotland

Population	5,200,000
Size	30,414 square miles
Capital	Edinburgh, population 453,000
Government	Constitutional Monarchy
Religion	Church of Scotland
Language	English and Gaelic

Scotland is best approached by the A68 where the Border is crossed at **Carter Bar** (1,300 feet up). The lowland towns of **Jedburgh, Melrose, Selkirk,** and **Galashiels** (home of Sir Walter Scott) are well worth seeing.

North of **Edinburgh,** after crossing the big Forth Road Bridge, you can join up with the M90 to Perth then the A85 which will take you through to **Dundee**. The city is nothing spectacular, but nearby, at a place called **Glamis,** is one of the better castles in Scotland.

Scotland is a place where you can enjoy the countryside – particularly the famous Highlands. In these heather-covered hills you will recognize the colours of the traditional tartans and you will notice a sense of spaciousness which you can't find elsewhere in the British Isles. Scotland is half the size of England, but with only one-tenth the population.

To get the full flavour of this Highland Scotland, probably the best route you can take is north from Dundee up through **Spittal of Glenshee** and **Devil's Elbow** to **Braemar,** which is the big centre for the Royal Highland Gathering, with caber-tossing and hammer-throwing. This takes place on the first Saturday in September each year. Just a little farther on is **Balmoral Castle,** still used by the British Royal Family for summer holidays. The Dee River, which runs through the Royal Estate, is well stocked with trout if you care to indulge in a little high-class poaching.

Farther north at **Huntly** you can join up with the A96 which curves around the coast towards **Inverness,** a pleasant town with a cathedral and a museum containing relics of the Jacobites. It's known as the Highland Capital and sits at the northern end of **Loch Ness,** home of the monster which *everyone* in Scotland has seen except the scientists. Just outside Inverness is **Culloden,** site of the famous battle of 1746 when Bonnie Prince Charlie's Jacobites were defeated by the Hanoverians. You can visit a small museum housed in a contemporary farm dwelling, and see the burial mounds of the various clans. If you make it on a drizzly day (you probably will), you'll get a real feeling of how the Moor must have been on the day of the battle.

North again and you're heading for **John o' Groats,** the northern counterpart of England's Land's End. The towns of **Wick** and **Thurso** are interesting and quite different from towns in the south.

If you take the western route back south, you'll be travelling through some of the loneliest country outside Northern Scandinavia. It's the real moor country with peat-bogs and little else. I remember passing through one 'town' which consisted of a signpost, one house, one hotel, and then another signpost. How the two establishments supported each other is a difficult question to answer. The whole area is beautiful if you enjoy a little loneliness. Be warned that the hitching can get really bad between **Tongue** and **Ullapool**.

South of Ullapool and you're in the land of mountains and lochs – the best part of the Western Highlands. See the tropical gardens (yes tropical!) at **Inverewe** and then continue through **Gairloch** and alongside Loch Maree, perhaps the loveliest of all the lochs. The road south continues through uninterrupted and outstanding scenery until you come to **Fort William** which is on Loch Linnhe and backed by the 4,406 foot Ben Nevis Mountain. Twenty miles farther south again and you're at **Glencoe,** scene of the Massacre of 1692.

Down the A82 and A84, through a whole lot of nice country and you arrive in **Stirling,** historically one of the most important cities in Scotland. Have a look at Stirling Castle, ex-home of the Royal Mint, and a great visit. A couple of miles north are the ruins of **Cambuskenneth Abbey,** while south is **Bannockburn** where Robert the Bruce defeated King Edward in 1314.

The next city you come to is **Glasgow** which is worth a day to look over the Art Gallery, Museum of Transport, and the thirteenth-century cathedral. Also have a look at Provand's Lordship, the oldest house in the city, dating from 1471. With two universities (Watt, of steam-engine fame, attended Glasgow University) the city is a good place to meet people.

South of Glasgow on the A77, is **Ayr**, and a couple of miles outside is **Alloway**, birthplace of Scotland's favourite poet, Robbie Burns. The cottage in which he was born in 1759 is now a completely restored monument. Inside you can see original manuscripts, letters, and objects associated with Burns.

Stranraer is where you can jump a ferry for Northern Ireland (see **Northern Ireland**). East along the A75 and you come to **Castle Douglas** with the huge Threave Castle nearby. Then you come to **Dumfries** where Burns died in 1796 and is buried. Then, just before you cross back into England, you come to **Gretna Green**, once famous around the world as the place where young people ran off to get married.

★**Highland Games** Main places for Highland Games are Fort William, Mallaig, Crieff, Glenfinnan, Edinburgh and Braemar. The games are usually held in July, August, or September and feature the famous caber toss as well as traditional dancing and music. Ask the Scottish Tourist Board.

★**Edinburgh Festival** The famous International Festival of Music and Drama is held every year in August/September.

Edinburgh: where to sleep

A bed in Edinburgh costs from around £1.50 at the youth hostel to about £3.75 at a boarding house or in a cheap hotel. Breakfast is normally included.

Youth Hostels at 7 Bruntsfield Crescent, Edinburgh 10 (Tel: 447 2994) and 18 Eglinton Crescent, Edinburgh 12 (Tel: 337 1120).

YMCA at 14 South St Andrew Street (Tel: 556 4304).

YWCA at 4 Randolph Place (Tel: 225 1875). Women only.

Manor Club at 12 Rothesay Place (Tel: 225 2134). It's cheaper if you can get into a room with three or four beds.

Winkler Guest House at 41 Albany Street (Tel: 556 1140). Another small place. Ring first.

Kiloran Guest House at 17 Leamington Terrace (off Bruntsfield Place) (Tel: 229 1789).

For help in finding a cheap place try the Edinburgh Tourist Information and Accommodation Service at 5 Waverley Bridge (Tel: 226 6591).

For sleeping rough, take a bus out to Holyrood Park.

Edinburgh: where to eat

£1.20 should handle any hunger problems. And remember, as in London, if you're ever really broke, you can survive very well (survive, though scarcely thrive) on fish 'n' chips.

The YWCA and YMCA both serve well-priced meals. (Addresses in **Where to sleep**.) If you like to make lunch your main meal of the day you can have good feeds at any number of pubs and small restaurants for around £1.00. Try:

Milnes Bar at 35 Hanover Street.

Woolworth's opposite Waverley Station in Princes Street.

Students' Refectory at 9 Chambers Street. Open July through October. Dinner served (very cheap) from 5–7 p.m.

Macvities at 4 South Charlotte Street. The ground floor snack bar is the cheapest place to eat of the three restaurants in the building.

Bombay Tandoori Restaurant at 14a Nicolson Street, 10% student reduction.

Lothian Restaurant at 16 Drummond Street. Cheap curry meals.

Edinburgh: what to see and do

THE CASTLE The huge military complex which dominates Edinburgh. Entrance free, but costs to go into the museum. Good place for overall view of what is a beautiful city.

JOHN KNOX'S HOUSE at the foot of High Street. Entrance charge. Closed on Sundays.

NATIONAL GALLERY OF SCOTLAND on the Mound. No entrance fee. Some good stuff.

THE OLD TOWN This is the area between the Castle rock and Holyroodhouse. It's the old quarter of Edinburgh which settled itself around the protective castle. Holyroodhouse was the home of several Scottish sovereigns, including Mary Queen of Scots. You can still see the room where Rizzio, her Italian secretary (and possibly, lover), was murdered in front of her eyes in 1566.

DEACON BRODIE'S TAVERN at the corner of Bank and High Streets, is a little touristy, but you can meet some good types there. Deacon Brodie was the evil man who inspired R. L. Stevenson to write *Dr Jekyll and Mr Hyde*. Prices OK.

THE TRAVERSE THEATRE CLUB is a sort of pub-cum-theatre-cum-art-gallery. Membership fee. Worth visiting to meet people and for general good talk.

FLANNIGAN's at 92 Rose Street, North Lane. Live music. Nice people. No grog. Usually lots of ladies. Opening days and times are erratic. 75p admission Sunday to Thursday and £1.25 on Fridays and Saturdays.

MUSEUM OF CHILDHOOD at 38 High Street. Four floors devoted to all the quaint paraphernalia of childhood. Strangely evocative. Worth a visit if you're in the right mood. Entrance fee.

ALTERNATIVE EDINBURGH If you're going to be in town for an extended stay you'll get some good tips on bread-line living if you buy *Another Edinburgh* (£1.00), published by the University Student Publications Board, 1 Buccleuch Place, Edinburgh. It has chapters on Eating, Sleeping, Seeing Edinburgh for Nothing, etc, etc.

Transport in Edinburgh
The bus service is the main means of public transport. It will take you everywhere.

Addresses

Main Post Office (for Poste Restante) at corner of Waterloo Place and North Bridge.

American Express at 139 Princes Street (Tel: 225 7881).

Edinburgh University Students' Association at Bristo Street (Tel: 667 0214).

Scottish Tourist Board at 5 Waverley Bridge (Tel: 332 2433).

US Consulate at 3 Regent Terrace (Tel: 556 8315).

Northern Ireland

Population　1,500,000
Size　　　5,452 square miles
Capital　　Belfast, population 425,000

Government Constitutional Monarchy
Religion Protestant
Language English

Crossing to Ireland is done cheapest by jumping the ferry in **Stranraer** (Scotland) and crossing to **Larne** which is just a few miles north of Belfast. Cost on this route is around £2.20. Other routes are from Liverpool (England) to Belfast (costing about £5.00); Heysham (England) to Belfast (about £4.80); and Ardrossan (Scotland) to Belfast (£4.00).

In the six counties of Northern Ireland (known also as Ulster) the main stopping points are the capital, Belfast, the Giant's Causeway and the ancient city of Londonderry.

Belfast is a city of markets. Smithfield is the big one. It's open every weekday and sells whatever you want to buy. Chichester Street, May Street and Oxford Street are three others, but they mostly sell food. Friday is the day at May Street and Chichester Street when they hold the junk market, somewhat reminiscent of London's Portobello Road, but not as touristy.

Buildings worth looking over include City Hall and Queens University. The Museum and Art Gallery are OK to wander through, but a better display is at the Ulster Folk Museum which gives you a good idea of what Irish life was like in centuries past. It's located eight miles from Belfast on the A2 Belfast–Bangor road and is built along the same lines as the big open air museum at Skansen in Sweden. (See **Scandinavia** and **Finland**.) While you're out that way you can see **Stormont**, until 1972 the seat of the Irish Government.

Carrickfergus, on the coast between Belfast and Larne, is a lobster-fishing port and the site of a big Norman castle. Gory story attached to the castle tells that during a siege, which came as the result of a war with Scotland, the garrison was so badly starved that they ate thirty Scottish prisoners. These days Carrickfergusians prefer sea-food.

You reach the **Giant's Causeway** via the A2, following it up through Larne and **Ballycastle**. The Causeway is one of *the* natural wonders of the world. It's a weird formation of basalt rock which was caused by volcanic action millions of years ago. At least that's how scientists tell it. The legendary explanation of the creation of the Causeway makes more sense. It tells that a gigantic Irishman, Finn MacCool, heard of a Scottish giant Finn Gall and decided to fight him to find out who was the better man. So he built the Causeway and walked over to Scotland. He found Gall's house and entered. He found Mrs Gall sewing and saw a huge body sleeping on a bed. He asked if it was her husband and she said her husband was out and that the sleeping figure was her two-year-old son – at which MacCool lost his cool and hurtled back to Ireland scared out of his wits at the thought of how big Finn Gall must be. They say he ripped up the Causeway as he returned so that Gall couldn't come over and get him. And that explains why there's so little of it left.

Londonderry, forty-odd miles farther on from the Causeway, is the second city of Northern Ireland and the one most laden with history. It was founded with the building of an Abbey in AD 540 and has been a magnet for strife ever since. Before the year 1200 it had been attacked by Danes and Normans and burned seven times. In 1556 it was the headquarters of a rebellion and destroyed by a huge explosion from the city ammunition magazines. In 1608 it was burned again. And then in 1689 a terrible siege which lasted 105 days resulted in the death of 7,000 defenders. The City Walls, which saw much of this, date from the 1600s and (incredibly!) are preserved intact. At St Columb's Cathedral you can see relics of the great siege, and the modern Guild Hall contains other objects related to the city's past.

Those are the three main places to visit in Northern Ireland, but almost wherever else you go you run into pockets of Irish history, mostly so old or so bloody that now there is scarcely anything left to see.

Warning! Travelling in this country can be dangerous. Think twice before you hop the boat to Larne.

Hitchers' tips and comments
I would advise anyone hitching in Ulster not to question the troubles. Any hitcher with relations in, or connected with the British army should think twice before going. But if you still wish to hitch there it can be a great place. The Republic is different again, the people are more friendly and helpful. *Sent by a British soldier who didn't supply his name. K.W.*

Ireland (Eire)

Population	2,975,000
Size	26,600 square miles
Capital	Dublin, population 860,000
Government	Republic
Religion	Roman Catholic
Language	Gaelic and English

For me, the Republic of Ireland is more interesting than the North.
The people are more relaxed and perhaps that is why the countryside
seems more beautiful. And there's much more to see. To get to the South,
you can cross over from the North with scarcely any formalities. Or, if
you're crossing over from England, the ferry routes are as follows:
Liverpool (England) to Dublin (costing about £14.00), Holyhead (Wales)
to Dun Laoghaire (about £11.25), Fishguard (Wales) to Rosslare
(about £11.50), or Swansea (Wales) to Cork (about £17.00).

The Irish have a saying, 'Everyone is an Irishman and those that ain't
are wishin' that they were'. If you check down the list of the top twenty
names in Ireland (see page 85), you'll see how many of us *do* have Irish
blood in the family. This strange fact derives from the exodus of the Irish
from their country to escape the great famine of the early 1800s and the
desolation which followed it. In less than eighty years the population
dropped from eight to four million, and many of those four million
expatriates went to America and the British colonies and took with them
not only their family names but also the names of their towns which have
become household words in the English language. Limerick, Killarney,
Tipperary, Blarney, Galway, Cork – and plenty of others.

Kilkenny is a tiny city of 13,500 and known as the capital of medieval
Ireland. Its castle, dating from the thirteenth century, is a beauty, and
contains a large collection of manuscripts and also, in the old stables, the
Kilkenny Design Workshops where you can see examples of Irish craft
and design. St Canice's Cathedral dates from the thirteenth century
as does the Dominican Church. The Dunmore Caves, seven miles north of
Kilkenny are supposed to have been the scene of a big massacre during
Viking times. Towards the end of August Kilkenny stages an Arts Week.
Well worth a visit if you're in the area and so inclined.

Cashel, between Kilkenny and Tipperary, is, after **Tara,** which is six
miles south of Navan in County Meath, the most important historical site
in Southern Ireland. Tara, in ancient times, was the capital of Ireland
and the seat of the Irish kings. However, little remains to be seen today
and it's scarcely worth the visit unless you're an archaeological or history
crank. At Cashel, though, there is plenty to see. It's a town of 3,000 people
dominated by the dramatic Rock of Cashel, a 200-foot-high outcrop of
limestone crowned by ruins. The town was the seat of the Munster kings
from AD 370 to AD 1101 and also a place where St Patrick preached.
It's said that it was in Cashel that he used the shamrock as an illustration
of the doctrine of the Trinity, thus establishing forever the national symbol
of Ireland. On the Rock, you can see a round tower dating from the
tenth century, the cathedral, the hall of the Vicars Choral, and

King Cormac's Chapel. (A story tells that the first cathedral on the site was burned down in 1495 by the Earl of Kildare. The Earl later apologized and explained to Henry VII that he'd done so because he'd thought the archbishop was inside.)

Cork is the third city of Ireland and perhaps one of her prettiest. Best things to see are the streets around the quays (it's a riverside city), Christ the King Church, designed in 1930 by an American and an outstanding piece of modern architecture, and the School of Art which is a good place to see some modern Irish painting. If you're musically-minded, a few pence allows you to play a tune on the historic Bells of Shanden Steeple.

Five miles out of Cork is **Blarney**, a tiny village of less than 1,200 people. The town boasts a fine old castle, and on the outside wall of the highest tower is the world-famous Blarney Stone. The payment of a small coin buys you the privilege of performing a contortionist act to kiss the stone, and, the deed being done, you are blessed forever with 'the gift of the gab'.

Wandering up through Killarney, by **Dingle Bay** to **Tralee** you reach the village of **Adare** (eleven miles south of Limerick). The exact origins of Adare are unknown, but it has survived, at least, since the reign of Henry II, when it was occupied by the Anglo-Normans. Even so, its population is still only 550. The point about Adare is that it's a perfect place to rest up a day or two, providing you like peace and quiet. Many travellers claim the village is Ireland's prettiest. Sights to see in and around Adare include the ruins of the Trinitarian Abbey and the Augustinian Abbey; the Franciscan Friary; the Desmond Castle which dates from the twelfth century; and the Adare Manor, residence of the Earl of Dunraven. If you can hustle up some tackle, try the first-rate brown trout fishing on the Maigue River.

The city of **Limerick** is more famous for the making of fine lace than the invention of dirty verse. See King John's Castle and St John's Cathedral. In the old city Exchange (only the front wall remains) was a pedestal known as 'The Nail' where merchants paid their debts – from which came the expression, 'paying on the nail'. The Nail in question can be seen at the Limerick Museum.

Galway, a city of 29,500, sitting on the famous bay of the same name, is a pleasant place with a long history. The Church of St Nicholas dating from 1320 is said to have been visited by Columbus on his way out to the Americas. Lynch's Castle dates from the same year and was the mansion of a city judge, part of whose story is told in a skull and cross-bone memorial erected in the Old Jail: 'This memorial of the stern and unbending justice of the chief magistrate of this City, James Lynch

Fitzstephen, elected mayor AD 1493, who condemned and executed his own guilty son, Walter, on this spot.'

Galway is a good place to catch Gaelic sports. The Pearse Stadium is where you can see Hurling or Gaelic Football. Summer is when the Feiseanna are held – festivals of Irish singing and dancing. And if you're in town between June and October, don't miss the salmon at Salmon Weir Bridge, over the River Corrib.

Galway was once described as the most Irish of all Irish cities. See the annual Galway Fair and believe it. It's held at the end of July or the beginning of August. Check with tourist offices.

★**Horse-drawn caravan travelling** Hitchers with a little spare time might be interested in this idea which is beginning to become popular – hiring a four-berth caravan with horse and covering a lazy 12–15 miles a day. Cost is around £75–£115 a week – which split four ways isn't too bad. As you can do your own cooking and sleep by a campfire or in the caravan, it works out around the same as hitching and sleeping in hostels. Five people in the caravan works out a fraction cheaper per head. With food and sightseeing you could expect to pay out £40–£50 per person, per week. Three addresses to contact concerning the hire of caravans are:

Mr Joe O'Reilly,
Blarney Romany Caravans,
Lancaster House,
Western Road,
Cork (Tel: (021) 20088/9).

Mr D. Wall,
Lough Gill Caravans Ltd,
Drumlease, Glebe House,
Dromahair, Co Leitrim (Tel: (071) 74141).

Mr T. G. Macnamara,
Shannon Horse Caravans,
Adare,
Co Limerick (Tel: (061) 43 844).

★ **Trace your ancestors** If you think your family is Irish and you want to trace some relatives or find out more about your ancestors, then your visit to Ireland is the ideal time to do it. The Irish Tourist Board will send you a free pamphlet on the subject if you write them, but in the meantime, here are some basic facts you should attempt to find out before you leave home: (a) the full name of your emigrant ancestor; (b) any background information as to his trade or social standing; (c) his religion; (d) the name of the county and town from which he came. With that information you have a good chance of finding out something about your family.

Just in case you're wondering if you *do* have Irish ancestors, here are the top twenty surnames in Ireland listed in order of frequency of occurrence:

Murphy	O'Brien	Reilly	Kennedy
Kelly	Byrne	Doyle	Lynch
Sullivan	Ryan	McCarthy	Murray
Walsh	Connor	Gallagher	Quinn
Smith	O'Neill	Doherty	Moore

Dublin: where to sleep

Hostels and student residences are cheapest, of course. Hotels and guest houses usually cost between £4 and £4.50 sometimes including breakfast. Below is a list of student accommodation.

Divinity Hostel at Braemor Park, Dublin 14 (Tel: 90 55 06). Men only. Open last half of July and through August to mid-September. Outside of town.

Trinity Hall at Dartry Road, Dublin 6 (Tel: 97 17 72). Open March and then from June through September. Outside of town.

Youth Hostel at 39 Mountjoy Square, Dublin 1 (Tel: 74 57 34). Open from 1st April to 30th September.

Youth Hostel at 78 Morehampton Road, Donnybrook, Dublin 4 (Tel: 68 03 25).

YWCA at Radcliff Hall, St John's Road, Sandymount (Tel: 68 45 21) and at Lower Baggot Street (Tel: 76 273).

These are some lower priced hotels and guest houses and bed and breakfast places:

Mrs A. Haire at 73 Dollymount Park (Tel: 33 36 95).

Mrs M. Dunwoody, Eldar at 19 Copeland Avenue (Tel: 33 90 91).

Mrs A. Hunt, Chez-Nous at 7 Kincora Drive (Tel: 33 38 97).

Mrs J. Creagh, St Aidan's at 150 Clonliffe Road (Tel: 37 67 50).

Mrs J. Murnane at 56 Castle Avenue (Tel: 33 64 02).

Mrs M. Dempsey at 35 St Anne's Road (Tel: 30 48 77).

Mrs E. Byrne-Pool, Sea Front at 278 Clontarf Road (Tel: 33 61 18).

Mrs M. Lumley, 59 Hollybank Road (Tel: 37 62 66).

For full information on all accommodation see the people at the
Irish Student Travel Service, 17 Anglesea Street (Tel: 77 81 17) or contact
Dublin Tourism at 14 Upper O'Connell Street and 51 Dawson Street
(Tel: 74 77 33).
  For sleeping out try around Phoenix Park and the race-course.
Fair amount of police around as the park is also the residence of the
President of Ireland. But it spreads over 1,700 acres, so you should
find a spot OK.

Dublin: where to eat

You can make a good meal in Dublin town for around the £2.20 mark –
and remember that like the British, the Irish have a big thing about
fish and chips. You can gorge yourself stupid on them for £1.00.

Newman House at 86 St Stephen's Green. This is the restaurant attached to
the university where the local students eat. Great lunches and very cheap.
Closed August. You probably won't be asked for a student card.

The Buttery at Trinity College. Another student haunt. Cheap.

Stag's Head at 1 Dame Court and across the road, the Stag's Tail. Lunch is
served between 12 and 2. It's big, it's hot, and it's about £1.90. Good places
for main meal of the day.

Bewleys Cafés Ltd at 10/12 Westmorland Street, 78/79 Grafton Street and
12/13 Sth Great Georges Street.

Hijak's Wine Bar at Lr O'Connell Street.

The Coffee Inn at 6 South Anne Street.

The Country Shop at 23 Saint Stephen's Green North. Lunches only and
good value.

Many hotels in Ireland and the British Isles offer counter-lunches and
dinners. Stand-up pub lunches rarely cost more than £1.00 or £1.20 and are
filling enough to count as the main meal of the day.

Dublin: what to see and do

DUBLIN CASTLE in Castle Street. Thirteenth century. Hangout of the English until they were removed (ask in any pub for details of the removal). Small entrance charge to see the *State Apartments*, but the *Heraldic Museum* is free. *City Hall* adjoins the castle.

THE GENERAL POST OFFICE in O'Connell Street was the headquarters of the Irish Volunteers during the Insurrection of 1916. It was destroyed during the fighting but is now rebuilt.

THE CUSTOM HOUSE at Custom House Quay is the city's finest piece of architecture. Destroyed during the War of Independence, but restored to its former Georgian elegance.

GUINNESS BREWERY at St James Gate, is the home of the famous 'drop'. You're welcome to visit between 10 a.m. and 3 p.m. Monday to Friday for a tour of the premises – and a free sample of the product. See the Brewery Museum.

THE NATIONAL MUSEUM at Kildare Street. Fine collection of Irish antiquities.

MUNICIPAL GALLERY OF MODERN ART at Parnell Square. Nice collection of modern Irish works.

NATIONAL GALLERY at Merrion Square West. Collection of old masters.

TRINITY COLLEGE LIBRARY at Trinity College in College Green is a very important library containing 800,000 volumes plus many manuscripts, including *The Book of the Kells* which is considered to be one of the world's most beautiful illuminated manuscripts. No charge.

THE JOYCEAN MUSEUM at Martello Tower, houses manuscripts, photographs, etc, relating to Ireland's greatest writer. Take a Number 8 bus from O'Connell Bridge and get off at Sandycove. Costs about 20p each way, 30p admission charge, less with a student card.

ST MICHAN'S CHURCH in Church Street offers a somewhat unique sight. In the vaults are bodies which have lain for centuries without decay. You can see these and, if you want, shake hands with a gentleman known as 'The Crusader', a few pence for the privilege.

ST PATRICK'S CATHEDRAL in St Patrick's Street. Fine old building dating back to the twelfth century. Jonathan Swift (*Gulliver's Travels*) was Dean of St Patrick's from 1713–45. Fans can see the tomb.

You can spend a very pleasant day wandering around PHOENIX PARK. (Plus, as I've said in the Sleeping section, you can find some good places to kip down.) You can watch horseracing at the *Racecourse* for free if you can find a way in, for over £2 if you're rich enough to pay. You can visit the *Zoo*, one of the oldest in Europe. With a bit of luck you might find some Gaelic football. With extra luck you'll find plenty of the opposite sex wandering around. Especially Saturday afternoons and Sundays.

MOORE STREET MARKET: best place in Dublin to get an idea of what the Irish are really like. Great stuff and free. Saturday morning is best.

KILMAINHAM JAIL If you're interested in modern Irish history take buses 21, 23, 24 or 78 out to Kilmainham on a Sunday afternoon. You get a guided tour through what is the kernel of the modern Irish revolutionary spirit. It was here that those who signed the proclamation of the Easter Week Rising of 1916 were executed. The last political prisoner to be released from the jail (in 1924) was Eamon de Valera, the late President of Ireland.

DAVY BYRNE'S PUB at 21 Duke Street, was one of James Joyce's haunts. Now a good place to meet young Dubliners. HARTIGAN'S PUB in Lower Leeson Street is another good place to meet people.

MULLIGAN'S in Poolbeg Street is a good rough pub in the Irish tradition. O'DONOHUE'S at 15 Merrion Row is a place where would-be if they could-be folk-groups meet to try themselves on the customers.

THE BAGGOT INN at Baggot Street features live entertainment every night (reasonable entrance charge) and LINCOLN'S INN at 18 Lincoln Place is where the Trinity College mob drink and talk.

Transport in Dublin
Bus fares are cheap, so don't be afraid to use the excellent system. There's a ticket called the Youth and Educational Travel Concession ticket which allows unlimited travel on all Dublin buses and suburban trains within a thirty-mile radius of the capital. It is one of the best deals in Europe, but technically you're supposed to be engaged on an educational or cultural project. (Hitch-hiking is highly educational and an excellent way of getting yer culture. After all, you're writing a book, aren't you!) Apply at the Youth and Educational Executive (at the Dublin Tourism office) 51 Dawson Street, Dublin 2. If you're feeling energetic, try renting a bike. You can probably find one for about £2.50 a day, or cheaper on a weekly basis.

Student discounts

Reductions to some cinemas and theatres. Discounts on certain items at some of the department stores, and on tickets between Dublin and London. For information contact:

IRISH STUDENT TRAVEL SERVICE,
7 Anglesea Street, Dublin (Tel: 77 81 17).

Addresses

Main Post Office (for Poste Restante) at O'Connell Street, Dublin.

American Express at 116 Grafton Street, Dublin (Tel: 77 28 74).

Irish Student Travel Service at 7 Anglesea Street, Dublin (Tel: 77 81 17).

Tourist Information Office at 14 Upper O'Connell Street and 51 Dawson Street (Tel: 74 77 33).

British Embassy at 33 Merrion Road, Dublin 4 (Tel: 69 52 11).

US Embassy at 42 Elgin Road, Ballsbridge, Dublin (Tel 68 87 77).

Hitchers' tips and comments

Your suggestion for sleeping rough in Dublin's Phoenix Park is not to be recommended. If the police don't throw you out, the army will.
D. G. Mulvey, Dublin, Ireland

7 Europe

Europe can never bore you. It stretches 2,400 miles north to south,
3,000 miles east to west and contains some 35 different states. Its highest
elevation, Mount Elbrus in the Soviet Union, rises 18,468 feet, its lowest,
the Caspian Sea, also in the Soviet Union, plunges 92 feet below sea-level.
Its highest recorded temperature was at Sevilla in Spain with 124 degrees
Fahrenheit and its lowest was −61 degrees at Ust-Tsilma in Russia.

But the people are the thing. With its 600,000,000 citizens stacked in
150 to the square mile it is the most densely populated continent on the
planet. You may never manage to remember which city the Forum is in
or the gallery in which you saw the 'Mona Lisa', but you will certainly
remember the city in which someone did you a good turn.

You meet hitchers on the road when you're heading, for instance, towards
Austria and you ask if they've come from there. They tell you, sure. You
say, what's it like? And they tell you that they met this guy in a bar and he
bought them a drink and then went 40 miles out of his way to get them
on to the road they wanted. So you ask what Vienna is like and they tell you
there was this young kid in the market-place who stole apples for them
and that a cop came and chased the kid off and then pinched an apple for
himself and started talking about his son who was hitching down in Africa.

You ask good travellers about a country and they never wax romantic
about green fields or snow-capped mountains. They tell you about people.
And everyone has a country in Europe they like best because of how the
people were with them and everyone has a country they like the least
because they couldn't understand the people. There are 3,900,000 square
miles filled with people.

What you will want to do in Europe depends on who you are. If history
is your line, you can pursue history until it runs out your ears. If you're
an artist, you can visit so many of the world's great galleries that you'll go
cross-eyed. If you're a person with an ordinary job and a few months off
to wander the hundreds of thousands of miles of European roads, then
that's OK, too, because you can dip and choose as the mood takes you,
without feeling the pressure of having to visit that city or see such a gallery.

If you can wander in Europe with just the vaguest idea of your route and
enough money in your pocket and enough time up your sleeve to go as the
road takes you, then you're lucky.

And there's nothing more to say, because Europe will say it all itself. Enjoy.

France

Population	53,000,000
Size	212,821 square miles
Capital	Paris, population 10,825,000
Government	Republic
Religion	Catholic
Language	French

From England, about the cheapest way into France (or onto the Continent) is by the hovercraft service which runs between Ramsgate and Calais and Dover and Boulogne. Full-time students who are under 26 years of age and who have a student card can claim a substantial discount. Other main routes are Folkestone–Boulogne, Dover–Calais, Southampton–Cherbourg, Newhaven–Dieppe, Southampton–Le Havre. Dover boats also go to Zeebrugge and Ostend in Belgium.

St Malo, an old walled seaport badly bombed in the latter days of the war, and Dinan, inland on the River Rance, a citadel town with a medieval castle, are both beautiful, impressive, and well worth seeing. In Brittany, of the many colourful seaports, Concarneau and Lezardrieux are perhaps the most outstanding.

If you're heading straight for Paris, you might want to stop in at Rouen, the capital of Normandy. An old, old, city it retains an ancient look with timber-framed houses (actually only eighteenth century) and huge Gothic structures dating from the twelfth to the sixteenth centuries. The Fine Arts Museum contains a fine collection of work from the French schools, including a good display of Impressionists. Buildings worth looking at include the gigantic Notre Dame Cathedral and the Church of Saint Ouen. See also, the Great Clock on Rue du Gros-Horloge. Its workings date from 1389. The Place du Vieux-Marché is the public square in which Joan of Arc was burned at the stake on 30th May, 1431.

Around Paris, there are at least three places worth a visit. Chartres is the home of the 700-year-old Cathedral of Notre Dame (they're all called that) which Rodin the sculptor described as 'the Acropolis of Christendom'. The 371-foot-high structure can be seen from Montmartre, in Paris, on a clear day. And that's sixty miles away. The church took 200 years to build and its 137 stained-glass windows cover an area of 25,000 square feet. See also the house known as 'Picasiette' which is decorated with pieces of broken china set into cement. The work, which took 36 years and 29,000 hours, is a mosaic of Chartres itself.

Fontainebleau, thirty-seven miles south of Paris, is the site of the palace of the French kings. Begun in the twelfth century it was continually added to. You can go through various royal apartments, including Marie Antoinette's.

Versailles is only twelve miles out of the capital. On this trip you can see the palace of Louis XIV (the famous Sun King) and La Malmaison, home of Napoleon and Josephine.

Back in Normandy again, **Bayeux** is an old Norman town with yet another cathedral of Notre Dame (it means 'Our Lady'). See the famed Bayeux tapestry, 225 feet long, dating from the eleventh century and depicting the Norman conquest of England.

Near Bayeux, on the coast, is the site of the 1944 D-Day landings. You can visit the beaches – **Utah, Omaha, Gold, Juno,** and **Sword.** Plenty of things to see connected with the battle, including a museum of the invasion at the tiny village of **Arromanches.**

Mont St Michel, like the Alhambra in Granada, is claimed to be the eighth wonder of the world. Built on an island linked to the mainland by a road, the twelfth-century fortified town topped by its huge monastery looks quite unreal. And in springtime the *Grande Marée,* the big tide, comes rolling in from the English Channel at better than ten miles an hour, covering the road and completely surrounding the rock with water.

Pushing down to Tours, you go through **Le Mans,** scene of the big international car-racing events. **Tours,** a medium-sized city of around 100,000, is an old commercial centre and of no great interest. But from there, if you're interested, you can head into the château country of the Loire Valley. There are more than 120 of the old fortress homes in the valley, the most spectacular of them being at **Amboise** (catch the Son et Lumière if you have the time and money), **Chenonceaux, Azay-le-Rideau, Ussé,** and **Cheverny.**

Lyons, with more than half a million people, is the gateway city to the south. Founded in 43 BC it has a lot to offer. To start with there are 22 museums. Try the Museum of Fine Arts for Gauguin's 'Who are we? Whence do we come? Whither are we going?' – just a sample of what you can find there. The Museum of the History of Lyons is a fascinating visual description of what happens to a city during twenty centuries. The Museum of the French Resistance speaks for itself. On the Hill of Fourvière, which was the city centre in Roman times, you can see a Roman theatre and the remains of a temple. The main theatre seated 10,000 people. The Gothic Church of St Jean is surrounded by some of Lyons' oldest streets. Fourteenth- and fifteenth-century houses are still standing.

South of Lyons and a few miles west of the Rhône Valley is **Le Puy**. This weird city is a place of strange, steep, narrow streets and is surrounded by volcanic pinnacles. The Chapel of St Michel d'Aiguille sits on top of a 250-foot volcanic needle. The cathedral of Notre Dame de Puy has a façade of multi-coloured lava. Homely lady hitchers may be interested to know that Le Puy is world famous for its lace and that its Crozatier Museum contains a selection of same.

South of Le Puy, where the N86 joins with the N113 is **Nîmes,** the oldest Roman city in France. Roman ruins everywhere, including the huge Nîmes arena. The hitching can be pretty tough in this congested area, particularly in summer, though students heading for the university city of **Montpellier** help out a lot.

Inland from Montpellier you travel through **Hérault,** the largest wine-producing area in the world. You see square miles of vineyards stretched out on every side.

There are at least two cities in this province worth visiting; **Albi** because of its Lautrec Museum which contains the largest collection of Lautrecs in the world – some 500 paintings and sketches, right from the first the artist ever made – and, south of Albi, **Carcassonne,** one of Europe's most memorable landmarks. The old medieval **Cité** remains intact and completely walled. From the distance it looks like some gigantic 20th Century Fox movie lot. Within the walls you get a complete picture of what life was like eight or nine centuries ago. The road south of Carcassonne leads to **Andorra (see Luxembourg and the Small Countries).**

Over the other side of the Rhône you have **Avignon,** the Papal Seat from 1309 to 1403. See the Palace of the Popes and dozens of other monuments from that period. **Arles,** south of Avignon, is where Van Gogh lived and worked. **Aix-en-Provence,** where Cézanne worked, was founded by the Romans in 123 BC as a thermal resort.

Marseilles, the big port of southern France, is the country's oldest city, dating from 600 BC when it was founded by the Phoenicians. Much of the old city was destroyed in the Second World War, but there are still plenty of good areas to wander in. Around the Vieux-Port are some of Europe's grottiest and most interesting streets. Out in the bay stands the **Château d'If** where the Man in the Iron Mask is said to have been imprisoned and from where Alexandre Dumas' fictional Count of Monte Cristo made his

dramatic escape. If you want to visit the Château (good trip), disregard the prices on the launch operator's placards and bargain like hell. A group of people should be able to cut the price per head nearly by half.

East of Marseilles is the expensive (and slow hitching) area of the French Riviera. South of Montpellier is the road to Spain, with the La Junquera road carrying more traffic than the Port Bou road, though the latter is prettier, taking you down the Costa Brava.

★ **Rent-a-Ride** Ever get that never-gonna-get-a-ride feeling? Well snap out of it. Your French hosts have the problem licked! You get on the phone, tell them where you're going and they get you in touch with a driver who is going your way. But you'd better have a high bank balance to match those low spirits, because the service is going to cost you 50 francs annual subscription plus shared petrol costs.

Here's the full story as described by the French Tourist Board's interesting *Young France* brochure (ask for it at any major French Tourist Office): 'Although it is not recommended as a means of transport, hitch-hiking is certainly the cheapest way to travel. We hope that you know the rules of the game and we would point out that hitch-hiking is forbidden on motorways (autoroutes) but not on slip-roads or at "péages" (where motorists pay their tolls).

'To avoid all the difficulties you might already have encountered on the roadside, a fantastic new service has just been created and several French organizations will put drivers and passengers in touch with each other; so contact the representatives of the "Fédération Nationale des Associations de stop organisé" at the following addresses:

Provoya at 14 rue du Faubourg Saint-Denis, 75010 Paris (Tel: 246 00 66). Open from 9 a.m. to 8 p.m. from March to September.

Provoya at 3 rue Merientie, 13005 Marseilles (Tel: (91) 48 01 70). Open from 4 p.m. to 7 p.m. from Monday to Friday all year round.

Allauto at 13 rue Faidherbe, 59000 Lille (Tel: (20) 52 96 69). Open from 4 p.m. to 6 p.m. from Monday to Friday and from 10 a.m. to noon on Saturdays.

Stop Voyages at 15 rue Saint François, 33000 Bordeaux (Tel: (56) 92 76 12). Open from 3 p.m. to 7 p.m. from Monday to Friday and 10 a.m. to 1.00 p.m. on Saturdays.

Univoya at 14 rue Terral, 34000 Montpellier (Tel: (67) 72 22 27). Open from 10 a.m. to 8 p.m. all year round. Also, but not belonging to this association:

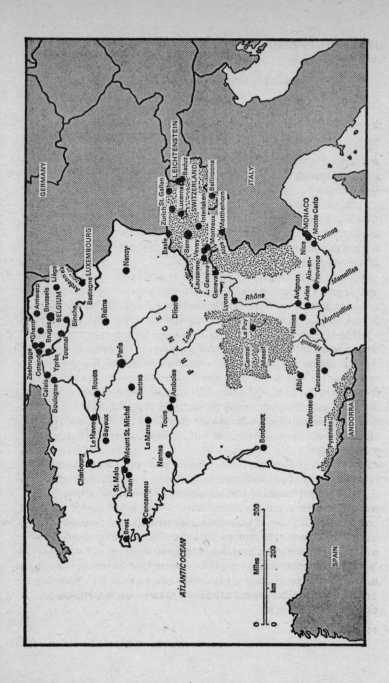

Dauphine Information Jeunesse at Jardin de Ville, 38000 Grenoble
(Tel: (76) 87 79 04).

' You will be asked to pay an annual subscription and share petrol expenses. Or if you catch French radio and mainly RTL between 9 p.m. and 12 p.m. every day except Sunday, Max Meynier will put you in touch with really "sympas" lorry drivers with whom you can travel. His telephone number in Paris is 720 22 11 and his broadcast *Les Routiers sont sympas*.'

★ **Corsica** You can reach Corsica by ferry from Nice, Marseilles or Toulon in France, or from Genoa in Italy. Cheapest crossing is from Nice.

The island is one of the Mediterranean's largest, over 100 miles long and 50 wide. And with a high average temperature throughout the year (57·4°F average through January and February) it's as good a place as any to hole up for a few days during winter. But be warned, it's expensive. Keep in the backstreets for eating and sleeping or you're going to get hit with jet-set prices.

If you like mountain scenery you'll be in your element, because this is a truly spectacular landscape (Mount Cinto, for instance, reaches nearly 9,000 feet!). Top towns are **Ajaccio, Bastia** and **Bonifacio. Ajaccio,** the capital, was the hometown of Corsica's most illustrious citizen: Napoleon. Visit the Maison Bonaparte, his birthplace and old family home which is now a museum. More Napoleon stuff to be seen in the Palais Fesch museum and in the Musée Napoléonien at the Town Hall. Wander around the old fishing harbour. Usually plenty of people around the cafés facing the harbour, but watch the prices. You can get stung if you aren't careful. **Bastia's** main attraction, in my opinion, is the beautiful old town. Great if you're a back-alley man. See also the museum, once the palace of the Governors of Genoa, and the port with its super-luxury ocean cruisers. (Some of them may need crew, so keep your eyes open if you're looking for a job.) The old fortified town of **Bonifacio** simply must be seen to be believed. Plenty of people claim it as the prettiest of all Mediterranean ports. 'Strangest' might be a better adjective. Have a look, anyway, and decide for yourself. History and art nuts should take the chance to drop in on the Bronze Age fort at **Cucuruzzu**. It's one of the best preserved in Europe. Also see the magnificent medieval frescoes at **Sermano di Bozio** which is in the centre of the island, near the ancient capital, **Corte**.

Camping out is permitted just about anywhere on the island, and with the high-cost of hotel rooms you might as well get used to the idea. You can camp wild or pitch a tent at an organized site at Ota, Ajaccio, Corte, Calvi or Uccaini.

★If you want to get on with French girls, pass yourself off as Scottish or Irish. If it doesn't work, don't tell me, tell Roger Brown. He claims it's true in his interesting *Travellers Survival Kit Europe* (Vacation-work, 9 Park End Street, Oxford).

Paris: where to sleep

French youth hostels cost around 25 francs (except in Paris where they are more expensive) and cheap hotel singles about 45 francs. If you're in a group of two or three, you can take double or triple rooms and cut hotel costs to around 38 francs a person. With French hotels, more than any others in Europe, *always* ask, after you've been quoted a price, if they don't have something a little cheaper. Top-floor rooms in cheap Parisian hotels which don't have lifts are quite often two or three francs cheaper – but naturally the proprietors try and get rid of their expensive rooms first.

★The following list of student accommodation has been supplied by the Centre d'Information et Documentation de Jeunesse. You can contact them at 101 Quai Branly, 75-Paris 15e (Tel: 566 4020).

1er arrondissement
Centre International de la Jeunesse at 20 rue J. J. Rousseau (Tel: 236 8818).

4e arrondissement
Hôtel des Jeunes 'Le Fauconnier' at 11 rue du Fauconnier (Tel: 277 8585).

Hôtel des Jeunes Maubuisson at 12 rue des Barres (Tel: 277 6753).

5e arrondissement
Foyer International des Etudiantes at 93 Boulevard St Germain (Tel: 033 4963). For girls only. Open July, August, September only.

Foyer Franco-Libanais at 15 rue d'Ulm (Tel: 633 4760). 15 July to 15 September only.

6e arrondissement
Association des Etudiants Protestants de Paris at 46 rue de Vaugirard (Tel: 033 31 49).

9e arrondissement
Union Chrétienne des Jeunes Gens (YMCA) at 14 rue de Trévise (Tel: 770 9094). Half-board compulsory.

11e arrondissement
Maison Internationale des Jeunes at 4 rue Titon (Tel: 371 9921/2).

12e arrondissement
Centre International de Séjour de Paris at 6 avenue Maurice Ravel
(Tel: 343 1901). Half-board compulsory. Ask for dormitory.

13e arrondissement
Maison des Clubs UNESCO at 43 rue de la Glacière (Tel: 336 0063).
For ages 16 to 25 only. July and August.

14e arrondissement
Foyer International d'Accueil de Paris at 30 rue Cabanis (Tel: 589 8915).
Half-board compulsory.

20e arrondissement
M.J.C. Théatre des deux Portes at 46 rue Louis Lumière (Tel: 797 2451).

Following is a list of hotels which are amongst the cheapest you will find
in the centre of Paris:

Hôtel Sully at 48 rue Saint Antoine (Tel: 278 49 32).
Métro to Bastille.

Hôtel At Home at 7 rue Thénard (Tel: 326 78 36).
Métro to Saint Michel.

Hôtel du Gros Caillou at 6 rue du Gros Caillou (Tel: 551 24 56).
Métro to Ecole Militaire.

Hôtel de la Tour Eiffel at 17 rue de l'Exposition (Tel: 705 50 31).
Métro to Ecole Militaire.

Hôtel du Bon Marché at 22 rue Saint Placide (Tel: 548 10 67).
Métro to Saint Placide.

Hôtel Joigny at 8 rue Saint-Charles (Tel: 579 3335).
Métro to Bir Hakeim.

For further information concerning student accommodation talk to the
people at Accueil des Jeunes en France, 12 rue des Barres, Paris 4e
(Tel: 272 7209).

To sleep rough try along the banks of the Seine beneath the Louvre.
There are usually some people sleeping there. (But see Marcel Thomas'
letter at the end of the chapter.) Other best bets are the cemeteries, with
the one at Montparnasse being handy to the centre. Cops don't seem to
worry rough-sleepers in Paris as long as they're quiet, though I imagine
mood varies with the political climate.

Another tip for sleeping: word has it that many of the churches in Paris are left open at night and that the priests don't mind if someone takes a pew.

To repeat: most rock bottom hotels come out at around 40 francs a single, but if you gang up with one or two others to take a double or triple, the per-person price drops a little.

Paris: where to eat

It's hard to find a decent meal in Paris for under 25 francs. For a filling, cheap restaurant meal expect to pay 25–30 francs, unless you are a student who can take advantage of student facilities, or a youth hosteller. For the average hitcher in Paris on a tight budget, someone who wants to stay on for a few days, it's necessary to buy food from shops and make picnic meals. But that's no hardship. A loaf of French bread, a slab of cheese and pâté, a piece of fruit and a bottle of wine will come out around 12 francs, and you can sit yourself down by the Seine or in the Luxembourg Gardens and it's nice enough. Invest another franc and eat your food with a cup of coffee at a sidewalk café and it's the nicest way of eating a meal in all of Europe.

Student Eating There are plenty of restaurants in Paris where students can get full meals for about 15 francs. For a complete list of addresses and for further information contact the Organisation pour le Tourisme Universitaire at 137 Boulevard St Michel. Métro to Port Royal, or telephone 326 60 97. Here are eight samples from the full list:

Le Mabillon at 3 rue Mabillon. Métro to Mabillon.

Le Bullier at 39 Avenue Georges Bernanos. Métro to Port Royal.

Le Centre Albert Châtelet at 6 rue Jean Calvin. Métro to Censier Daubenton.

Le Mazet at 5 rue Mazet. Métro to Odéon.

Les Mines at 270 rue Saint Jacques. Métro to Port Royal.

Le Censier at 3 rue Censier. Métro to Censier Daubenton.

Le Grand Palais at Cours la Reine. Métro to Champs-Elysées-Clemenceau.

The above are all classified as university restaurants. They are open 11.30 a.m.–2 p.m. and 6.30 p.m.–8 p.m.

Latin Cluny Self-Service Cafeteria at 98 Boulevard St Germain.

La Petite Source at 130 Boulevard St Germain.

Restaurant Jean at 132 Boulevard St Germain.

Grand Restaurant St Michel at 10 Boulevard St Michel.

La Source at 35 Boulevard St Michel.

Cafeterias Tuesdays to Saturdays only. *Galeries Lafayette* and
Au Printemps, both on Boulevard Haussmann, which is just at the back of
the Opéra (Métro to Opéra). Good meals for about 25 francs if you stand
up. More to sit.

Just about all of the little streets on the left side (with your back
to the river) of Place St Michel – like rue de la Harpe, or rue St Severin –
have cheap eating places. Head for the restaurants with the longest queues
outside because those are the ones with the best meals for your money.
A lot of students eat in this area and there are usually plenty of people
hanging around the fountain in Place St Michel, so you'll have no trouble
getting directions to the current best place.

   Here are some samples where you should be able to make a decent meal
around the 30 franc mark:

In rue de la Hachette: **Ristorante Pizza Pino** (number 8), **Crêperie
Restaurant** and **La Chameru Gourmand** (both numbered 13), **Restaurant
Bar Pino** (number 18), **Crêperie** (number 21), **Le Minos** (number 22),
Bar El Beida (no number).

In rue Xavier Privas: **Restaurant au Bon Couscous** (number 7), **Privas**
(number 9), **Restaurant du Bon Coin** (number 10), **Restaurant Belle Etoile**
(number 15), **Restaurant Long Van** (number 20), **Restaurant Le Latin**
(number 22).

In rue St Severin: **Restaurant le Vieux Paris** (number 9),
Viet Huong (number 14), **Au Petit St Michel Restaurant** (number 34).

In rue de la Harpe: **Les Balkans** (number 3), **Restaurant Chinois, Le Sérail**
(both at number 7), **Restaurant Chinois Nan-wa** (number 12), **Café-bar
Tout Va Bien** (number 19), **Nuit de Chine** (number 31).

Also at the corner of rue de la Harpe and St Severin, there's a great
take-away sandwich bar called **Pâtisserie du Sud Tunisien**.

Next best eating area, though not as colourful, nor with such a young
crowd, is in the Marais on the Right Bank – the section bounded by
rue de Rivoli, rue de Temple and the Boulevard Beaumarchais.

Paris: what to see and do

JEU DE PAUME: at the Jardin des Tuileries. Admission charge, but half price Sundays. World's greatest collection of Impressionist paintings.

LOUVRE in rue de Rivoli. Admission charge except Sunday when it's free. Great collection of paintings and sculpture. Closed Tuesdays.

RODIN MUSEUM rue de Varenne 77. Entrance charge, but half price Sundays. Rodin is considered by many to have been the greatest sculptor since Michelangelo. Closed Tuesdays.

EIFFEL TOWER in Champ de Mars. There are three platforms on the 1,033-feet-high tower, and it costs to go to each of them. By the time you reach the top you're in for more than 15 francs but you have a great view of Paris.

GEORGES POMPIDOU NATIONAL CENTRE OF ART AND CULTURE stands on the Plateau Beaubourg, bounded by rue Rambuteau and rue de Renard. Nearest Métro: Rambuteau. Open daily except Tuesday. The Centre is the result of an attempt to bring together all forms of cultural expression. Thus, under one roof, you can visit the National Museum of Modern Art, featuring work by dozens of top painters including Matisse, Miro, Picasso and Chagall; The Public Information Library with one million books, films, records, slides etc; the Institute for Research and Coordination in Acoustics and Music; the Centre of Industrial Creation; the Children's Workshop; the Cinémathèque, which tells the entire story of motion pictures, etc. In addition, anything up to forty exhibitions and demonstrations are held each year in this fantastic building which to some is a gem of modern architecture and to others, a sewer on stilts. A day pass costs around 12 francs. Entry free if you're under 18. Don't miss the happenings in the plaza in front. On the right day it's the best entertainment in Paris, and all free. Great place to meet people.

FREE VIEW OF PARIS from the roof of the *Samaritaine Department Store* on rue de Rivoli. You're ten floors up, so you can see plenty. Another good view over the city is from Sacré Coeur which surmounts the Butte Montmartre. (When this church was built, the architects found that the soil of the Butte was incapable of supporting the weight of the building so they had to push the foundations right through the hill. Consequently, Parisians say that if the hill were removed the church would be left standing.) In summer, young Parisians often meet on the steps of the Basilica. Whether they will this season, is another thing. Worth checking though.

MUSEE DE CLUNY 6 place Paul-Painlevé. Nearest Métro: St Michel. Admission charge. Open daily except Tuesday. A collection of some 25,000 works of art including painting, sculpture, carving, metal work, fabrics, ancient furniture, porcelain and glass, all housed in one of the city's most beautiful old buildings. Closed Tuesdays.

LUXEMBOURG GARDENS Métro to Gare du Luxembourg. Gardens (free) in which is contained the huge Luxembourg Palace which was built between 1615 and 1620 for the mother of Louis XIII. The palace was used as the headquarters of the Luftwaffe during the World War II German occupation of Paris. Usually plenty of people wandering about the gardens if you're looking for company.

SEWERS Enter from the south end of the Pont C'Alma on the Quai Bronly, near Place de la Résistance. About a twenty-minute barge trip through the sewers from the Place de la Concorde to Madeleine. Check with people for ever-changing time schedules unless you're between May and June when trips usually take place at 2, 3, 4, and 5 p.m.

PLACE PIGALLE This was once the centre of Bohemian Paris (now MONTPARNASSE is more the place), but these days Pigalle and Boulevard de Clichy are neon-lit tourist traps, full of clubs like the famous *Moulin Rouge* (you can see the show for about 40 francs if you sit at the bar and hold your drink tight), third-rate strip-joints full of drooping boobies, half-baked sex shops and handbag-swinging prostitutes who case you with a smiling eye. (The pros, by the way, aren't always what they seem. Paris fuzz did a big round-up recently and found that a large percentage of the ladies were, in fact, gentlemen.) But it's a great free show and if you're lucky you'll be able to watch some expert fleecers in action against the slow-witted tourist cult.

NOTRE DAME CATHEDRAL One of the classic sights of Paris. Worth looking through. Also try and make it up the Tower for a good view. Entrance charge for the Tower, but half price on Sundays. Closed Tuesdays.

VICTOR HUGO'S HOUSE is in the beautiful Place des Vosges which is buried in the Marais area. (Just a few minutes' walk from Place de la Bastille.) Fans of the old gent – and quite a gent at that – will enjoy the pilgrimage. Those not interested in literature will probably enjoy the square anyway. It's like stepping back a couple of centuries.

NAPOLEON'S TOMB at the Hôtel des Invalides. Take the Métro to Ecole Militaire. You'll see the granite sarcophagus in the Crypt. Inside are six coffins, one within the other. In the last is the Emperor. See the room which contains his personal relics, including his death-mask, his hat and his sword. Don't miss the nearby *Army Museum* (at the *Hôtel des Invalides*) which has one of the world's best collections of swords, bows, guns, cannon and other would-be problem solvers.

MONTMARTRE CEMETERY Enter from Avenue Rachel. Free. Interesting trip through a very strange scene. Some graves are crowned by monuments as big as houses which must have cost tens of thousands of francs to build. Quite unlike English or American style cemeteries. Zola is buried there, as are Stendhal, Berlioz, Offenbach, Delibes, and the son of Alexandre Dumas. The MONTPARNASSE CEMETERY is another free, weird trip. Enter on the rue Froidevaux. Famous people buried there include Saint-Saëns, de Maupassant and Baudelaire. A third is PERE LACHAISE CEMETERY, entrance on Boulevard Menilmontant, where you can see the graves of Rossini, Balzac, and Oscar Wilde.

MARKETS: free. There are several worth a visit. The BIRD MARKET at Place Louis-Lépine, open Sundays 9 a.m. to 7 p.m. The DOG MARKET at 106 rue Brancion open Sundays 1 p.m. to 4 p.m. The CLOTHES MARKET at Carreau du Temple, open all week, except Monday, from 8 a.m. to 7.30 p.m. and on Sundays 8 a.m. to 1 p.m. The FLOWER MARKET at the east side of Madeleine, open every day except Monday, from 9 a.m. to 7.30 p.m. The FLEA MARKET, the biggest in the world with four miles of open stalls and shops, at Porte de Clignancourt, open all day Saturday, Sunday and Monday. The STAMP MARKET at Avenue Gabriel and Avenue Marigny, open Thursday, Saturday, Sunday 8 a.m. to 7 p.m. HORSE, DONKEY, AND MULE MARKET at 106 rue Brancion, open Monday, Wednesday, Friday 9 a.m. to 12 midday.

THE CATACOMBS at Place Denfert-Rochereau. Small charge. October 16th to June 30th, first and third Saturdays at 2 p.m. July 1st to October 15th, every Saturday at 2 p.m. Originally the catacombs may have been a Roman quarry. Back in the 1780s, the city authorities were clearing an ancient cemetery and moved the bones into the catacombs. Some workmen took it into their heads to do a little interior decorating with the skulls – and you can still see the result of their efforts. The catacombs were also used as Resistance headquarters during the war.

PLACE ST MICHEL One of the best places to meet students is at the Place St Michel in front of the fountain showing St Michel with the Devil.

LES CAVES These famous Parisian institutions where you fight the haze of cigarette smoke and drown in the music are expensive. Entrance to most is in the vicinity of 15–25 francs, the price usually including one drink and you don't have to buy another. If you do they cost 8–12 francs each. But you meet some great people, hear some nice music, and have a very real chance of latching onto someone of the opposite sex. If you can afford it, try:

CAVEAU DE LA HUCHETTE at 5 rue de la Huchette. (Métro: St Michel.)

LE CHAT QUI PECHE at 4 rue de la Huchette. (Métro: St Michel.)

TROIS MAILLETS at 56 rue Galande. (Métro: St Michel.)

LE RIVER BOAT at 67 rue St André des Arts. (Métro: St Germain des Prés.)

USED BOOKS Try Shakespeare and Company at 37 rue de la Bûcherie (just a couple of minutes walk from Boulevard St Michel). One of Europe's most interesting multi-lingual shops. Owner George Whitman gives out cards which tell that the shop is 'The Free University of Paris', and 'To those who cherish freedom, practise equality and seek justice – welcome!'

Transport in Paris

With many of the major sights within half an hour of each other, Paris is a good walking city. Just as well, because the Métro (the underground railway) and the bus system are expensive. If you're going to be in town any length of time buy a *carnet*. On the Métro, for instance, a *carnet* will give you 10 tickets for 12 francs. (Make sure you get second class.) Bus prices are about the same as the Métro. Rich hitchers can buy a special 4-day tourist ticket for 38 francs which gives unlimited travel on the Métro, plus on city and suburban buses. It's not a bad deal when you consider you can go as far afield as Versailles! Richer hitchers expecting to be in town for a week can buy a 7-day ticket for 63 francs. If you have that sort of money present yourself and your passport at any RATP office. (There's one at Place de la Madeleine and another at 53 Quai des Grands Augustins.)

Bicycle rental is very expensive. Around 30 francs for the first day, about 15 francs each subsequent day. *Plus* you need an enormous 250 franc deposit.

Hitchers' tips and comments

I found the *Hitcher's Guide* fascinating. I can't wait for my next trip! I was disappointed that you left out the French Alps. I stayed in Grenoble for three weeks and I assure you it's worth visiting.

Some things in the area worth seeing are Collégiale St André, heavily war-damaged 13th-century church, one of the oldest in the area; Olympic Stade de Glace, ice arena where figure-skating competition was held (also Tremplin de Saut, the Olympic ski-jump near the village of St Nizier, fantastic views from there of the Alps and Grenoble); ruins of the Bastille and Grenoble's Téléphérique, you can spend hours exploring the ruins of the ancient prison, tunnels and city walls; Château de Vizille, south of Grenoble. Has nice formal gardens and a beautiful trout-filled lake (no fishing). Charles de Gaulle slept there.
David McDermot, University of Pittsburgh, USA

Best time to get from Paris to the South in one hop is to be there on the day the Big Vacation starts (in August) and everybody leaves for their holidays. Autoroute 1 is the main line of escape. Take a bus to the main feeder just near Orly Airport. Watch that you get the dates right. There seems to be a sort of vacuum period of bad hitch for a week after the big exodus.
Clive Gill, Birchington, England

People coming from Mont-St-Michel should stop a night at the small youth hostel in Fougères. It's a really nice little city. At the youth hostel there's a Golden Book (already up to volume 2) in which there's stacks of information written down by all the hitchers who've gone through.
Jurgen Bischoff, Gelsenkirchen, Germany
Jurgen is the guy who is working on the hitch-hiker's initiative (see letters on How to Hitch). It's a great idea. If you can help, why not write to him? K.W.

Greetings from the Fastest Thumb in the West! In Paris don't sleep on the Ile de la Cité. You'll get ripped off. Try the woods called Bois de Boulogne where there are wooden shelters to keep the rain off. Take Métro 2 to Porte Dauphine.
Bernd Vahle (Phallus), Bochum, Germany

Camping in Paris – for 40p a night at the pleasant site in the Bois de Boulogne. Don't walk from the Métro station (5 km), get a suburban train from St Lazare station in central Paris to Suresnes, walk down the hill, over Port de Suresnes and the camp site is on your left – about 10 minutes walk from the station. Suresnes station also has trains to Versailles.
Simon Calder, Coventry, England

A word of advice for anyone visiting Paris – unless you're absolutely stranded, as we were, stay away from the new Hostel at Choisey-le-Roi.

It's a rip-off. I know Paris is supposed to be expensive but 35F a night is a bit much, to say nothing of the 4F it costs to get there, or the 20F fine if you use a sleeping-bag.
D. G. Mulvey, Dublin, Ireland

With reference to your comments on grape picking where you say 'most of this work is of very temporary nature and badly paid' I would like to recount our experience in Beaujolais (north west of Lyons). We worked on two farms for a total of 14 days and were paid F820 each. We were woken at 6.30 a.m. for breakfast; tea or coffee and bread and jam. Work started between 7.30 a.m. and 8.00 a.m. and we worked intil 12 noon. Sometimes there was a break in the morning of 15 minutes for bread, cheese, chocolate and a drink. Wine, water and squash were available for the asking. Lunch was a massive affair eaten in traditional French fashion with each course being eaten separately. Wine flowed like a river. Work started at 1.30 p.m. and finished between 6 and 7.30 p.m. Dinner was excellent – plenty to eat and drink. Some might regard the sleeping and toilet facilities as being rough. You slept at the farms in a bed or on the floor – most places have hot water and showers. The working day is 10 hours, rarely more. The pay was F58 per day. If it rained you didn't work and you didn't get paid but you got your bed and food. We must add that the work is hard and dirty particularly when it's wet.

All in all it was a thoroughly enjoyable experience – you eat and drink well, can meet some pleasant and interesting people and you can save money because you have no expenses. On some farms (the ones we worked on) cigarettes were on the house. We would recommend the grape harvest (*Vendange*). Beware of organizations like the one we contacted which gave us a vineyard address and a starting date. They charged £11 each and told us they'd send us the information via a Poste Restante address. After much phoning and hassling we got an address but not a starting date which was important because the harvest was a month early this year.

We think that the best thing to do would be to visit an area in early September, get yourself fixed up with a farmer and drift off until the *Vendange* starts. Sometimes you can work on afterwards. Two people we know have got jobs for three months and one year – the exception rather than the rule.
Gail Pemberton and David Griffith, Lyons, France

Anywhere in France if you order a coffee, make sure it's a *petit* otherwise they serve you a super de luxe version at a price to match.

In Paris for crashing rough your book suggests the banks of the Seine near the Louvre – forget it! I slept there with a fellow English guy and

several others and we were wiped out at 5 in the morning by a bunch of very professional heavies. They woke us up but we couldn't stand up. I was rolled for about £60 cash, stripped of valuables, watch, ring etc. Even lost me Levis and travelling the Métro in underwear isn't funny! Everyone lost something so I suggest that spot gets black-listed in the next edition.
Marcel Thomas, Horndean, England

On Paris you failed to mention a mass of cheap hotels directly outside of the Port de Vincennes subway stop.
Lynne Hoffman and Judith Zorfas, Canada and USA

Just south of Paris, not too far from Porte d'Orléans, is the Rungis, an enormous fresh food market. Lorries leave here for all over Europe.
Chris Moore, Bedford, England

If you're passing through Lyons, an excellent place to kip is in an elevated shopping area next to Lyons Perrache station. It is totally enclosed, heated, and chairs are provided. It's just a big indoor shopping area. Sleeping bags are not allowed, but they're not needed.
   If drinking wine in a bar or restaurant, emphasize *vin ordinaire*. I got ripped off for some expensive wine, and you're obliged to pay.
John Heywood, Devon, England

There was hardly a town in France that I passed through that didn't have an approved campsite. These can work out quite cheap although not as cheap as out on the road. They have several advantages; they are safe as there is always somebody about to watch your stuff; they have hot showers; and there is usually a supermarket nearby where you can get decent grub for a decent price.
Paul Lawrence, Belfast, Northern Ireland

Underneath Louvre and Eiffel Tower Gardens always rest your head on your kit and tie your pack to your sleeping bag.
Nicholas M. Steven, Sherborne, England

Student discounts
Reductions to all state museums and galleries, to certain other museums and galleries, plus to some theatres, cinemas and clubs. Check with: 137 Boulevard St Michel, Paris 5e (Tel: 326 60 97).

Addresses

Main Post Office (for Poste Restante) at 52 rue du Louvre, Paris.

American Express at 11 rue Scribe, Paris (Tel: 073 42 90).

Organisation pour le Tourisme Universitaire (l'OTU) at 137 Boulevard St Michel, Paris 5e (Tel: 326 60 97).

Office de Tourisme de Paris at 127 Champs Elysées, Paris (Tel: 720 90 16).

US Embassy at 2 Avenue Gabriel, Paris (Tel: 265 74 60).

British Embassy at 35 rue du Faubourg Saint-Honoré, Paris 8e (Tel: 266 91 42).

Belgium

Population	9,800,000
Size	12,000 square miles
Capital	Brussels, population 1,200,000
Government	Constitutional Monarchy
Religion	Roman Catholic
Language	French, Flemish, and some German. English widely spoken

Entry into Belgium from England is by ferry from Dover, Felixstowe, Folkestone or Hull to either Zeebrugge or Ostend. The single-fare price is about £10.

A Jetfoil service (fast but expensive) also runs between Port of London and Zeebrugge.

Principal cities after Brussels are **Liège, Bruges, Ghent** and **Antwerp**.

Ostend is one of the country's largest seaside resorts and even though it has 186 hotels and caters to the very solid tourist type it's a rather likeable place – one day at a time. The port is nice and there are a few things to see, but don't stop there if you're pushed for time.

Bruges, just a dozen or so miles inland from the sea, is one of the big art centres of Belgium and one of the most unspoiled medieval cities in Europe. The most important commercial city in Europe during the thirteenth and fourteenth centuries it is now one of the most popular for tourists. See the old market square and the 275-foot-high belfry with its treasure-room and 11,400 lb Triumph Bell. See the Basilica of the Holy Blood where they keep what is believed to be a drop of Christ's blood – and if you're in town on Ascension Day (Ascension Day is a moveable feast held in May) catch the famous Procession of the Holy Blood. To see paintings by Brueghel the Younger, van Eyck and Bosch, drop into the Groeninge Museum. If you don't have a student card and feel like visiting each of the 16 museums and galleries in Bruges, you can buy a special discount card from tourist offices or museums.

If you're interested in exploring the infamous Flanders Fields of the First World War visit **Ieper** (or **Ypres**). The town stands in the middle of the old battlefields 50 kilometres south of Bruges.

Ghent, 30 kilometres down either the E5 or the N10 from Bruges, is known as the City of Flowers, and every fifth year (1970–1975–1980) hosts the Ghent *Floralies*, a huge international flower show. The other four years you can visit St Bavo's Cathedral, the Castle of the Counts (see the horrifying collection of instruments of torture), the Castle of Gerard the Devil (not as good as the Castle of the Counts, but it has a better name) and see the Ghent Museum of Fine Arts for a fantastic collection of Flemish paintings. Have a look, also, at Mad Meg, a fifteenth-century cannon, 17 feet long, and weighing 16 tons, which used to spit out stone balls weighing 750 lb. (In 1978 I heard on the grapevine that a group in Ghent were considering starting a scheme whereby hitchers bought petrol tokens to offer drivers in exchange for rides. Anyone heard more?)

Antwerp, the world's leading diamond centre, is not a madly exciting city to my mind, but if you're going that way, drop in and see Rubens' house where the famous artist lived and worked. The Museum Mayer Van Den Bergh has a good collection, including 'Dulle Griet' by the mystical Mr Brueghel. Sea-going types might be interested in the National Maritime Museum and, talking of the sea, it's interesting to note that even though Antwerp is 50 miles from the ocean it's the world's fourth largest port. It has 30 miles of docks along the banks of the Scheldt River (which drains into the sea) and those docks see 50,000 barges and 10,000 ocean-going ships tie up each year. Try the barges for possible river rides. It's done quite often by hitchers who drop the hard word into the right soft ear. The port also boasts a wild night-life.

Halfway between Antwerp and Brussels on the E10 is **Breendonk** where the Belgians have kept intact a Nazi concentration camp. Nasty to look at and a sledge-hammer reminder of what 'people' are capable of doing.

Binche, between Mons and Charleroi, is the scene of one of the wildest carnivals in Europe every March, culminating on Shrove Tuesday – Pancake Day. Great show if you can make it; fancy dress (Peruvian), flour bombs, more booze than you've seen in your life and lots of single ladies and gentlemen guarantee that it's a swinging show. You'll probably need a full day to rest after it, so budget accordingly.

Tournai, 80 kilometres from Brussels on the N8, is a town of 35,000 which dates from AD 275 and mainly for those interested in history and architecture. For instance, its five-steepled Romanesque church is considered one of the finest in the world, while the Belfry is the oldest in the country. Of particular interest are the ancient houses which dot the city.

Bastogne, on the N4 near the Luxembourg border, is a tourist centre for the Ardennes area. It's famous as the town where, during the Battle of the Bulge, when the Germans had the American forces surrounded and sent a man under truce to ask them to surrender, the American commander answered 'Nuts', thus leaving the German translator with an untranslatable word.

Waterloo, just south of Brussels, is the battle-site where Napoleon met his you-know-what. In the town's main street you can visit Wellington's headquarters and a museum, while on the battlefield itself you can see Napoleon's headquarters and other museums and memorials.

Liège is yet another of Belgium's important art cities, and if you visit don't miss the sixteenth-century Palace of the Prince Bishops, the Museum of Fine Arts or the Museum of Walloon Life which concentrates on life in Liège during past centuries.

Hitch-hiking is OK in Belgium, though the big main highway through from Ostend to Brussels – the E5 – can sometimes prove to be a trap. However, with any luck you'll meet someone on the ferry who is taking a car over and you'll be right on your way. Be warned that the Belgians are amongst the fastest and worst drivers in the world.

Brussels: where to sleep

Expect to pay 190 francs even for hostels and as much as 375 francs for a cheap room. Make sure VAT and 16% service fee are included.

CHAB at 6 rue Traversière (Tel: 219 58 16).

Hotel des Etudiants at 14 rue des Etudiants (Tel: 539 07 25).

YMCA at 31 rue Duquesmoy (Tel: 513 47 55). Men only.

YWCA at 43 rue St Bernard (Tel: 538 09 84). Women only.

International Youth Home at 21 rue du Congrès (Tel: 218 48 53). Take student card.

Centre International des Etudiants at 26 rue des Parme (Tel: 537 89 61). Ask for dormitory.

Cité Universitaire at 22 Avenue Paul Héger (Tel: 647 10 56).
Open August 1st to September 15th.

Hôtel des Touristes at 11 rue du Marché (Tel: 217 64 37).

Hôtel Osborne at 67 rue Bosquet (Tel: 537 92 51).

Ballon Nord at 24 rue de Brabant (Tel: 217 54 87).

Résidence Botanique at 171 rue Royale (Tel: 217 82 20).

Hôtel Ruche Bourse at 1 rue Grétry (Tel: 218 58 87).

Hôtel Sabot d'Or at 5 Boulevard d'Anvers (Tel: 217 48 69).

Hôtel Du Merlo at 2 avenue Fonsny (Tel: 538 15 69).

Hôtel Sainte-Anne at 1a Boulevard Jardin Botanique (Tel: 218 35 19).

Hôtel Alfa at 144 rue Defacqz (Tel: 537 04 19).

For help finding hotels contact the Brussels Information Office at rue
Marché aux Herbes. For help in locating student accommodation try the
MUBEF at 61 rue Belliard.

For sleeping rough there's Parc de Brussels, the Botanic Gardens or
the Parc Josaphat. But be warned – the word is that the Belgian police are
coming down hard these days.

Brussels: where to eat

As in most of Europe a good filling meal will cost 140–200 francs in
a cheap restaurant or perhaps less if you use student facilities or chain
cafeterias.

Cité Universitaire at 22 Avenue Paul Héger.

YWCA at 43 rue St Bernard. Dinner served between 7 and 8 p.m.
Women only.

YMCA at 31 rue Duquesmoy. Dinner between 7 and 8 p.m. Men only.

Galeries Anspach (department store) at Boulevard Anspach. Closes 6 p.m.

Sarma (department store) at 17 rue Neuve. Closes 6 p.m.

Au Bon Marché (department store) at Place Rogier. Closes 6 p.m.

Le Breton, student café at 49 rue des Drapiers.

Chez Georges at 24 rue des Chapeliers.

Restaurant Hubert at 33 rue du Progrès.

Youth Hostel at Poststraat 91–93.

Brussels: what to see and do

THE GRAND' PLACE This is the heart of Brussels and has been since medieval times. Originally it was a market-place and is still used as such in the mornings. Sunday morning is the scene of a bird market. The *Hôtel de Ville* (or Town Hall) is one of the oldest and most beautiful of the buildings on the square. A few francs gets you in for a tour and another few lets you climb the tower for a great view of Brussels. Directly opposite Hôtel de Ville is the *Maison du Roi*, a restored sixteenth-century building housing the Municipal Museum.

FLEA MARKET at Place du Jeu de Balle. Every day from 9 a.m. to 1 p.m. Best days, Saturdays and Sundays.

THE OLD MARKET at Place du Grand Sablon. Mostly antiques (swords, furniture, rare books, etc). All day Saturday and also Sunday morning.

MANNEKEN-PIS in rue du Chêne, near the Grand' Place. A small statue of a small boy taking a small leak. Not really worth seeing, but like the Mermaid in Copenhagen, you gotta go and have a look.

MUSEE D'ART ANCIEN at 3 rue de la Régence. Free on Wednesday, Saturday and Sunday afternoons. Tremendous collection of Flemish art. This is where you can get a head full of Bosch and Brueghel.

THE BRUEGHEL MUSEUM at 132 rue Haute. Strictly for serious Brueghel fans, but for them it's going to be a real trip.

NEW POL'S JAZZ PLACE at 23A rue de Stassart. Live jazz, silent movies, friendly people. About 30 francs entrance and 30 francs a beer. Closed Sundays and Mondays.

CLUBS Try along Avenue de la Toison d'Or (between Chaussée d'Ixelles and Porte Louise) for fairly cheap prices and a fairly good chance for some action.

MUSEE DE CINEMA at 9 rue Baron Horta in the Palais des Beaux-Arts. This is a museum of the cinema which also shows several classic movies in the original language each night. Costs about 50 francs a movie, and you might catch an old one you've been hunting for. There are 12,000 titles in the archives. (Tel: 513 41 55).

DRUG HELP CENTRE Infor Drogue at 4 Place Quêtelet will help if you need it. Day number 218 28 28. Night number 736 36 36.

YOUTH INFORMATION CENTRE Try Infor Jeunes, 288 rue Royale (Tel: 736 36 36) for information on just about anything. Including drug problems and legal aid.

Transport in Brussels
Bus and tram tickets are expensive enough, but if you're in town a few days prices will really add up. So try investing in a six-journey card or a weekly ticket (Monday to Friday). Each offers big discounts; buy them at stations.

Student discounts
Special reductions to most museums, galleries, theatres and cinemas throughout the country. Information from:
MUBEF,
61 rue Belliard, Brussels 4 (Tel: 513 07 12).

Addresses

Main Post Office (for Poste Restante) at rue des Halles, Brussels.

American Express at 22–24 Place Charles Rogier, Brussels (Tel: 219 01 90).

Tourisme des Etudiants et de la Jeunesse (MUBEF) at 61 rue Belliard, Brussels 4 (Tel: 513 07 12).

Brussels Information Centre at 61 rue Marché aux Herbes, Brussels (Tel: 513 89 40).

Belgian National Tourist Office at 61 rue Marché aux Herbes, Brussels (Tel: 513 90 90).

US Embassy at 27 Boulevard du Régent, Brussels (Tel: 513 38 30).

British Embassy at 28 rue Joseph II, Brussels (Tel: 19 11 65).

Hitchers' tips and comments
Brussels. Cafés really expensive. Stick to picnic meals. Good place to rest is railway station lounge – soft leather couches.
Malcolm Frankland, Glaslum, England

It is illegal for an unmarried couple under 21 to camp together or stay in a hotel room together! (Punishable by 3 years prison).
Simon Calder, Coventry, England

Holland

Population	13,875,000
Size	15,892 square miles
Capital	Amsterdam, population 759,000
Government	Constitutional Monarchy
Religion	Protestant and Roman Catholic
Language	Dutch. A lot of English spoken, especially in the cities

Usual form of entry to Holland is by road after having taken the ferry to France or Belgium.

After Amsterdam, the most important cities to see are Rotterdam and The Hague.

Rotterdam, with its 750,000 inhabitants, is the largest port in Europe and the second largest in the world. Its 47 kilometres of dockside is worth going down to see. Waalhaven Dock is the largest artificial harbour in the world. For a great view over the port, climb to the 383-foot-high lookout on the 600-foot Euromast (if you can afford the heavy entrance charge) – but avoid the restaurant, it's expensive. The Boymans-van-Beuningen Museum claims to be the richest in Holland after the Rijksmuseum in Amsterdam. If it's half as good it's doing well. For a look at a building of a different sort, try the largest one in Western Europe. The Groothandelsgebouw, or wholesaler's building, is 220 metres long, 84 wide, and 43 high. In it are 300 offices, a restaurant, meeting-halls, a post-office, bowling alleys plus lots more, including a staff of 5,000. Another interesting feature is its 1½ kilometres of road – inside! – leading to various indoor parking facilities. Americans might be interested in seeing Delfshaven, embarkation point of the Pilgrim Fathers in 1620.

The Hague, just a few short miles up the E10 from Rotterdam, has a lot more to offer. To start with, the Municipal Museum has a fine line-up of modern art, including the world's largest collection of Mondriaan. The Dutch Postal Museum will keep philatelists happy for hours. To see one of the most unusual (and largest) paintings in the world, drop in on the Mesdag Panorama, while for a somewhat ghoulish hour go to the Prisoner's Gate to see the collection of instruments of torture.

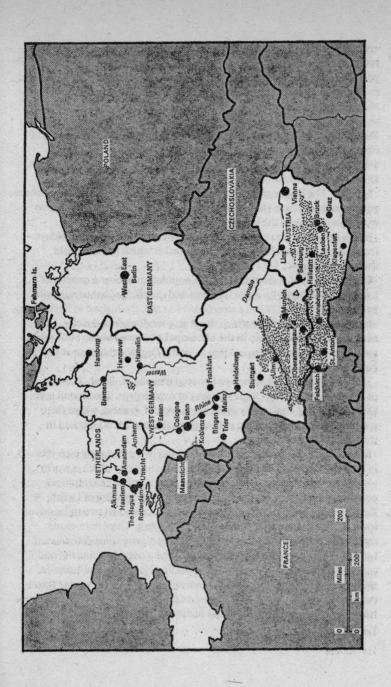

A suburb of The Hague, but with a character of its own, is the seaside resort of **Scheveningen**. The long, long beach is the ideal place to sleep while you're visiting The Hague and a marvellous place – on sunny days – to make contact with sun-bathers of the opposite sex. The Pier is a sideshow-type place jutting 1,200 feet out into the sea and makes for pleasant evening walking. The Fishing Harbour is a riot of smells just about any morning. Don't miss the miniature town of Madurodam. It's built over an area of four acres, complete with two miles of railway track, houses, castles, churches, and even an airport, all constructed perfectly to a 1/25th scale. Open April to September.

North of The Hague and a few miles from Amsterdam, is **Haarlem**, where you can see the Frans Hals Museum and the Great Church of St Bravo which houses one of the largest organs in the world.

North again and you come to **Alkmaar** where the big sight on Fridays from April to September is the Cheese Market which has been held there for centuries.

Utrecht, south of Amsterdam, with a population of over a quarter of a million, is dotted with ancient houses and canals. Its Cathedral, built between 1254 and 1517 has a steeple 360 feet tall, the highest in the country, and it's a great place from which to get an overall view of the city. Try, also, to see the Viking ship in the Municipal Museum. Music buffs might want to try the 'From Musical Box to Barrel Organ' exhibition at the National Museum.

For Van Gogh fans there are two special treats in Holland. The first, of course, is at the Van Gogh Museum in Amsterdam. The second is at **Otterlo National Park,** a few miles north-west of **Arnhem**, where there is another large and excellent collection of the man's work housed in the Kröller-Muller Museum.

Maastricht, right down in southern Holland in the enclave which juts in between Germany and Belgium, is an industrial city which is worth visiting for two reasons. First, because as a result of its geographical position, it uses three languages and has a strange mixture of Dutch, Belgian, and German customs; and second, because just two miles out of town are the Roman Catacombs of St Pietersberg. These man-made catacombs bored into a huge limestone hill comprise some 200 miles of tunnels. Thousands of people have visited them over the centuries and carved their names in the soft walls, including Napoleon and Voltaire.

★**Hitching** Hitching in Holland is generally good – you can cross the entire country in a couple of hours – but remember that if you want to travel fast you must keep to the big highways. Holland is one of the most densely-populated areas in the world and it's very easy to get trapped on a village to village, town to town tour if you stay on the small roads. (Not that there's anything wrong with that if you have the time to spare!) The same rules apply on the highways as on the German autobahns – no hitching! You must grab your ride on the exit or entrance roads. Cops in white Porsches are around to make sure you do just that.

★**Tulips and windmills** There used to be 9,000 working windmills in Holland. Now, unless you know where to look, you can travel through the entire country without seeing one. The place to go is **Kinderdijk**, a few miles east of Rotterdam, where the largest concentration of those still remaining can be found. The tulips can be seen at their best around early May – acres of them. Best areas are between **Leiden** and **Haarlem**. If you specifically want to see them you should avoid the big roads and plot a route which will take you through the small villages west of the N99.

★**Hitching barges** This is becoming a more and more popular method of off-beat travel – but you must have plenty of time if you want to do a complete trip. Rotterdam is the place to start and from there you can go right through the Rhine into Switzerland. Just ask a barge captain – some will tell you to go to hell, but plenty won't. Most charge for food, some don't. If, because of the time factor, you decide you can only afford one day aboard, you'll have much less trouble finding a boat.

Warning! Two readers have written in warning about the drug scene in Holland. The gist of it is this . . . people are lulled into a false sense of confidence because everyone in Amsterdam seems so free and easy. When they try their same tricks in the provincial towns they get busted so fast their heads spin. Take care!

Amsterdam: where to sleep

Sleeping prices are high in Amsterdam – even the youth hostel costs 15 guilders – but the blow is softened a bit when you discover that the price always includes a breakfast guaranteed to set you on your feet for the day. Most of these breakfasts are large enough so that you can take a portion away with you and use it as a lunchtime snack. Generally, expect to pay between 18 and 30 guilders for bed and breakfast in a hotel.

Youth Hostel Stadsdoelen at Kloveniersburgwal 97 (Tel: 24 68 32).

Fat City at O.2. Voorburgwal 157 (Tel: 020-226 705).

Hotel Adolesce at Nieuwe Keizersgracht 26 (Tel: 26 39 59). Ask for dormitory.

Hotel Schreierstoren at Geldersekade 10 (Tel: 22 43 70). Ask for dormitory. And good luck to you.

Hans Brinker Stutel at Kerkstraat 136 (Tel: 22 06 87). This one is very good, but also pretty expensive. About 20 guilders even in the dormitory.

Youth Hostel Vondelpark, Zandpad 5 (Tel: 14 17 44).

Hotel Cok at Koninginneweg 30 (Tel: 79 66 53).

Hotel Groenendael, Nieuwendijk 15 (Tel: 24 48 22).

The Shelter, Barndesteeg 21–25 (Tel: 25 32 30). No breakfast. Ask for dormitory.

Adam & Eva at Sarphatistraat 105 (Tel: 24 62 06). Ask for dormitory.

Hotel de Beurs, Beursstraat 7 (Tel: 22 07 41).

Eben Haëzer at Bloemstraat 179 (Tel: 24 47 17). Ask for dormitory.

H88 at Herengracht 88 (Tel: 24 44 46). Closed in winter. Ask for dormitory.

Hotel Clemens, Raadhuisstraat 39 (Tel: 24 60 89).

Kabul Student Hotel at 42 Warmoesstraat (Tel: 23 71 58).

Hotel Brian at Singel 69 (Tel: 24 46 61).

Hotel Anja at Singel 97 (Tel: 24 16 17).

Hotel Astoria at Martelaarsgracht 15 (Tel: 24 71 80).

Hotel Ronnie at Raadhuisstraat 41 (Tel: 24 28 21).

Hotel Schirmann at Prins Hendrikkade 23 (Tel: 24 19 42).

Hotel Schröder at Haarlemmerdijk 48B (Tel: 66 272).

Hotel de Westertoren at Raadhuisstraat 35B (Tel: 24 46 39).

Hotel Hiller at Herengracht 129 (Tel: 24 21 18).

Hotel Galerij, Raadhuisstraat 43 (Tel: 24 88 51).

Hotel van Onna at Bloemgracht 102 (Tel: 26 58 01).

Hotel l'Avenir at Joh. Verhulststraat 132 (Tel: 79 47 17).

Hotel Grégoire at Nic Maesstraat 77 (Tel: 72 95 67).

It's worth remembering that student hotels in Holland are generally open to anyone, with or without student credentials, as long as they look *something* like a student.

Also, if you're travelling with someone, double rooms work out cheaper per person than singles.

For help with all accommodation problems, contact the VVV Tourist Information Office at Stationsplein which is open every day of the year until 11 p.m. In 1978 they operated **Sleepin** 1 at Looiersgracht 35 (Tel: 22 94 02) and **Sleepin** 2 at Rozengracht 180 (Tel: 23 58 71) – both huge dormitories of 800 and 550 beds respectively. Cost was 5 guilders. You brought your own sleeping bag. Check VVV for current addresses and price.

Also ask them for *Use-it*, a free weekly newspaper published throughout June, July and August and featuring money-saving advice on accommodation and restaurants for travelling youth (that's you!).

Sleeping rough should be no problem. Julianapark, Vondelpark and Beatrixpark are your best bets. (The cops don't bite if you don't.) If you prefer to be completely legal try the Youth Camping Grounds at: **Zeeburg**, Ijdijk (A'dam-Oost) (Tel: 94 66 88).
Vliegenbos, Meeuwenlaan 138 (A'dam-Noord) (Tel: 36 88 55).
(Both cost around 5 guilders.)

Amsterdam: where to eat

Beds are expensive in Amsterdam and so is food. Expect to pay as much as 10–12 guilders for the main meal of the day. If you're eating breakfast away from your hotel, try *ontbijtkoek* which is a little cake. Try, also, the little pancakes called *poffertjes*.

The Chinese and Indonesian Restaurants in the Binen Bantammerstraat near Central Station. Good filling meals. The lunchtime specials are the best deals.

Van Dobben at Korte Reguliersdwarsstraat, 5–9. Sandwich shop. Cheap.

Restaurant Alleman at Sweenlinckstraat 23.

Kow Loon at Singel 498. Very cheap Oriental-type food.

De Drie Musketiers at Thorbeckeplein 12.

Hema Department Store Cafeteria at Nieuwendijk 174.

Vami Restaurant at Kalverstraat 171.

VGK Restaurant at Spuistraat 4. Open Monday to Friday and closes 7 p.m.

Ta Dung at Bethaniendwarsstraat 10. Chinese and dirt cheap.

Restaurant Leto – Plate service at Haarlemmerdijk 114.

Quick Snackbar at the corner of Martelaarsgracht and Nieuwendijk 50. An automat place where you can fill yourself for 8 guilders.

H88, at Herengracht 88. Cheap.

Coffee Haesje Claes at Nieuwe Zijds Voorburgwal 320.

Indonesian Restaurant Sukasari at Damstraat 26.

Buddha's Belly at Rozenstraat 145. Indian food.

De Lantaan at 2e Const. Huygenstraat 64.

Kosmos at Prinshendrikkade 142. Macrobiotic food at reasonable prices.

Amsterdam: what to see and do

THE STEDELIJK MUSEUM in Paulus Potterstraat is probably the greatest museum of modern art in Europe. The collections are superbly displayed and unbelievably good. De Kooning, Mondrian, Miro, Degas, Cézanne, Chagall, Picasso . . . you name it. Admission charge but half price on Sundays.

VAN GOGH MUSEUM on Museumplein. A mind-bender! Don't miss it!

THE RIJKSMUSEUM is just a couple of hundred yards from the Stedelijk. Admission charge, but half price on Saturdays and Sundays. This museum houses a superb classical collection. Particularly strong on Rembrandt (they have his 'Night Watch'). Also Vermeer, Goya, Tintoretto, Hals, Rubens, Jan Steen, etc.

THE WATERFRONT AREA Free and fascinating. Set in amongst the streets and alleys of the Zeedijk/Nieuwmarkt area is Europe's vastest collection of bars, dives, queer-shops, clubs, cafés, and brothels. No point in describing it all – just get down and have a look round about 11 at night. (The prices go as low as 30 guilders for which you get fifteen minutes of what is mostly indifference.)

MOVIES Shown in original language. Plenty of first-run American and English shows. Prices lower than in most capital cities.

REMBRANDT'S HOUSE at Jodenbreestraat 4. Admission charge. Rembrandt lived here for twenty years. It contains a large collection of his etchings and drawings.

THE HOUSE OF ANNE FRANK at 263–265 Prinsengracht. Admission charge. This is where Anne Frank, the young Jewish girl who wrote the famous *Diary*, lived with her family in total isolation and secrecy for two years during the German occupation of the city. In 1944 the family was betrayed, the Gestapo arrested them and they were sent to a concentration camp where Anne died. The secret apartment has been preserved in its entirety. A permanent exhibition on contemporary anti-semitism is displayed in the building.

FREE BEER! FREE FOOD! The Heineken's Brewery at Van der Helststraat 30 give guided tours of their establishment at 10 in the morning, Monday to Friday. At the end of the tour there's free beer, free cheese and sometimes free cigarettes. I hear, though, that in summer the breweries are asking a small fee which is donated to UNICEF.

CANAL TRIPS generally cost about 7 guilders and are a fine way of seeing Amsterdam if it's your first day there (and if you can put up with the same jokes being cracked by the same hostess in four different languages!). Trips last about an hour. You'll see the boats and advertisements near the Central Station.

FLEA MARKET at Waterlooplein. Every morning except Sunday. Good for second-hand clothes.

MUSEUM AMSTELKRING at 40 Oude Zijds Voorburgwal is more popularly known as 'Our Lord in the Attic'. This strange church is completely camouflaged and hidden within the top floors of several old canal houses. It was built during the Reformation when the Roman Catholics were having trouble with the authorities.

WORLD'S NARROWEST HOUSE Said the coachman to his boss, 'Sir, if only I had a house as wide as your front door.' Said the boss, 'You shall.' The result is at Singel 7 – the house of Mr Tripp's coachman.

Transport in Amsterdam
Cheapest way to travel around is by trams and buses. You can buy one to three day tickets priced at between 4 and 7.50 guilders.

For the rental of bicycles try Koenders, Utrechtsedwarsstraat 105
(Tel: 23 46 57) who rent them for 6 guilders a day.

Student discounts

Reductions to some theatres, cinemas, galleries, museums, restaurants,
and nightclubs. For information, contact:
NBBS STUDENT CENTRE,
Damrak 87, Amsterdam (Tel: 22 32 42).

Addresses

Main Post Office (for Poste Restante) at NZ Voorburgwal 182,
Amsterdam.

American Express at Damrak 66, Amsterdam (Tel: 62 042).

NBBS (Netherlands Bureau for Foreign Student Relations) at Damrak 87,
Amsterdam (Tel: 22 32 42).

NBBS at Rapenburg 6, Leiden (Tel: 4 39 41).

Amsterdam Tourist Office (VVV) at Rokin 5, Amsterdam (Tel: 26 64 44).

US Consulate at Museumplein 19, Amsterdam (Tel: 79 03 21).

British Consulate-General, Joh. Vermeerstraat 7, Amsterdam
(Tel: 73 61 28).

Hitchers' tips and comments

Dutch officials seem to be tightening up. Constant demands to know how
much money you have, whether you have return ticket to your country of
origin.
D. F. Dickson, London N4

The canal trips from opposite Heineken Brewery are cheaper, especially
for students, than from outside central station. 'Amstel toerist' is the name
of the line.
Richard, New Zealand

Sleeping rough in Amsterdam is illegal now so take care.
John Eames, Bognor Regis, England

Travellers entering Holland at Enschese from Germany, beware! Customs officials frisk long-hairs. And if one has insufficient funds it's back to Germany.
Malcolm Frankland, Glaslum, England

West Germany

Population	60,000,000
Size	(excluding West Berlin) 95,742 square miles
Capital	Bonn, population 150,000
Government	Federal Republic
Religion	All denominations
Language	German. Some French and English understood

There's a lot to see in Germany, but I'll start by mentioning something which you *can't* see unless you're in Europe in 1980, 1990, or 2000. This is the famous Passion Play which is held in the village of **Oberammergau** every ten years. The Play, which is performed by the villagers and which attracts crowds from all over the world, was first staged in 1634 after the village prayed that the Black Plague which was ravaging Europe at that time should spare the tiny town. It did. From then on the play was performed every decade until 1934 when Hitler stopped it. It was resumed in 1950 and the most recent performance was in 1970.

  Ulm, which is about 100 kilometres north-west of Oberammergau, is a city of 100,000, large enough to be interesting but small enough to walk in. It's fairly representative of what you'll find in Germany. Clean, spacious, and dotted with ancient landmarks (many rebuilt since the devastation of World War II bombing). The city, birthplace of Albert Einstein, houses a fourteenth-century Gothic cathedral with the highest stone church tower in the world – 528 feet.

  To the west of Ulm is the beautiful **Black Forest** area – ideal for slow village to village wandering.

  Heidelberg is the favourite German city of thousands of tourists. Celebrated in songs and plays it still seems to cling longingly to the memories of its past. It's the home of Germany's oldest and most famous university, founded in 1386. Visit the Red Ox, an old student inn, which was the scene of many a duelling challenge. You might also go and see the thirteenth-century castle which houses the Apothecary Museum and the famed Heidelberg Tun, a gigantic beer barrel which holds 221,726 litres – or about 50,000 gallons.

Continuing on up the Rhine you reach **Frankfurt** where you can see Goethe's House and Museum and the Stadel Art Institute which displays a good collection of European paintings.

Bingen am Rhein, just west of **Mainz** (which holds a wine festival in August and September) is a wine-town crowned by Klopp Castle. Climb up there for great views over the Rhine Valley.

Koblenz, at the head of the twisting, turning vineyard-lined Mosel Valley, is a city of 100,000 and another wine-centre. Its big landmark is the Ehrenbreitstein Fortress. If you have time, try and catch a river barge from Koblenz which will take you down along the Mosel to **Trier** (just near the border with Luxembourg) which is the oldest town in Germany and one of the oldest in Europe. Lots of Roman ruins to see. Whether you hitch a barge or a car, the Mosel trip is worthwhile. (Also possible to find grape-picking work in this area around September.)

North-west of Koblenz is **Bonn**, capital of the Federal Republic, birthplace of Beethoven (see his house and the museum), and home of Poppelsdorf Castle. A few kilometres farther on is **Cologne** (or Köln) which was founded by the Romans in 32 BC and badly battered by the Allies in the last war. See the famous cathedral (if you can stand the sight of yet another) which dates from 1248 and is one of the largest Gothic buildings in the world.

North of Cologne is the huge industrial complex centred on **Essen**. A nightmare of converging autobahns and twisting ring-roads, for me it's one of the ugliest areas in Europe. Getting in and out of the various towns and cities without spending money is virtually impossible. It's a hitch-hiker's hell on earth.

Hamelin, way, way from all that and just south of **Hannover,** is a pleasant town of 60,000 which contains some of the best examples of timber-façaded houses in Germany. It was, also, the home of the legendary Pied Piper who is supposed to have led invading rats away from the town to the sound of his pipes and then, when he wasn't rewarded by the townspeople, to have caused the children to follow him in the same way. In the summer there is a Pied Piper procession through the streets every Sunday around 11 in the morning.

Bremen, 42 miles inland on the Weser River, is the oldest seaport in Germany. The old part of the city is great for wandering. In the eleventh-century St Peter's Cathedral you can see 500-year-old mummies preserved in a lead-lined vault.

North of Bremen is **Hamburg** (population 2,000,000), which was terribly damaged in the Second World War. Her citizens have completed an amazing job of rebuilding. There are half a dozen museums worth looking through – especially the Kunst und Gewerbe which features arts and crafts dating back to the Middle Ages. But outdoing all the galleries and museums in the visitor stakes is the district of St Pauli where 300,000 souls per month go to enjoy themselves in the most up-to-date red-light district in the world. As *Time Magazine* described it, you can 'swing into an underground garage, park, choose a fräulein at a discreet *Kontakthof* (contact court), then take an elevator to one of two six-storey, modern sexscrapers named Eros Centre and Palais d'Amour'. Poorer types still go to streets like Herbertstrasse, just off the Reeperbahn, where sex is dished up like ham and eggs but at a slightly higher price.

Whichever road you take north of Hamburg leads you into Denmark. For ferry prices from **Fehmarn Island** (Puttgarden), see **Scandinavia and Finland**.

★**Happenings** Germany is filled with festivals and concerts. The famed *Munich Oktoberfest* is mentioned below. Some others to look out for are: *The Great Marksmanship Contest* at Hannover in July; *The International Fair* at Frankfurt, March and September; *The Pied Piper of Hamelin Festival* at Hamelin, June to August; *The Christmas Fair* at Nuremburg, in December; *The Killing of the Dragon* at Furth-im-Wald in August; *The Bach Week* at Ansbach in July and *The European Weeks* at Passau in June and July.

★**Auer Dult** This is a fantastic flea market of both junk and antiques which is held only three times a year in Munich's Mariahilfsplatz. Approximate times are April/May, July/August and mid-October. If you're looking for an unusual souvenir from your European trip, this'll be the place to find it. Check with German Tourist Office in any major city for exact dates from year to year.

★**Oktoberfest** The world-famous Munich beer festival draws thousands from all over the world – including Australians who have earned themselves a bad name in Munich ever since the year a gang of them got stoned on the suds and hi-jacked a street-car. These festivities last 16 days and end on the first Sunday in October. Precise details from any German Tourist Office.

★**Buy a ride**! Feeling lazy? Want a break from hitching? From Munich you can buy a ride in a private car to a score of destinations through

Mitfahr-GmbH, Lämmerstrasse 4, 8 Munich 2 (Tel: 594561/63 or 592510). People driving between, say, Munich and Essen, inform the company when they are going, saying they want to take a passenger to share petrol costs. The company finds the passenger and takes a commission. Typical prices: Munich–Barcelona, 90 marks; Munich–Berlin, 48 marks; Munich–Paris, 50 marks; Munich–Zurich, 27 marks. You can even buy insurance and pay a booking fee! It mightn't be hitching, but it's a good idea.

Munich: where to sleep

Outside of youth hostels, which in Germany cost around 11 marks, there are not many cheap beds. Even student accommodation costs about 13 marks. In cheap hotels be prepared to pay around 28 marks.

Youth Camp at Kapuzinerholzl (Tel: 14 14 300). Tram No 21 from Main Railway Station (North) to Botanischergarten. About 5 marks a night. Open July and August.

YH Jugendherberge at Wendl-Dietrich Strasse 20 (Tel: 13 11 56). Closed from 15th December to 15th January.

YH Jugendgästehaus, Miesingstrasse 4 (Tel: 72 36 550/72 36 560).

Newman-Haus at Kaulbachstrasse 29 (Tel: 28 50 91). Students only.

Haus International (Jugendhotel) at Elisabethstrasse 87 (Tel: 18 50 81/83). Ask to share in 6-bedded rooms.

YMCA-CVJM-Gästehaus at Landwehrstrasse 13 (Tel: 55 59 41).

YMCA John Mott Haus at Theo-Prosel-Weg 16 (Tel: 18 85 24).

Übernachtungsheim at Goethestrasse 9 (Tel: 55 58 91). Girls only.

St Paul's Kolleg at Paul-Heyse Strasse 18 (Tel: 53 74 36). Ask for dormitory. Men only.

Kolping-Haus at Adolf Kolping Strasse (Tel: 59 38 59).

For help in finding student accommodation contact the MUNICH STUDENT TRAVEL SERVICE at Luisenstrasse 43, 8 München 2 (Tel: 52 50 55), or try **Jugend Informationszentrum** at Paul-Heyse-Strasse 22, 8 München 2 (Tel: 53 16 55). For help in finding hotels contact the *Verkehrsamt* next to the main railway station. For sleeping out try the parks on the banks of the Isar River, or the huge park up behind the Haus der Kunst.

Remember that as in most of the big European cities you can drop your per-person bed costs considerably by taking a double or triple room in company with others.

Munich: where to eat

It's no problem to feed yourself for around 6-8 marks in Munich and the following list names some places where you can do just that:

Mensa Universität at Leopoldstrasse 13. Student card required.

Mensa Technische Universität at Arcisstrasse 17 (Tel: 28 61 15). Student card required.

Donisl Pschorr-Gaststatte at Weinstrasse 1 (Marienplatz).

Picnik at Leopoldstrasse 29.

Cornelius Schüler Bufeteria at Bayerstrasse 13.

Herties Department Store (Cafeteria) at Bahnhofsplatz.

Kaufhof Department Store (Cafeteria) at Karlsplatz.

Wienerwalds (Chain Group). There are 41 of them in Munich.

Good meals – carefully chosen – will cost you around 9 marks. Try: Leopoldstrasse 44, Herzogstrasse 25, Frauenstrasse 4, Lindwurmstrasse 48.

Ratskeller at Marienplatz 8.

Munich: what to see and do

DEUTSCHES MUSEUM One of Europe's great museums and the largest science and technical museum in the world. Plenty of buttons to push and a bonanza for anyone who can recognize a wheel when they see one. Admission charge. Half-price with student card. On the Isarinsel.

ALTE PINAKOTHEK at Barerstrasse 27. Featuring paintings of the fourteenth to eighteenth centuries, including some great ones. Huge collection of Rubens and works by Velasquez, El Greco, Leonardo, etc. Entrance charge, but free on Sundays.

NEUE PINAKOTHEK One of the three galleries in the Haus der Kunst at Prinzregentenstrasse 1. Fine collection of French Impressionists. Admission charge, but free on Sundays.

SCHLOSS NYMPHENBURG Take Tram 21 from Dachauerstrasse.
This palace was built between 1664 and 1823 as the German kings' summer
residence. A huge and remarkable complex in the Baroque-Rococo style
sitting in 500 acres of sculptured gardens. Tough entrance fee which
is halved if you carry a student card. (The place was used as a setting
in *Last Year in Marienbad*.)

DACHAU CONCENTRATION CAMP Take the S-Bahn to the town of Dachau,
then the Dachau-Ost bus to the camp. The place was once the best
organized slaughter yard in the Third Reich.
It implants in your mind once and for all that those figures in history
books were people.

FREE BEER! FREE FOOD! Take Tram 4, 1, 11 or 21 to the Löwenbräu
Brewery at Nymphenburgerstrasse 4. English language tours through the
premises are conducted weekdays in summer from about 9.00 a.m. Tour of
considerable satisfaction for those interested in beer production and of
great fascination to the hungry. Free beer and bread and sausage served
after you've done the rounds.

THE GLOCKENSPIEL The performing clock on the tower of the town-hall.
Animated figures do the usual stuff at 11 a.m. each day.

BEER HALLS With southern Germany's 1,600 breweries producing about
a quarter of the world's beer supply you have to enter into the spirit of the
thing – and you do that in the beer halls. Entrance is free, except to certain
sections where there is entertainment, and a half litre stein costs about
3 marks. Try the *Hofbräuhaus* at Platzl 9 and the *Platzl* across the street.
Two others worth a look-in are the *Löwenbräukeller* at Stiglmaierplatz and
the *Mäthaser Bier Stadt* at Bayerstrasse 5 which claims it can seat no less
than 5,500 beer-swilling customers.

DRUGSTORE at Wedekindplatz. Music and lots more.

Transport in Munich
The Munich transport system includes trams, buses, underground
trains (*U-Bahn*) and surface trains (*S-Bahn*). Tickets are expensive. Cost
depends on length of journey. A 24-hour ticket allowing you to use all
four systems in the city area costs around 6 marks.

Student discounts
Reduced tickets to theatres, cinemas. Reduced tickets or free entry to

State-run galleries and museums. Cheaper entrance to fairs and exhibitions. For information contact:

MUNICH STUDENT TRAVEL SERVICE,
Luisenstrasse 43, 8 Munich 2 (Tel: 52 50 55).

Crossing East Germany to West Berlin

The best hitching route into West Berlin is along the big Hannover–Berlin autobahn which crossses the east-west border at Helmstedt. This is the fastest route to Berlin from the industrial complex of Dortmund, Essen, and Dusseldorf and the track most businessmen from those areas follow. But whichever road you take through East Germany, the following information is pertinent.

Foreigners are not permitted to hitch-hike on East German roads.
Because of this you have to stop a car in West Germany which will take you right through to Berlin. This is one time when a placard stating your destination will come in handy. Petrol stations near border-crossing points are a good place to grab rides, but wherever you set yourself up remember that the West Germans do not permit hitch-hikers to stand on the side of the autobahn and the roads are continually patrolled. You can only hitch on the entrance – or *Einfahrt* – of an autobahn.

The following information comes from a pamphlet issued by the West Berlin Tourist Information Office.

REQUIREMENTS

1 German and foreign nationals: passport. A transit visa is issued at the checkpoints.
2 When driving by car: car registration papers, green international insurance card and initial plaque indicating nationality.
3 Make sure you car has enough petrol for driving through before entering the German Democratic Republic.

CURRENCY

The amount of West German marks and foreign currency allowed is unlimited. It is forbidden to take East German marks.

CHECKPOINTS BETWEEN WEST GERMANY AND EAST GERMANY
Trains
Büchen–Schwanheide
Helmstedt–Marienborn
Bebra–Gerstungen

Ludwigsstadt–Probstzella
Hof–Gutenfüerst

Cars
Lauenburg–Horst
Helmstedt–Marienborn
Rudolphstein–Hirschberg
Herleshausen–Wartha
As a rule foreigners must also pay for a liability insurance in addition
to fee for visas.

Berlin: where to sleep

The price structure is roughly the same as for Munich.

Youth Hostels at Berlin 19, Bayernallee 36 (Charlottenburg)
(Tel: 305 30 55). Berlin 28, Hermsdorfer Damm 48 (Hermsdorf).
Tel: 404 16 10 for bookings.

Jugendgästehaus at Berlin 30, Kluckstrasse 3 (Tiergarten) (Tel: 261 10 97).

Studentenwohnheim Hardenbergstrasse at Berlin 12, Hardenbergstrasse 34
(Tel: 31 12 1). Open March 1st to April 30th and from July 15th to
October 15th. Students only. Men only.

Pension Schaumann at Schaperstrasse 14 (Tel: 881 52 37).

Gästehaus Elton at Pariserstrasse 9 (Tel: 883 61 55).

Adam-Von-Trott-Haus at Berlin 39, am kleinen Wannsee 20
(Tel: 805 34 91). (A fair way out of town.) Open February 15th to April 15th
and from July 15th to October 15th.

Bahnhof Mission at Bahnhof Zoo (in the central railway station).
Cheapest place in town outside the youth hostels and it's more central.

YMCA at Einemstrasse 10 (Tel: 261 37 91). Groups of men only.

YWCA at Isarstrasse 12 (Tel: 623 19 95). Groups of women only.

Pension Christine at Uhlandstrasse 142, Berlin 31 (Tel: 87 30 46).

Pension Masovia at Clausewitzstrasse 2, Berlin 12 (Tel: 883 62 78).

Centrum Pension at Kantstrasse 31, Berlin 12 (Tel: 31 61 53).

For help with student accommodation, talk to the German Student
Travel Service at Berlin 12, Hardenbergstrasse 9 (Tel: 312 10 42).

The *Verkehrsamts* people at Europa Center will sort out hotel problems for you and charge two marks – unless they help you into hostel or student accommodation in which case it's free.

For sleeping out in Berlin it's best to move half an hour out of the city – there are a hell of a lot of police and uniforms around. Try anywhere around the Wannsee or the Grunewald – though these places are going to cost you a mark or two to reach on public transport. If you want to sleep out in the city, you should check with locals.

Two camping grounds are, **Kohlhasenbruck** at Neue Kreisstrasse (Tel: 805 17 37), and **Kladow** at Krampnitzer Weg 111–117 (Tel: 353 27 97). The first is open only from April to September, the second all the year. Both are cheap and both have good facilities.

Berlin: where to eat

Same price structure as Munich.

Studentenhotel Berlin at Meiningerstrasse 10. Dinner served from 6 until 8 p.m.

Kadewe Department Store at Wittenbergplatz.

Wienerwalds (Chain group). Some of the more than a dozen addresses are:
Kurfürstendamm 68,   Schildhorn 42,
Schlossstrasse 1,   Moselstrasse 1.

Kantine (in the Town Hall) at John F. Kennedy Platz. Open to the public from 2 to 4 p.m. Worth going. Full meals for under 6 marks.

Pohlmann's Gaststatten. A chain of very cheap eating places where you can fill up for well under 6 marks. Addresses are:
Kantstrasse 85,   Wilmersdorferstrasse 30,
Droysenstrasse 1,   Mullerstrasse 164,
Corner of Fritz Reuterstrasse and Maxstrasse.

Bilka Department Store at Coachimstalerstrasse 5. The cheap, fixed menu meal is only served until 6 p.m.

Piccolo Taormina is a little pizza joint on Uhlandstrasse just one hundred yards up from the Kurfürstendamm and on your right (beneath the sauna place). They do a pizza snack and plenty of cheap Italian meals. Lots of kindred spirits haunt the place.

Hardtke's at 26 Meinekestrasse does a good and reasonably cheap three-course meal from about 1 o'clock until 3.

Kuba at Schaperstrasse 12 is one of Berlin's cheapest Chinese places. Student hangout – or used to be.

Quick at Kurfürstendamm 230 is an automat joint where you can eat for around 6 marks.

Sausage stands. You can find them all around town – indeed, all around Germany. A couple of big sausages with bread for about 2·50 marks apiece fills you up well if you're short of money.

Berlin: what to see and do

KAISER WILHELM GEDACHTNISKIRCHE in the Kurfürstendamm. A new and very beautiful church standing beside the war-gutted shell of the old. The West Berliners call the ruin, 'The Hollow Tooth'.

CHECKPOINT CHARLEY at Friedrichstrasse brings back memories of the Cold War when it was a real freeze. Near Charley is the MUSEUM OF THE WALL which offers vivid testimony of escapes and shooting incidents around the Wall.

DAHLEM MUSEUM at Arnimallee 23–27. This is one of Europe's greatest galleries and if you like paintings, don't miss it. All classic stuff, nothing after about 1800. Rembrandt, Brueghel, Dürer, El Greco, Goya. And it's all for free. Closed Monday.

BERLIN ZOO beside Tiergarten. Europe's largest zoo, with more than 3,000 mammals and 8,000 reptiles, including – in the excellent aquarium – Europe's largest collection of crocodiles. Student card gets you in cheaper.

CHARLOTTENBURG PALACE at Luisenplatz. A day's outing in itself if you're an art-lover. The seventeenth-century palace is the home of half a dozen galleries and museums, including the Department of Egyptian Antiquities where you can see the famous 3,300-year-old bust of Queen Nefertiti. The museums are all free but it costs to go into the palace and the Mausoleum. Closed Friday.

BRANDENBURG GATE which separates the East and West zones of the city.

NIGHTLIFE Try the *Big Eden* at 202 Kurfürstendamm. It costs you about 5 marks to enter, which includes the first drink, and all drinks after the first are 5 marks. It's a big, big disco which can hold 2,000 people – many of whom are looking for partners. Last I heard was that unescorted girls could enter free. Try also the *Big Apple* at Bundesallee 13 (disco, not too expensive).

Transport in Berlin

The subway is the cheapest way around. There are two systems – the U-Bahn run by the West Berliners and the S-Bahn run by the East Berliners. Both lines operate in both the West and the East. The S-Bahn is a little cheaper.

Best deal in town, though, is the 17-marks Touristenkarte which gives you unlimited travel on all buses and the U-Bahn subway lines within the city for four days or 9 marks for two days. Buy it at the Berlin Public Transport Office at Potsdamerstrasse 188, or at the Zoo Station at Hardenbergplatz.

Student discounts

For details of what's available contact:

GERMAN STUDENT TRAVEL SERVICE,
West Berlin 12, Hardenbergstrasse 9 (Tel: 312 10 42).

How to get to East Berlin

At the time of writing, crossing into East Berlin for a day's sightseeing is no problem. Easiest way to do it is to present yourself with your passport to Checkpoint Charley on Friedrichstrasse.

There is some red tape to go through, but nothing that should take more than twenty or thirty minutes. Anyone who is worried about going into the East sector (perhaps someone whose family came from there recently) can cover themselves by registering with the West Berlin authorities at the checkpoint and stating what time they expect to be back. If they have not returned soon after that time, something is done about it.

People going in in cars must have the vehicle's registration papers, green-card insurance and, for the sake of economy, enough petrol to see them through the day.

Everyone who enters the Eastern sector on foot or in a private vehicle is obliged to buy 8 East German marks. These 8 marks cannot be changed back into D-marks. If you don't spend it you'll have to donate it to an East German charity. Unspent money which is changed in excess of 8 marks may be changed back into other currencies.

Foreigners must leave East Berlin by midnight by the same checkpoint by which they entered.

(One hint I can give anyone who is going over to the East for a one-day trip is to carry as little stuff as possible. I went through on the Underground to the Friedrichstrasse station with a shoulder-bag stuffed with my usual assortment of notebooks, city maps and tourist information. The customs' guy (complete with pistol and looking like something out of a spy movie) spent ten minutes going through every piece of paper I was carrying and then spent a further five minutes carefully leafing through the last edition of this book which was covered in notes for new info. The whole long process was punctuated by him asking questions in German – which I don't understand – and me muttering away in English – which he didn't understand. But he smiled when he'd finished.)

Warning! Rules and regulations regarding crossing from West Germany to East Germany and from West Berlin to East Berlin are liable to change at any time. Best to check with tourist offices before you start the trip.

East Berlin

There are three major information offices in East Berlin where you can get city maps and sightseeing data. They are located at the Berolina Hotel in Karl-Marx-Allee, next to the S-Bahnhof at Alexanderplatz, and at Friedrichstrasse 162.

Sights to see include the complex of galleries and museums on Museum Island; the Museum for German History on Unter den Linden (a museum which displays its goods with a political bias – very interesting); the Memorial to the Victims of Fascism and Militarism also on Unter den Linden; and, perhaps as the biggest sight, the streets and department stores of the city itself.

To meet up with East German students, drop into the Humboldt University on Unter den Linden and find your way to the canteen around lunchtime. You'll get a cheap meal and some interesting conversation.

If you've come in by Underground to Friedrichstrasse, you can get a quite good and cheap enough meal in the station restaurant. It's a good way of blowing any East German marks you have left before leaving. (You can buy your homeward-bound ticket with West German marks.)

Addresses

Main Post Office (for Poste Restante) at Munich, Postamt 32, Bahnhofplatz 1.

Main Post Office (for Poste Restante) at Berlin 12, Postant Berlin, Bahnhof Zoo.

American Express at Munich, Promenadeplatz 3
(Tel: 22 81 66).

American Express at Berlin, Kurfürstendamm 11
(Tel: 881 43 33).

Munich Student Travel Service at Munich 2, Luisenstrasse 43
(Tel: 52 50 55).

German Student Travel Service at Berlin 12, Hardenbergstrasse 9
(Tel: 312 10 42).

German Student Travel Service at Hamburg 13, Schluterstrasse 18
(Tel: 45 44 09).

Tourist Information Office at Munich, Rindermarkt 5
(Tel: 23911).

Tourist Information Office at West Berlin, Europa-Center
(Tel: (030) 21234).

British Consulate-General at Munich, Amalienstrasse 62
(Tel: 39 40 15).

British Embassy at West Berlin, Uhlandstrasse 7
(Tel: 30 95 293).

American Embassy at Munich, Koeniginstrasse 5 (Tel: 23 011).

American Embassy at Berlin, Clayallee 170 (Tel: 83 24 087).

Hitchers' tips and comments

Crossing to East Berlin: In your bit on this subject you don't mention
that receipts must be obtained for all money spent in East Berlin. The
officials don't tell you either, until you're coming back.
D. F. Dickson, London N4

Here's something for people who are stony broke. How to sleep in Munich
for 20 pfennig. First go to the main *bahnhof* until you're kicked out around
midnight. Then walk the streets until around 3.30 or 4.00 a.m. Then go
to Karlsplatz, go into the toilets, plug in your 20 pfennig and go to sleep.
Note that the WC is closed around midnight until around 4.00 a.m.

For free food in Munich, go to the student cafeteria while they're serving.
Go to the kitchen and ask if you can have the left-overs as they come back
from the cafeteria. (I've done it four times and haven't been refused yet.)

I like the book a lot, and wish I'd known about it before I came to Europe, but that's life (and life can really screw you – 76 hours from Liverpool to London, mostly in the rain, and I look almost completely straight, too).

The only adverse comment I have is your German pronunciation key. Personally, I think it's the shits. Other than that, far out. Keep on trucking.
Richard Walker, Seattle, USA

The English 5p piece is the same size as the German mark piece and Swiss 1 franc piece. Thus feed the 5p into a 1 mark change machine on stations and hey presto, 25p.
Lesley Kountaff, South Africa

If you sleep rough on the banks of the River Neckar in central Heidelberg watch out for the rats – they're like cats!
Jonah, Neath, South Wales

If you're really broke, go to Marienplatz underground station and hang around the sausage stands. You can make a good meal on other people's leftovers.
Hugh Dunne, Dublin, Ireland

Luxembourg and the Small Countries

There exist in Europe a number of independent or semi-independent countries which are complete anachronisms. They are mini-countries which have little business existing in this hurly-burly century, but somehow they survive. Most of them have fewer citizens than the Ford Motor Company has workers. The countries are Luxembourg, Monaco, Andorra, Gibraltar, San Marino, and Liechtenstein.

Luxembourg with its 999 square miles of territory and population of 333,000 is the largest of these countries. Its modern history as a Grand Duchy began in AD 963 when a nobleman took over the ruins of a Roman fort which sat on a huge rock over the Alzette River, and built it into a castle. By the thirteenth century the country was one of the strongest in Europe and embraced an area 500 times the size it is today. Then the empire fell and its power diminished. Because of its central location it became an axiom that whoever controlled Luxembourg controlled the Continent. As no power could tolerate another having this advantage, an agreement was made at the London Congress of 1867 which guaranteed the independence of the country and demanded that the fortress be made inoperative.

In the city of Luxembourg, with its population of 90,000, the things to see include the remains of the fortifications (the castle is known as 'The Hollow Tooth') and some of the 21 kilometres of underground passages cut into solid rock. The fortifications, the city's 80 bridges and its cathedral, are all illuminated during the summer.

In Luxembourg cigarettes are about the cheapest in Europe outside of Spain. Good place to stock up in, especially if you're heading up north into expensive Scandinavia. Luxembourg currency (francs) has the same value as Belgian money.

The 188 square miles of **Andorra** sit high in the Pyrenees between France and Spain. Her 16,000 citizens speak Catalan, French, and Spanish and trade in Spanish pesetas and French francs.

Legend says the country was founded by Charlemagne in AD 784. The present co-Principality dates from 1278 and is under the joint suzerainty of the President of France and the Bishop of Urgel in Spain. A feudal toll is still paid each year, one year to the French, the next to the Spanish. In 1968 the Bishop of Urgel received 900 pesetas in cash, plus 6 hams, 12 chickens, and 24 cheeses.

After tourism, which brings in plenty of cash owing to the practically duty-free state of its shops, tobacco is one of the big businesses. Cigarettes are about the same price as in Spain. Liquor is cheaper. Petrol, if you're driving a van, is cheaper than in either France or Spain – so fill up.

In this weird little place which boasts that it is the smallest country in the world and which is locked in by 8,000-foot snow-capped peaks, they have reached one state of affairs towards which you can only wish other countries would strive. The 1969 Defence Budget was £2 ($4·00). This gross expenditure bought bullets for the police force's pistol practice and shotgun shells for the mountain gamewardens.

Hitch-hiking both in and out of the place can be hard. It's all up and down or curves and the roads are narrow. Unless you want a long, long walk pick yourself a nice position and stay there with your thumb propped in the air.

★**Shopping** Prices are good on things like cameras, film, radios, cassettes, tapes, etc. But on decent-sized purchases (say, over £15) you can still get 10–20 per cent off by asking. The bigger the purchase the more chance of the discount, so it's worth shopping with friends and getting all the things you want on the counter at the one time so you've got better bargaining power.

Monaco with its 23,500 inhabitants stacked into an area of 368 acres on France's Côte d'Azur is a Principality governed by Prince Rainier, the gentleman who married the American screen actress Grace Kelly – now Princess Grace.

The Principality has been independent since 1415 and has been ruled by the Grimaldi family (of which the current Prince is a member) since 1297. Many efforts have been made to destroy its independence, the most recent being in 1963 when De Gaulle blockaded the state in an effort to make it fall in line, economically, with the rest of France. Prince Rainier held out until a 90-page document was signed by both parties guaranteeing, in part, that Monaco's citizens would continue to enjoy their tax-free status.

The State makes a good half of its income from tourism. Way over a million tourists visit each year, most to soak up the sun and sample the delights of the rich Mediterranean life-style. Some go to play at the famous Casino, all hoping that they'll be the second person to break the fabulous bank of Monte Carlo. If you want to play the wheels, good luck to you, but it's strictly for hitchers expecting an inheritance!

For such a small place (small, but it has the greatest population density in the world) there is plenty to see. Not to be missed is the fantastic Oceanographic Museum. If you expect to be hitting the area around May, check with a tourist office for the exact dates of the *Grand Prix de Monaco*, one of the most exciting races in the car-sport world. Other sights include the quite good collection of paintings in the National Museum of Fine Arts and the Prince's palace.

Note that the hitching is slow all along this area during summer. (And has been for the last three editions!)

Gibraltar perches right on the end of the Iberian Peninsula, and, at the time of writing, is the object of negotiations between the English and the Spanish. As a result the famous Rock can only be reached by air or sea. The Algeciras ferry has been cut off, which means that to get there by sea you now have to travel to Tangier in Morocco and then from Tangier to Gib, and then, when you want to leave, you reverse the whole thing. Many dollars and many miles later you come to journey's end; a journey which used to cost nothing as you walked across the Spanish/Gibraltar land frontier.

Gib has an area of $2\frac{1}{4}$ square miles and a population of 25,000. The huge Rock is 1,396 feet high and you can walk up or, if you're feeling rich, take the cable-car. Whichever way, go. On a clear day, the view from the top goes clear across to the Atlas mountains in Morocco. Halfway up is where you can see the famous Barbary apes who are said to have arrived in Gibraltar by way of a secret tunnel from Africa. The superstition is that if the apes ever leave Gib, then British rule will come to an end. The British, with typical thoroughness, have the apes on garrison strength and feed them daily rations. Be warned that the beasts bite. I know. I've been bitten. The population of Gibraltar is a weird mixture of Genoese, Maltese, Spanish, British, and Arab. The people's temperament seems to be somewhere between that of a Spaniard and an Englishman. Everyone is bi-lingual in Spanish and English and can change languages without batting an eyelid.

The name Gibraltar comes from the Arabic *Gibel Tarik*, or Tarik's Hill. Tarik was Tarik-ibn-Zeyad the Moor who started the invasion of Spain near Gibraltar in AD 711. Today there are several Moorish ruins to be seen, including the Castle, the Wall and the Baths. Other sights include St Michael's Cave in which occasionally there are held Rock (so to speak) concerts, the Gibraltar Museum, and the Trafalgar Cemetery in which sailors killed at the Battle of Trafalgar are buried.

For cheap eating try Smoky Joe's just off Main Street. It's an English truckie-style café. For cheap sleeping go to TOC 'H' at the opposite end of Main Street.

Warning! Being partly tax-free, prices in Gib can be amongst the lowest in Europe for luxury items like cameras and tape-recorders. But since the Spanish-Gib border was closed tourism has dropped badly and many shop-keepers have raised their prices. I've seen cameras in Main Street shop windows marked at higher prices than in the centre of London. Prices can also vary as much as 20 per cent between different shops. Make sure you're getting value before you put your money on the counter – and bargain hard.

San Marino, completely surrounded by Italy, is the oldest state in the world, dating from the fourth century. Its official title is The Most Serene Republic of San Marino. With a population of some 17,000 and an area of 238 square miles, its big industries revolve around tourism and postage stamps. Tourism brings in 1,000,000 visitors each year. The big sight is the city of San Marino itself, which sits 2,200 feet above and just inland from the Adriatic Sea. Have a look at the Rocca Fortress and the Palazzo Valloni.

Liechtenstein, sitting between Switzerland and Austria, covers an area of 62 square miles and has a population of 20,000. It's just big (or small) enough to provide a pleasant day's walk so that you can at least say you've been through a country on foot.

The state was founded in 1719 and gained independence in 1806 after a spell as part of the Holy Roman Empire.

Vaduz, the capital, is a huge metropolis of 4,000 souls, including a Prince who lives in a castle on a hill above the town. The town itself is very much tourist-orientated. It has to be because Liechtenstein is much too pleasant a place to worry much about industrialization. Postage stamps, however, are big deal in this tiny land and any wandering philatelists should have a look at the excellent Philately Museum in the capital. Also check over the local Art Gallery which has better stuff in it than you might imagine.

Hitchers' tips and comments
A bit about Gibraltar. As it's so small there's a shortage of accommodation and beds are pretty expensive with the notable exception of the Continental Hotel. Mostly 'freaks and a few humans' (quote from Gib police). The manager is Monty. A great guy.
Writer requests no credit (England)

To get out of Andorra into Spain, the best bet is to take the St Julia bus to the end of the line, then walk to the petrol station just past town. It has a big parking lot and average waiting time for a ride out is about ten minutes.
David Fremon, Palatine, USA

Switzerland

Population	6,333,200
Size	15,941 square miles
Capital	Berne, population 146,820
Government	Federal Republic
Religion	Roman Catholic and Protestant
Language	French, German, Italian, and the little used Romansch are the national languages. Some English spoken in cities

Berne is the capital of Switzerland, but **Zurich** is the largest city and perhaps the best to wander in for a few days. After those two, the towns to visit are Geneva, Lausanne, Lucerne, Basel, and St Gallen. In the south are the big mountains which are famous the world over – Monte Rosa at

15,023 feet, Dom at 14,920 feet, Matterhorn at 14,780 feet. And there are the high alpine passes – Umbrail at 8,218 feet and Bernina at 7,643 feet – and the long, long mountain tunnels – Simplon, stretching 12¼ miles and St Gotthard, 9 miles.

The mountains are beautiful, but when you're up that high it can be very cold so keep an eye on the weather. A good route if you're chasing snow and glaciers, is to head out from Lausanne to Interlaken (an out-and-out tourist town, but in a beautiful situation) and take, in turn, Highways 6, 20, and 2 down to Bellinzona near the Italian border. This route takes you through some spectacular scenery which is a good cross-section of the mountain country. You cross the Susten Pass at the 7,299 foot level, catch a glacier just near there, and then climb to the St Gotthard Pass at nearly 7,000 feet. It's an exhilarating trip, especially if you can do it on a blue-sky day. (It usually rains!)

Geneva, which is where most hitchers enter Switzerland after a French tour, is a good introduction to the country – and a hint of what to expect price-wise. It is slick, one hundred per cent modern, and beautiful the way a jet-plane is. It's no place for us cheap-skate hitchers. The youth hostels are usually full during the summer, so if you're thinking of staying it's worth booking in advance. Sights to see include the *Jet d'eau* on the lake, a fantastic spout which hurls water 400 feet into the air; the Palais des Nations, the United Nations European home; and the museum of Art and History which contains a beautiful display of Impressionist and post-Impressionist work. Music buffs may like to visit the Museum of Old Musical Instruments. Philosophers shouldn't miss the Rousseau Museum.

The *Youth Hostel* is on Rue des Plantaporrets (Tel: 29 06 19). If you don't have your Hostel Card it'll cost you nearly double. The *YMCA–YWCA* is at 9 Avenue Sainte-Clotilde (Tel: 24 42 93). Ask for the dormitory and if you can do without sheets you'll save a couple of francs. *Centre Mazaryk* at 11 Avenue de la Paix (Tel: 33 07 72), is cheap enough, but make sure you don't get the breakfast-included price. The *Salvation Army* has a hotel *for men* at 1 Rue Baudit (Tel: 33 77 04) and a hotel *for women* at 14 Rue de l'Industrie. There's cheap eating at the *YMCA–YWCA* and at the *Restaurant Universitaire* at 2 Avenue du Mail, *Cité Universitaire* at 26 Avenue de Miremont, the *International Student Club* at 6 rue de Saussure and at *Résidence Internationale* at 63 rue des Paquis.

Lausanne, just a hop, step, and jump from Geneva along the fast autoroute, is a city of 137,800. Like Geneva, it sits on Lake Léman. But for me it offers more charm than many other Swiss cities because it is not a big international or business centre. The cathedral is worth a visit, as is the Old Episcopal Palace of the Bishops of Lausanne.

Just outside of town is the village of **Vevey**, a pretty lakeside spot which has seen more than its share of famous people. Courbet, Byron, Hugo, and Rousseau all made visits or lived there at one time or another. A couple of miles farther on is **Montreux**, famous for its International Music Festival held each September. Nicknamed the 'Swiss Riviera', Montreux and its surrounds have been on and off with the international set for a century – and that, along with the Casino in town, should give you an inkling of the sort of money that's floating around. But outside of town, the Castle of Chillon is worth a visit.

If you head to **Interlaken** (Highway 20) after Montreux, you have a choice of travelling south on the mountain trip previously mentioned, or going up to **Berne**, the capital. With 146,800 people, it's a small city, but it has enough to keep you amused for a day. The Clock Tower is the principal attraction, one of those jobs which put on a complete stage-show each hour. Don't miss the Bear Pit for a show of a different type (real bears). For a good view over the attractive Old Town, visit the public park called the Rose Garden. In here you may also find a place to lay your head (and if you can't, try down by the river).

Lucerne, on Highway 10 from Berne, is small (67,600) and perhaps the prettiest of all Swiss cities. It is the site of another International Music Festival, in late August, and also of the Great Lakeside Evening Festival, in late June. Two things to see, if the subjects interest you, are the Swiss Transport Museum, which features wheeled monstrosities from all ages, and Tribschen, a house where Wagner lived and worked. Glacier Garden is a favourite with the tourists but, without a doubt, the nicest thing to do in Lucerne is wander around the old section near the strange Chapel Bridge.

Basel, north of Berne and north-west of Lucerne, is Switzerland's second largest city. Situated exactly on the junction of France, Germany, and Switzerland, you have a nice choice of direction after you've seen the sights. The ancient cathedral, surrounded by medieval houses and standing beside a beautiful square, is nice to wander around, while the Art Museum holds one of the world's outstanding collections of Holbein as well as a superb display of modern works. The Zoo is considered one of the world's best. Sitting on the Rhine, it is also the home of the Swiss Navy – not a joke after all – the Navy consisting of river transport vessels. Late February or early March is the time of the three-day Basel Carnival, known as the *Fasnacht*.

St Gallen, in the north-eastern corner of the country, is about the same size as Lucerne. It's a pretty town, but its sights are of a specialist nature. It is built around a huge Baroque cathedral which contains the famous Abbey Library, a collection of 2,000 ancient manuscripts and nearly 2,000 more very old printed books.

Hitching in Switzerland is no great problem although you might find it slow in the back-wood areas. Major cities are well linked by fast highways, and the student population is flush enough to own its own transport – and they seem to be helpful in offering rides.

Remember that many of the high passes are not used during the winter months. If travelling between November and February, be sure to check ahead of yourself. Good maps like Michelin tell which passes you can expect to be closed, and the Swiss National Tourist Office in London hands out a leaflet called 'Switzerland by Car' which offers complete information on alpine passes.

★**Buying money** You can find good rates of exchange in Switzerland on most 'soft' currencies, e.g., Turkish lira, Moroccan dirhams, etc. Sometimes you can buy up to 20 per cent cheaper so it's a good investment if you expect to be spending time in the 'soft' currency countries. But remember that most of those places have a limit on the amount of money you are permitted to carry across their borders . . . in fact, most of them practically force you to break the law.

★**Drugs** If you need help with a drug problem (support, that is, not supply), talk to the people at DROP-IN at Dufourstrasse 181 (Tel: 55 53 11), open 8 a.m. to 8 p.m.

Zurich: where to sleep

Try and keep out of hotels in Zurich or, for that matter, anywhere in Switzerland. They are fantastic places, clean, comfortable, with all mod-cons, but at an average 30–35 francs for a night for a single, they're budget-wreckers. Unless you're fairly well-heeled you should try and sleep rough or at least stick to hostels or other special facilities. And even then, student hostels can cost you as much as 14 francs. Most of the ones listed below are bargains by Swiss standards, but try and ring before you go to the place you choose. Because of the high prices of normal hotels the budget places are often booked up.

Youth Hostel at Mutschellenstrasse 114 (Tel: 45 35 44). Ask for dormitory, because there are also double-rooms (at double the price per person).

Touristenlager at Limmatstrasse 118 (Tel: 42 38 00). Ask for dormitory. Open May–September.

Studentinnenhaus at 16 Freudenbergstrasse (Tel: 34 75 00). Open summer only. For women only. Cheaper with student card.

Foyer Hottingen at 31 Hottingerstrasse (Tel: 47 93 15). Girls or married couples only. You must be in by midnight.

YMCA at Sihlstrasse 33 (Tel: 25 86 73). Men only.

YWCA (Martahaus) at 36 Zähringerstrasse (Tel: 32 45 50). Women only.

Hotel Beau Site at 40 Dufourstrasse (Tel: 32 11 47).

Hotel Italia at 61 Zeughausstrasse (Tel: 241 43 39).

Hotel Rothaus at Sihlhallenstrasse 1 (Tel: 241 24 51).

Hotel Splendid at 5 Rosengasse (Tel: 34 58 50).

Hotel Limmathof at 142 Limmatquai (Tel: 47 42 20).

Any hotel problems can be sorted out at the Tourist Office, Bahnhofplatz 15 (at the Main Station). The same office can also give you information on locations and costs of half a dozen camping grounds in the area – which, in summer, can help you save a packet. **Campingplatz** at Seebucht Seestrasse 557 (Tel: 45 16 12), reached by taking Bus 61 or 65 from Bürkliplatz to Grenzsteig, is open May to September and costs around SFr 3·50. Showers extra. Believe me, it's as good a deal as you'll find in the city.

  For roughing it, you might find a spot by the Zurich-See between Mythen-Quai and General-Guisan-Quai. Otherwise, best bet is out around the Dolder sports park.

Zurich: where to eat

7 francs should handle things and for that you can get some good food. As in most cities, it's wise to keep an eye open for the chain restaurants and cafeterias. In Zurich, best bets are: **Migros, Silberkugel,** and especially the **Stadtküche Zurich** (or Zurich's People's Kitchens). These, for anyone on a limited budget, are perfect. There are eleven of them and the addresses are:

Selnaustrasse 46,	Bederstrasse 130,
Untergraben 4,	Luggwegstrasse 27,

Schipfe 16,   Sihlquai 332,
Nordstrasse 101,   Zentralstrasse 34,
Neunbrunnenstrasse 4,   Mühlebachstrasse 180,
                               Dufourstrasse 146.

Other places to consider are:

Studentenheim at Clausiusstrasse 21. Closed Sundays mid-July to mid-September and Easter and Christmas.

Rheinfelder Bierhaus at 19 Marktgasse.

Culmann at Culmannstrasse 1. (This one is a student haunt.)

Wellenberg and **Biber** at Niederdorfstrasse 10 and 7. Specialize in vegetarian and south-east Asian food.

Catalana at 8 Glockengasse. Spanish restaurant.

Kantorei at 2 Neumarkt. Popular with student-types.

Select Café at 16 Limmatquai.

Weisser Wind at 20 Oberdorfstrasse.

University Restaurant at 10 Künstlergasse.

Cafeteria of the Institute of Dentistry (Zahnärztliches Institut) at 11 Plattenstrasse. Closed mid-July to mid-August.

Another excellent chain where you can eat for 5 or 6 francs if you choose carefully is run by the Zurich Women's Association. They are:

Karl der Grosse at 14 Kirchgasse

Rütli at 43 Zähringerstrasse

Seidenhof at 7–9 Sihlstrasse

Olivenbaum at 10 Stadelhoferstrasse

Zurich: what to see and do

SWISS NATIONAL MUSEUM on Museumstrasse, near Main Station. No entrance fee. Good run-down on the history of Switzerland.

RIETBERG MUSEUM in the Reiterpark. Free. One of Europe's great collections of non-European art.

KUNSTHAUS on Heimplatz. Good collection of Swiss art and large collection of moderns. High entrance charge but less on Mondays and evenings.

GROSSMÜNSTER near City Hall. The largest Romanesque church in Switzerland. Said to have been founded by Charlemagne.

OPFELCHAMMER at Rindermarkt 12 is one of the city's oldest beerhalls. Prices are OK (though avoid the expensive restaurant next door). Good place to meet people. Try also the *Bierhalle Wolf* at 6 Rindermarkt. For jazz, *Casa Bar* at Münstergasse 30 is fine, while for dancing try *Club Zabriskie-Point* at Leonhardstrasse 19 or *Hazyland* in the Kongresshaus. If you want to meet up with local students go to the *International Student Club* at 1 Augustinerhof, but you'll have to show a student ID card to get in.

CINEMA Anything made in English will probably be shown in English – with up to three (German, French, Italian) sub-titles on the screen. For programme info from cinemas, theatres and concert halls ask for the Zurich Weekly Bulletin, available free at the Tourist Office (Bahnhofplatz 15).

FLEAMARKET Held every Saturday between 8 a.m. and 4 p.m. on Bahnhofstrasse towards the lake. There's also a CURIOSITY MARKET held Thursdays between 9 a.m. and 9 p.m. in the Rosenhof, the small square between Limmatquai and Niederdorf.

Transport in Zurich
Best way, for a day of sightseeing, is to buy the special day-ticket for 3·50 francs which allows you unlimited travel right through until midnight. If you expect to be in town for a couple of days, buy special discount booklets. Check at tourist office about this.

Student discounts
Half-price for some concerts, cinemas, and theatres. Reduced admission to galleries and museums. Discounts in many large stores. For information, contact:

SWISS STUDENT TRAVEL OFFICE,
Leonhardstrasse 10, 8001 Zurich (Tel: 47 30 00).

Addresses
Post Office (for Poste Restante) at Kasernenstrasse 95–97, Zurich.

American Express at Bahnhofstrasse 20, Zurich (Tel: 211 29 30).

Schweizerischer Studentenreisedienst at Leonhardstrasse 10, 8001 Zurich (Tel: 47 30 00).

Tourist Office at Bahnhofplatz 15, Zurich (Tel: 211 40 00).

US Consulate at Zollikerstrasse 141, Zurich (Tel: 55 25 66).

British Consulate at Bellerivestrasse 5, Zurich (Tel: 47 15 20).

Hitchers' tips and comments
Basel. Sign-posting for getting out of the city is terrible. I walked in a complete circle, wasting two hours. When you reach the Football Stadium, keep right ahead for Lucerne road – don't turn left!
Malcolm Frankland, Glaslum, England

Basel. For hitching to Lucerne, Zurich or Berne, hitch at the beginning of the highway to pick up traffic from Germany and France (and Switzerland of course). If you hitch at the slip road in the town (1 km from start of highway) you'll only be getting local traffic and no lifts. I met an American who'd been stood there 6 hours. I waited another 2 before discovering the start of the highway. He got the train. It wasn't a lack of cars, but they were all local. Anyway Switzerland is slow compared to Germany.
Capt'n Clem, Bristol, England

Austria

Population	7,500,000
Size	32,374 square miles
Capital	Vienna, population 1,700,000
Government	Federal Republic
Religion	Roman Catholic
Language	German. Some English and French spoken

A pleasant morning's walk through Liechtenstein (see *The Small Countries*) and then a quick hitch and you're in **Feldkirch**. That's as nice a way as any of entering Austria. Feldkirch is an old-world kind of town. Her 17,000 inhabitants move slowly and don't seem to give a damn about anything. See the tenth-century Schattenburg Castle.

The Innsbruck road takes you through some really great country (*Sound of Music* all the way), including the 5,000-foot Arlberg Pass near St Anton, a famed ski-resort with Europe's oldest ski-school.

Innsbruck is 700 years old and, many say, Austria's most beautiful city, though in my opinion, Salzburg could lay a pretty solid claim to that title. Innsbruck was Winter Olympics city in 1964 and those interested in snow sports might like to see the Olympic Speed Skating Oval, the Bergisel Olympic Ski Jump, and the Olympic Bobsleigh and Toboggan Runs in Igls. Anyone heading down into Italy from Innsbruck will go over the famous Europe Bridge, the highest in Europe, 897 yards long and standing 624 feet above the river bed. In the city itself see the Imperial Palace, the Museum of Tyrolese Art, and the Alpine Museum at Emperor Maximilian's Arsenal.

The fastest way to **Salzburg** (population 120,000) is along the E17 which cuts briefly across Germany at **Bad Reichenhall** (a town with a local reputation for its healing mineral springs). Sitting beautifully on a plain and backed with huge mountains, Salzburg's focal point is the twelfth-century Hohensalzburg Castle. The Franziskanerkirche Cathedral is worth a look, as is the superbly presented Carolino Augusteum Museum. Mozart fans will know that the musician was born in Salzburg and will want to see his house and museum. They should note that the city holds a Mozart Week each January (exact dates may vary from year to year) which features the Vienna Philharmonic Orchestra. Then, of course, there's the fantastic Salzburg Music Festival which is held every July and August.

Hallstatt is a tiny village of about 2,000 people a few kilometres off the Salzburg–Graz highway. Apart from being the ideal place to get a whiff of rural Austria it offers the added attractions of the Hallstatt Museum which features prehistoric objects found in various tombs, and the Dachstein Caves which you reach by cable railway.

The road now takes you through the lushness of Styria, over the 2,500-foot Schober Pass, through the towns of **Leoben** and **Bruck** (and precious few others) until you arrive in **Graz** which, with 250,000 people, is Austria's second largest city. Things to see include the fantastic Arsenal with the world's largest collection of medieval armour (30,000 pieces in all), the ornate mausoleum of Emperor Ferdinand II, the Castles which you reach by cable-car, and several important galleries and museums.

Two main roads run south of Graz. The 67 leads you into Yugoslavia (only 40 kilometres away) and the 70 goes to **Klagenfurt**, with side roads into Yugoslavia. The 70 then becomes the 100 and joins up with **Lienz**, a small Tyrol city crowned by a castle and as typical as they come. Here's the ideal place for any hitcher who has enough spare cash to take a few days off for some skiing. Thirty kilometres south of Lienz and you're in Italy.

Vienna: where to sleep

Prices fairly high. Student and hostel accommodation costs around 50–80 schillings per bed. Hotels? Count on paying 90–120 per head.

Don Bosco Turmherberge at Lechnerstrasse 12 (Tel: 73 14 94). Men only.

Meidling Kolpinghaus at Bendlgasse 10–12 (Tel: 83 54 87). Men only.

Jugendgastehaus Schloss Potzleinsdorf at Geymullergasse 1 (Tel: 47 13 12). Open March through October. Long way out.

Jugendgastehaus Hütteldorf at Schlossbergasse 8 (Tel: 82 15 01). Long way out.

Stadtherberg Esterhazypark at Schadekgasse 1 (Tel: 57 91 31). A good deal and interesting – it's an old wartime bunker which has been done up.

Katholisches Studentinnenheim at Servitengasse 3 (Tel: 34 34 09). Open from July 1st to October 20th. Students only. Women only.

Studentheim des Asylvereines der Wiener Universität (Vienna University Student Home) at Porzellangasse 30 (Tel: 34 72 83). Open July 10th to September 25th. Students only.

Hotel Adlerhof at Hafnersteig 7 (Tel: 63 29 61).

Studentenheim Rudolfinum at Mayerhofgasse 3 (Tel: 65 44 51). Students only. Men only.

For help with student accommodation talk with the people at SAS at Führichgasse 10 (Tel: 52 92 47). You'll find the city-run hotel-finding service at Schubert Ring 6 or at the South Station or West Station.
 For sleeping out try the golf-links on Hauptallee and the Prater Park, or Donaupark on the east side of the canal.

Vienna: where to eat

Count on paying 40–50 schillings in a cheap restaurant. But if you're a student, try the first two listings below and you'll eat dinner for around 25 schillings.

Mensa der Osterreichischen Hochschülerschaft at Führichgasse 10.
Students only. Dinner served from 6 to 10 p.m. Open during
student holiday periods only.

Mensa des Hauptausschusses at Universitätsstrasse 7. Students only.
Open all year except Easter and Christmas. Dinner served from 6 to 10 p.m.

Leopold Kainz at Wiedner Gürtel 16.

WOK's are chain restaurants. There are more than a dozen of them
in Vienna. Try:

Schonbrunnerstrasse 45,   Liechtensteinstrasse 4,
Mariahilferstrasse 85,   Schottengasse 1.

Cooking School. Just down from the WOK on Schottengasse. Only open
for lunch (12 until 2) and Monday through Friday. Cheap and good.

OK Restaurant at Karntnerstrasse 61. Very cheap.

Residenz Café at the Opera end of Mariahilferstrasse, where the shops end.
Also try eating at any of the wine houses and cellars. Prices will usually
be a bit more than 45 schillings, but the food is great. Don't forget to buy
Vienna pastry from the *Konditoreien.* Cheap enough and great breakfast
food, especially if you have a sweet tooth.

Vienna: what to see and do

SCHLOSS SCHONBRUNN is a huge Baroque palace containing more than
1,400 rooms. It was the modest summer residence of the Hapsburgs from
1695. Costs about 20 schillings for a guided tour in English, but less if
you're a student.

KUNSTHISTORISCHES MUSEUM at the Ring. Fine collection of masters.
Works by Rembrandt, Brueghel, Vermeer, Velasquez, etc.
Closed Monday. Admission fee.

HOFBURG was the official residence of the Hapsburgs. Lots to do. You can
visit the Imperial Rooms where Emperor Franz Josef lived, or
the *Schatzkammer* which contains the royal treasures, including the insignia
of the Holy Roman Empire and the sword of Charlemagne. Then there's
the famous Spanish Riding School (check with tourist office for
performance times) and the *Schweizer Kapelle* where the Vienna Boys Choir
perform each Sunday except in summer. It'd take you days (and some
expense) to get through the place if you wanted to see everything.

ST STEPHAN'S GOTHIC CATHEDRAL at Stephansplatz. Climb the tower for a tremendous view over the city and head down into the crypt and have a look at some skulls. Admission charge for both tower and crypt.

BURG KREUZENSTEIN is a moated medieval castle 30 minutes from the centre of Vienna. Take a train from Landstrasse.

KELLERS AND HEURIGE are wine cellars and wine gardens and were once – not so much now – an integral part of the life of the Viennese. But still good fun. Costs depend on how thirsty you are.

PRATER is an amusement park featuring the world's largest ferris wheel. No entrance charge to the grounds. Sometimes a good place to meet the opposite sex.

THEATRE for those who want a taste of the Vienna of old. Try the *Theater an der Wien* at Lehargasse 5 for operettas (standing room is cheapest).

DISCOTHEQUES *Voom-Voom* at Daungasse 1. *Tenne*, *Playboy*, and *Take Five* at Annagasse 4, 6, and 8. Admission charge includes the price of the first drink.

Transport in Vienna
Average price of a ticket on the street-cars is a high 10 schillings, but you can get a 20 per cent discount by buying five tickets at a time at *Tabak Trafic*.

Student discounts
Free entrance to public museums and reductions to theatres and cinemas. For information:
OSTERREICHISCHE HOCHSCHULERSCHAFT,
Führichgasse 10, Vienna 1010 (Tel: 52 66 63).

Addresses

Main Post Office (for Poste Restante) at Fleischmarkt 19, Vienna.

American Express at Kaemtnerstrasse 21, Vienna (Tel: 52 05 44).

Student Travel Service at Führichgasse 10, Vienna (Tel: 52 66 63).

Student Travel Service at Hildmannplatz 1a, Salzburg (Tel: 84 069).

Student Travel Service at Erlerstrasse 19–25, Innsbruck (Tel: 28 997).

Tourist Office at Stadiongasse 6–8, Vienna (Tel: 43 16 08).

US Embassy at Boltzmanngasse 16, Vienna (Tel: 34 66 11).

British Embassy at Reisnerstrasse 40, Vienna (Tel: 73 15 75).

Hitchers' tips and comments

Innsbruck. Don't try and walk out to the east. You face a seven-mile walk!
Good place to sleep is under the Brenner Autobahn above the Olympic
Stadium – good view of city lights. Keep out of pastry shops – too
expensive. Don't try sleeping in the centre of Salzburg. Police are on the
look out. Try out in the forest. It's only a couple of miles walk. Hope this
helps fellow travellers.
Malcolm Frankland, Glaslum, England

In Vienna tickets for the metro are cancelled by a machine so buy one
ticket and forget to feed it in thus moving around on the cheap. I kept it up
for 3 days – no hassles.
Marcel Thomas, Horndean, England

Italy

Population	55,000,000
Size	116,372 square miles
Capital	Rome, population 3,000,000
Government	Republic.
Religion	Roman Catholic
Language	Italian

The four most common entry routes into Italy are (1) along the French
Riviera to **Genova** (Genoa) (birthplace of Columbus), with its fantastic
harbour area, (2) in over the French Alps to **Torino** (Turin) where you
can catch the important Egyptian Museum and Museum of Ancient Art,
(3) from Switzerland through the Swiss-Italian town of Lugano to
Milano (Milan), or (4) through the Mont Blanc Tunnel.

Winter travellers coming in on the Turin route should note that the
Col du Mt Cenis on the French side of the border may be impassable
between December and May. Most of the passes in Switzerland (No 3 route
or any near it), like Simplon, Lukmanier, or Splugen may be closed
during the same months. Summertime travellers should remember that the
Riviera route is blanketed with family holiday cars from June through
August and that the hitching can sometimes be very, very slow.

Milan is not my favourite city. With a population of more than one and a half million it's big, dusty, noisy, and industrial, but there are many things to see, notably the church of Santa Maria delle Grazie which houses Leonardo da Vinci's famous *Last Supper*. The Gothic Duomo cathedral stands 357 feet high and has (if you're interested in such facts) 4,400 statues serving as decoration. About 300 lire gets you up on to the roof from where you see a fantastic view over the city and wax poetic to gargoyles if you feel so inclined. La Scala is the big stop for opera lovers. It's a superb theatre and features the best singers in the world. Cheapest way to view a show is to buy standing room. Museum fans will have a ball in Milan.

Right near La Scala is the Museo Teatrale which relates the history of the 150-year-old theatre, while the National Museum of Science and Technology (free on Sundays and Thursday mornings) has a Leonardo Gallery in which you can see models of Da Vinci's fascinating inventions. Then there's the Pinacoteca di Brera (free on Sundays) which Milan claims as the second gallery in Italy after Florence's Uffizi.

Finally, drop in on the thirteenth-century Castello Sforzesco, and the strange, ornate cemetery known as Cimitero Monumentale.

Halfway between Milan and Venice (Venezia) is **Verona** where you can see a well-preserved Roman amphitheatre, one of Italy's largest.

Venice may be the world's weirdest city. Built on a lagoon $2\frac{1}{2}$ miles from the mainland (but with a road connection) it spreads over 118 tiny islands. It is criss-crossed by more than 160 canals and, as no cars are allowed into the city, you either walk from place to place or jump a *vaporetto*, the small canal boats. Take a tip that Lines 1 and 3 might be slower than Lines 2 and 4, but they are cheaper. Big sights in Venice, apart from the city itself, include the Cathedral of San Marco and the Palace of the Doges, the Campanile, which offers a great view of the canal city (costs 500 lire) and the Gallery of Modern Art (great collection and free on Sundays). The Guggenheim Collection is an outstanding collection of twentieth-century painting and is free for the looking on Tuesdays and Fridays from 3 to 6 p.m. There is a special exhibition of young up-and-coming artists which is particularly interesting. For a look at some Venetian glass-blowers in action jump *vaporetto* No 5 at **Fondamente Nuova**, which for a few lire will take you out to the island of **Murano**. Another interesting island trip (leaving from the same place) is to **Torcello** with its old, old churches. If you're trying to find yourself a little company, try the Lido beach. To get there you take another boat ride. Once on the beach you'll have to pay around 1,000 lire for a dressing-room. But the possibilities, in summer, of finding some action, are enormous. If you find it and take it back to Venice with you, walk it on the **Rialto Bridge**

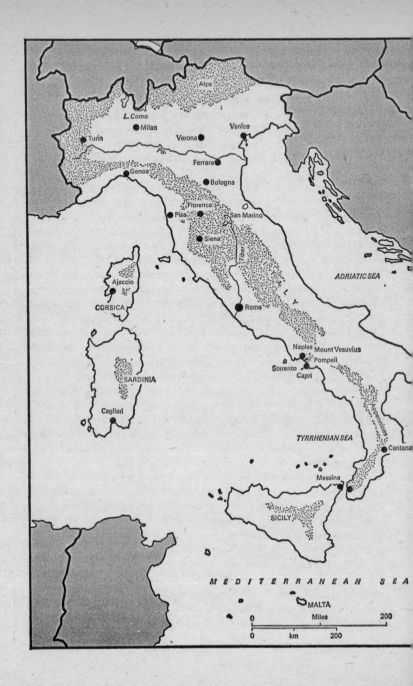

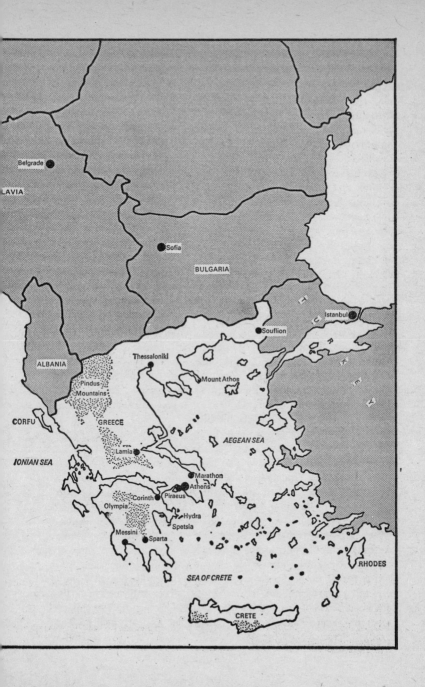

around 10 or 11 in the evening and listen to the music coming from the gondolas. The people *in* the gondolas are paying around 6,000 lire for the privilege.

Heading back across the country, you pass through **Ferrara** with its marvellous moated Castello Estense and its twelfth-century cathedral, and then through gracious **Bologna**, perhaps the best place in the country to try some good, cheap, Italian home cooking. See the Fountain of Neptune and climb the 320-foot Asinelli Tower for a great view over this ancient town.

Next big stop (there are plenty of nice villages in-between) is **Firenze** (Florence). Considered *the* great art city of the world, it's a natural target for thousands of students from all over the globe. Consequently, you have an excellent chance of finding someone who'd just love to accompany you on a tour. All museums and galleries in Florence are free on Sunday, otherwise it'll cost you up to 500 lire a visit (less on student cards, of course). With something like fifty places to visit in Florence you have to choose carefully what you want to see. Most people consider the Uffizi Galleries and the Pitti Palace indispensable. What else ? Try the Baptistry opposite the Duomo with its fantastic 'Door of Paradise' by Ghiberti, or the Piazzale Michelangelo from where you can look out over Florence and the Arno Valley. Visit Santa Croce, badly battered during the 1966 floods, but now restored. Drop in on the Medici Chapel where you can see Michelangelo's work adorning the tombs of the famous family. Try . . . well, pick it for yourself – free literature from the Tourist Office at Via Tornabuoni 15. There is so much to see and you will be surrounded by the masterpieces of so many famous artists that you may end up wondering if perfection isn't a trifle claustrophobic.

Pisa, just an hour or two west of Florence, where you can see the famous Leaning Tower. Its proper name is Campanile. It was begun in 1173 and leans 14 feet out of plumb owing to land subsidence during its construction.

South-east from Pisa is **Siena**, the most important town in Tuscany after Florence. Once again there are galleries and churches enough to keep you busy. But with a population of only 55,000 this beautiful old medieval city is small enough to wander in at leisure. Maybe a nice resting place before hitting the bustle of Rome. And if you're there in July or August, try and catch The Palio, a wild horse race around the square, run with the riders wearing medieval costume. (Exact dates from tourist office.)

After Rome, the next big 'must' is the Bay of Naples. **Napoli**, a city of one and a quarter million, has for centuries been subjected to earthquakes and volcanic eruptions, but the place just keeps on going. It is a marvellous town in which to wander – it's so 'Italian' that it's nearly a cliché. The two big things to see are the Castel Nuovo, dating from 1282, and the National Museum with its collection of ancient sculpture and important finds from Pompeii.

Pompeii is the greatest standing remnant of the Roman world. Once an important city of 20,000 people, it was completely buried by an eruption of Mount Vesuvius in AD 79. The memory of the place died in the succeeding centuries until the name became a mere legend. Then, late last century, it was rediscovered, and for decades the work of digging it out of millions of tons of dirt has continued. Now you can wander for hours in a complete Roman city – and it's weird. In some streets you see ruts in the cobbles from chariot wheels. In doorways you see grooves scraped into floors by the doors which once opened across them. And you can see the stone-entombed bodies of some of the citizens.

Herculaneum, close to Pompeii, is another city which was buried in the same eruption. Not as fascinating as Pompeii, but OK.

The villain of the piece, Mount Vesuvius, is a volcano 3,984 feet high. And it's still active. You can walk up to the top, if you're feeling fit, or take the expensive chair-lift if you're not, and then descend into the actual crater amongst the fumes drifting out from crevices. Interesting stuff.

Also in the Bay of Naples area is the famous resort town of **Sorrento** (beautiful and expensive) and the fabulous island of **Capri,** once the favourite haunt of old Emperor Tiberius (you can see the ruins of his palace). Don't miss the Blue Grotto if you can afford the couple of dollars that the excursion will cost you. To get to Capri, the cheapest way is to take a steamer from Naples. It'll cost you 2,500 lire or so return – but as it's a 1½-hour trip each way it makes for a fascinating day. If you want to hitch out to Sorrento (difficult because it's a built-up area), you can buy a return fare to Capri for around 1,200 lire. But you get a much better look at the bay by leaving from Naples.

The Island of **Ischia** is a rich man's place, but apart from private yachts and bikini-ed kittens, it's laden with plenty of sights to see. Return trip by steamer from Naples will cost you about 2,000 lire.

South of Naples and you're into Calabria which, though progressing fast, still tends to prefer a life-style unchanged for centuries. See, too, the Greek temples at Paestum.

You can cross into **Sicily** from **Reggio di Calabria** to **Messina** for about 500 lire. Once there, forget the Mafia. Just remember that Sicily (pop 5,000,000) is the largest island in the Mediterranean (10,000 square miles) and home of some of its richest archaeological finds.

Capital and chief port **Palermo** (pop 700,000) is an Arab-Norman-influenced city of baroque squares, running fountains and Florentine statues. Plus odd gentlemen wearing pink ties who try and sell you contraband watches or worse. See the 12th-century Palace of the Normans with its marble-floored Palatine Chapel and dazzling mosaics.

At **Segesta**, 35 miles west of Palermo, a desolately beautiful but unfinished Doric Temple dates back to the 5th century BC. Further south, at Agrigento's Valley of the Temples, a clutch of imposing temples overlook a labyrinthine on-site museum containing a superb collection of Greek art.

Syracuse (pop 100,000), 80 miles south of Messina, was the birthplace of Archimedes, who discovered the theory of water displacement whilst taking a bath. Once Syracuse was the most important city in the western world after Athens. Half-a-million people lived there. Today it's a stylish town, with baroque palaces, beautiful piazzas, and a seventh-century cathedral. The massive archaeological zone includes a Roman coliseum, well-preserved Greek theatre and interesting caves and catacombs.

Don't miss **Etna**, at 10,725 feet the highest volcano in Europe. You reach it by bus, funicular and foot from **Catania**, Sicily's second largest city, on the east coast. The walk from the funicular terminal to the summit takes one hour.

Warning! The Italians are tough on drugs and the word is out that they're using the old hippie type spy gimmick. So choose your friends carefully. If you're copped out and you're lucky you'll only get three years.

★**Hitching in Italy** Generally OK. There are a tremendous amount of *autostradas*, but I find I've always had more luck on the smaller roads. You're allowed to hitch on the *autostradas*, but the rules are the same as anywhere else in Europe. Namely, you can only pick up rides on entrance roads; hitching on the actual *autostrada* is a no-no and will result in you being turfed back to where you belong by the scores of patrolling *polizia*.

★**Crossing to Sardinia** From Genoa to Olbia will cost around 20,000 lire, one way. From Naples to Cagliari, the same but cheaper if you sit up in a chair all night. From Civitavecchia (north of Rome) to Olbia will cost about 13,000 lire one way.

Rome: where to sleep

In Rome expect to pay between 1,600–2,600 lire for student accommodation. Hotels and *pensiones* – cheap ones – will take as much as 3,500–4,200 lire from you unless you find a real bargain. Doubles and triples, of course, give you a good saving per head. Make sure you don't land in a place which insists that you pay full pension (bed and all meals) –

they may offer a good deal, but it won't be as much fun as eating out.
Incidentally, when you're arranging for your room or buying a meal
you'll find that speaking Spanish (if you've got some) will solve most
problems (unless you can speak Italian, in which case you can solve
all the problems).

Del Foro Italico Youth Hostel at Viale delle Olimpiadi 61, Flaminio, Rome
(Tel: 396 47 09). Fair way out of town.

Hotel Vanni at Via Treviso 31 (Tel: 85 93 54). 5th floor.

NBBS Hotel at Via dei Bichi 17, Forte Aurelio (Tel: 622 41 98).
Open June 16th to October 15th. Fair way out of town.

Casa dello Studente, Citta Universitaria at Via Cesare de Lollis 24
(Tel: 49 02 43). Ask for dormitory. Open June 21st to September 20th.

Pensione Cristallo at Via Montebello 114 (Tel: 47 98 10).

Pensione Melinelli at Via Montebello 114 (Tel: 47 03 27).

Casa Gizzi at Via Codorna 29 (Tel: 48 19 77).

Albergo del Popolo at Via Apuli 41 (Tel: 49 05 58). Women admitted from
July 1st to September 30th only. Otherwise men only.

For cheap *pensiones* (around 3,500 lire) head for Via Principe Amedeo
which is bang in the middle of town and two blocks to your left as you
stand at the front of and with your back to the Terminal Station (in Piazza
dei Cinquecento). The Via Palestro, a couple of blocks to the right of the
station, is another good area.

For help in finding accommodation go to the EPT information office
in the Terminal Station.

For sleeping rough, head into the gardens of the Villa Borghese –
you won't be alone! Second choice is the park at Colle Oppio,
near the Colosseum.

Warning! See hitch-hiker's letter at end of 'How to Survive' chapter.

Rome: where to eat

Expect to pay 1,800–2,600 lire for a good meal. To cut costs, remember
that in Italy, as in Spain, Greece, and France, bar-owners usually don't
object if you bring in a pile of food you've bought elsewhere to make a
meal – as long as you buy a drink or two in the process. In the

Colosseum/Colle Oppio area there are plenty of cheap food shops where you can buy in small quantities. The *Rosticcerie* and *Tavole Calde* are eating places which feature cheap, quick meals ideal for travellers low on lire.

Da Peppino at Via Castelfidardo 35 (couple of blocks to the right of the Terminal Station) is one of the cheapest places in town – but it's closed on Friday. All around that area to the right of the station is dead cheap.

Ristorante Peppino at Via dei Graci 5 near the Spanish Steps.

Mario's at Via del Moro 53. Just over the river near Ponte Sisto. Cheap!

Trattoria Marcello at Borgo Pio 87. (Near St Peter's.)

Trattoria da Mariani at Borgo Pio 92. (Near St Peter's.)

Imperiale at Via Flaminia 11.

Falconi's at Piazza dei Cinquecento 47, in front of the station.

For a bit of a splurge, you might consider some restaurants around the Fountains of Trevi. They will cost you about 3,500 lire for a really fine meal. Try *Ristorante Trevi* at Piazza Fontana di Trevi 101, or for something a little cheaper, but still nice, the *Trattoria da Quinto* at Via del Lavatore 42, just off the Piazza. If in this area, but not out for a slap-up meal, drop into *Rosticceria Trevi* just off the Piazza at Via San Vincenzo 30 where you can eat well for 2,200 lire.

Rome: what to see and do

THE ROMAN FORUM AND THE PALATINE Open every day except Tuesday. Entrance charge, but half-price on Sundays. Ticket gives entrance to both sites. The *Forum* was the heart of the Roman Empire, the place from which all roads started and the market and meeting-place of Rome's citizens. It is said that the site was first built upon, in wood, as far back as the sixth century BC. The *Palatine* is a low hill between the Forum and the Tiber and was the first of Rome's seven hills to be inhabited. At nights (check the tourist office for times) a 'sound and light' display is held in the Forum. It costs a lot to enter, but from the back of the Capitoline Hill (or Campidoglio), once the sacred hill of Rome, you can watch the display (even if you can't hear it all) for nothing. Also, on Campidoglio is the *Capitoline Museum* (entrance charge) which contains a fine antique collection, much of it related to Imperial Rome.

THE PANTHEON at Piazza della Rotonda is the best preserved of all Rome's ancient buildings. It was built in AD 27 and then, after being burned down, rebuilt by Hadrian in the second century AD. Various Italian kings, as well as the painter Raphael, are buried in the building.

THE VATICAN CITY The Vatican became an independent state led by the Pope as the result of a treaty signed on February 11th, 1929, between the Papacy and the Italian State. The City covers an area of 109 acres and has a population of 1,000. It has its own newspaper (*Osservatore Romano*), its own postal service, radio station, railway station, court of law, and its own diplomatic representatives. It imports food and exports a nebulous hope which affects the lives of millions around the world. It is an indispensable stop on a Roman tour. Principal sights in the City are the fabulous *St Peter's Cathedral*, the *Sistine Chapel*, the *Vatican Museum*, and the *Raphael Rooms*. Entrance to the last three costs the better part of 1,500 lire if you don't have a student card, but are free on the last Saturday of each month. Tickets for Papal audiences can be picked up at several points around Rome and in the Vatican – check at the tourist office about this. If you just want a quick look at the Pope, at noon most Sundays he gives a sermon from the balcony overlooking St Peter's Square.

COLOSSEUM The Colosseum was built between AD 70 and AD 80. The big inauguration show lasted 100 days during which 5,000 wild animals were slaughtered. Not too long after, the Romans graduated to watching people being killed. The Colosseum could hold 50,000 spectators. It is undergoing long-term restoration and is sometimes closed.

CHURCHES St Peter's is the main church to see, but others, all of artistic or historical interest, include, *Santa Maria degli Angeli*, *St Peter in Vincoli* (which houses Michelangelo's *Moses*), and *Santa Maria Maggiore*.

CATACOMBS Bus Number 118 from the Colosseum takes you out along the Old Appian Way and passes the *Catacombs of St Sebastian* and the *Catacombs of St Callistus*. Both are worth seeing. The Catacombs of St Callistus are considered the most important in Rome. Entrance charge to both.

MUSEUMS AND GALLERIES Amongst the many to be seen are the *Galleria Borghese*, *The Lateran Museum*, *The National Museum of Rome*, *The National Gallery of Modern Art*, and *The National Gallery of Antique Art*. If you only have time for one museum, then the *Vatican Museum* is considered amongst the most important.

THE TREVI FOUNTAIN at Via del Muratte. This is the place where, if you're romantically inclined, you toss a coin into the water and make a wish that you will soon return to Rome. If you're a hitch-hiker, you'll notice that a lot of young Italians have figured out how to get the coins back on dry land without getting their feet wet. They use magnets on a fishing line, hurl them into the water and slowly drag them back along the bottom. Guys using bigger and better magnets – I saw one a foot long and about an inch wide – bring in as many as five coins at a time. The fishing takes place just after dark and about an hour after it starts there aren't many coins left – so if you want to try it get there at the right time. (Beware of two things: the locals who don't like foreign competition, and the police who think it's all illegal.) Incidentally, I haven't seen fountain-dragging done anywhere else in Europe. Perhaps it hasn't caught on. It might be a good way of picking up pocket money. If you don't want to make money, go to the Trevi after dark during summer anyway. It's a great meeting place.

THE SPANISH STEPS These 137 steps lead off the Piazza di Spagna up to the church of *Trinita dei Monti*. Nearby is *Keats' House*, where the poet died in 1821. The Piazza, and the Steps, which in the eighteenth and nineteenth centuries were the centre of the English colony in Rome, are now the meeting place of American travellers visiting American Express for their mail. Good place to meet people and dig out information.

FLEA MARKET One of the better markets in Europe. It's at the Porta Portese and held every Sunday morning. There's a smaller market at Piazza della Fontanella Borghese held every afternoon (except Sunday) from 3 p.m. Mostly antique and imitation. Not as good as Porta Portese.

MOVIES Several cinemas around town show original version films. For information, buy the daily paper or a copy of the English-language publication *This Week in Rome*.

CONCERTS Check with tourist office for dates of concerts held outdoors in the Basilica of Maxeusis. Great setting with the cheapest seats around 900 lire.

Transport in Rome
Trolley-car and Underground tickets all cost around 100 lire. A flat rate of 150 lire operates for the bus system in Rome.

Student discounts
Reductions in all museums and art galleries, to some theatres and cinemas,

to some Sound and Light spectacles, and for goods purchased in some department stores. For information:

MINISTRY OF PUBLIC INSTRUCTION,
Viale Trastevere 76A, Rome.

Addresses

Main Post Office (for Poste Restante) at Piazza S. Silvestro, Rome.

American Express at Piazza di Spagna 38, Rome (Tel: 68 87 51).

State Tourist Office in station terminal.

Relazione Universitaire at 11 Via Palestro, Rome (Tel: 47 55 265) (for student travel).

Ministry of Public Instruction at Viale Trastevere 76A, Rome. (For matters relating to students).

US Embassy at Via Vittorio Veneto 119, Rome (Tel: 46 74).

British Embassy at 80 XX Settembre, Rome (Tel: 475 54 41).

Hitchers' tips and comments

Don't know how it is now, but it used to be that if the Italian fuzz picked you up in Rome, you got presented with a rail ticket to the frontier of your choice. After dark on the Spanish Steps used to be a good place to get lumbered and to get a free ticket out. ·
Mike Feeney, Haslow, England

In Venice forget the Youth Hostel unless you've already got fleas. If swimming off the Lido (and let's face it, if you swim anywhere else in Venice you've no right to call yourself human) you'll come out two shades of brown and only one shade is due to the sun. It's not too bad if you watch where you're going and can tell a jelly-fish from less desirable items.
Graham Harvey, Warminster, England

Anybody going to Italy should go along to the Automobile Association (AA) offices. For a small fee they will supply a museum entry card. The card allows free entry to any museum, art gallery or historical site run by the Italian Government.
B. J. Salmon, Birmingham, England

Special thanks to hitchers Sergio Berio and Giuseppe Giaume of Rome for comments on the Italian edition! K.W.

Spain

Population	34,364,000
Size	194,883 square miles
Capital	Madrid, population 3,147,000
Government	Monarchy
Religion	Roman Catholic
Language	Spanish is the official language but Catalan is spoken in the north-east, Basque in the Basque provinces on the northern coast, and Gallego in Galicia

Unless you have unlimited time, travelling in Spain presents one big problem – where to go! The cities in Spain which have become household words outdo those of any other country. Madrid, Barcelona, Pamplona, Segovia, Toledo, Sevilla, Granada, Salamanca, Málaga, Valencia, Alicante, Cartagena, Córdoba, Zaragoza, Bilbao, San Sebastián, Tarragona, Gerona. All names with which the mind has some vague association.

But after Madrid, if five cities must be chosen to see, then they are probably Sevilla, Granada, Barcelona, Toledo, and Málaga. They are my personal choices and I'm a little one-sided when it comes to Spain. I particularly prefer the southern region of Andalucia, the land of tiny white mountain villages, old and smelly bars and cafés, cheap wine, bullfights, and a to-hell-with-it philosophy which leaves plenty of scope for tomorrow to look after itself. Sevilla, Granada, and Málaga are all part of the south.

Barcelona, in the north, is Spain's second city, but vies with Madrid when it claims to be the most dynamic. Just south of the Costa Brava, it is the largest sea-port in the Mediterranean, and that, along with its population of two-and-a-half million, helps it to be about the liveliest city in the country. Things to see include Gaudi's fabulous *La Sagrada Familia* church and the apartment buildings he designed on the Paseo de Gracia. The museum of Modern Art, free if you show a student card, includes paintings by Dali and Picasso, while the Picasso Museum has many works from that artist's Blue Period. Up on the mountain called Montjuich (Bus 57 from the railway station) is a castle, which houses a Military Museum, and what is claimed to be the world's third largest amusement park (good place for meeting people). The mountain also offers superb views over the city. The **Pueblo Español** – the Spanish village – was built in the 1920s and contains examples of every type of regional architecture to be found in Spain. Barceloneta is the fisherman's and working-man's area of Barcelona where the really cheap cafés and bars are to be found.

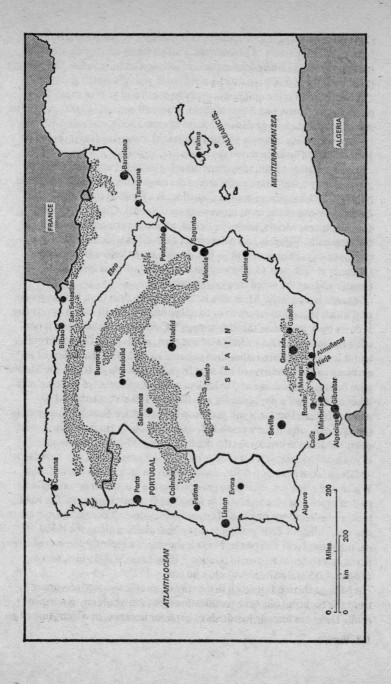

Just off Highway N11, 40 kilometres north-west of Barcelona, is the famous old monastery of **Montserrat**. This eleventh-century Benedictine building sits in a tremendous mountain location and if you feel like fighting it out with the 500,000 tourists who visit each year it's worth going up.

The coast road is the quickest way down south and goes through some good places. **Tarragona** is one of them. It's small enough (45,000 people) to wander around easily and it's one mass of monuments and ruins. It's one of the oldest cities in Spain and St Paul is said to have visited it during its Roman period and converted the locals to Christianity.

Heading farther south, towns worth seeing include **Peñiscola,** a small place of only 3,000 but perhaps one of the most beautiful villages in Spain. **Sagunto,** 22 kilometres south of Castellón, is a fortified town and historically one of the most interesting on the coast. Greeks, Romans, Carthaginians, Moors, and even El Cid, at one time or another, paid business calls. **Valencia** and **Alicante** are both cities which could take a couple of days of anyone's time, but if you have to keep moving then Granada is next stop. On the way through, you will pass through **Guadix** and see the weird troglodyte dwellings.

Granada is where the Alhambra is, but it's more than that. It's the sort of city which is good to return to or to tell yourself you will return to one day. It dates back to at least the fifth century BC and its crumbling age is one of its fascinations. Old streets twist and turn, weeds grow from the roofs, and it is commonplace rather than unusual to look through a door or an archway to find a courtyard left over from Moorish days. It was the Moors who built the Alhambra and to look over this reconstructed Arabian relic takes at least half a day, even for a swift visit. Tickets cost about 130 pesetas, but student cards will get you in for half-price. See also Sacromonte (go at night), one of the world's best operated tourist traps, where gypsies operate flamenco dives from the depths of all-mod-con cave-houses. If you want to sample what they're offering, be prepared to pay too much.

Málaga is the next stop if you decide to have a look at the Costa del Sol. Whichever route you choose to get down to the Costa can be a rough one so don't move too far after you've found a prime hitching spot. The road is either bend-ridden or has bad edges – which doesn't encourage motorists to stop. Villages worth looking at if you're travelling along the N340 include **Almuñecar** and **Nerja**. Nerja is the site of a recently discovered cave which has traces of human habitation dating back 20,000 years, and a 195-feet-high stalactite, the world's largest.

In Málaga there is not much in the way of specific sights to see, apart from the beautiful old Arab fortifications, but the whole city is a trip in itself. There are literally hundreds of bars, for instance, in which you can go berserk trying to taste the dozens of famous sweet wines which Málaga province produces. At 20 pesetas a glass it's a pleasant way to kill yourself.

Fourteen kilometres west of Málaga is the much-written-about tourist resort of Torremolinos. Fifteen years ago it was a not-very-attractive fishing village. Now it's a not-very-attractive city of super-skyscrapers packed with package tourists. For the hitcher its main advantage is that all year round there are people in town looking for partners. Best place to start the hunt is down on the Carihuela beach. Plenty of bars there with like-minded souls. Also great fish restaurants.

Another good thing about it is the *Torremolinos Secondhand Book Market* where you can pick up something to read real cheap. It's upstairs at 26 Calle San Miguel (the main shopping street). They also have a free notice board where people advertise for rides to Morocco, cheap airfares back to London, things to buy and sell, etc. They've offered a 20 per cent cash discount on second-hand books to any hitch-hiker who flashes his copy of the *Hitcher's Guide*.

From Torremolinos, the N340 continues straight down to Algeciras for ferry connections with Morocco (see **Morocco and North Africa**) and to Gibraltar (see **The Small Countries**). If time is available, a detour to **Ronda,** 50 kilometres into the Sierra de Ronda along the C339 is a nice trip. The city perches on the edge of a 600-foot-high cliff.

Sevilla can be reached by continuing along the N340 past **Cadiz** and then going north via **Jerez de la Frontera**, the sherry-producing area where there's plenty of free wine-tasting, or by going north-west from Málaga and meeting up with the N334 at **Antequera**. Sevilla with its population of half a million is the fourth city of Spain and so old that legend tells it was founded by Hercules. Like many other southern Spanish cities, it reached its zenith during the long Arab occupation and today one of the best things to see is the 320-foot-high Giralda Tower and the beautiful cathedral alongside. In the cathedral is a tomb said to contain the remains of Christopher Columbus. But the really big thing to see in Sevilla, apart from the city's own life-style, is the three-day-long *feria*, or fair, which is held each year around April when the entire population goes mad with bullfights, flamenco, and all things Spanish. The *feria* is heavily attended by tourists, but the Sevillaños tend to disregard them and keep to the business in hand. Check local or international Spanish tourist offices for exact dates of the fair and also of the *Semana Santa*, or Holy Week Fiesta, which precedes it.

Toledo, 70 kilometres south of Madrid, is said by the Spaniards to be that city which most perfectly includes all the most important elements of Spanish history. It is an historical and architectural monument to all that Spain has been, and in 1937 the entire city was declared a National

Monument. Toledo was the home of El Greco and the artist's house has been refurnished to imitate the style of his period. A gallery next door contains many important works. Around the corner from the house is the tiny church of Santo Tome which contains what many experts consider his best painting, *The Burial of the Count of Orgaz*. Other points of interest include the Gothic Cathedral which is claimed as the best in Spain, and the huge Alcazar, scene of a tremendous siege during the Civil War.

South of Toledo is La Mancha, Don Quixote country, and any fans of the sprightly gentleman can pick up a pamphlet from the tourist offices describing a trip through villages associated with the man's adventures.

From Sevilla, the E52 leads into Portugal for those heading for Lisbon, and the N630 leads north, joining with the E3 for those travelling to France. The four major cities on this route are all worth time if you can spare it. **Salamanca, Valladolid, Burgos** (home of the legendary El Cid), and **San Sebastian**.

(The cheap living ends at the border! Load up with cigarettes and wine before you cross into France!)

★**Drinkers** who think they can drink, drop into a bar and order yourselves an *anis seco*. For those who are less pretentious but who still want an alcoholic kick, try the *anis dulce*. To anyone who can drop six *anis secos* within an hour and furnish proof that he was still capable of crossing a road, a free copy of the next edition will be given.

Living winners from last year are:
Paul Le Butt of Frederictory, Canada (6 in 52 minutes); John Houston of Hull, England (6 in 38 minutes and 2 more before his hour was up) and Del Absolom of Cranham, England (6 in 60 minutes).

★**Bullfights** Tickets are quite expensive. Generally, a seat in the shade (*sombra*) will cost between 300 and 500 pesetas. Seats in the sun (*sol*) are cheaper, while standing room is cheapest of all. But as the fight takes about two hours it's worth investing in sitting space.

★**Fiestas** There's nothing quite like a Spanish fiesta, and you should try and visit one if you're anywhere near it. Here's a list of some of the more important fiestas, including the months they are usually held. You'll have to check with the Spanish Tourist Office to get exact dates as they change from year to year. *Cabalgata de Reyes*, the Fiesta of the Kings, is a parade held in most Spanish cities on the Eve of Epiphany in January. *Moros y Cristianos*, mock battles between Moors and Christians, are especially popular in the Levante area. Some of the best known are at Bocairente (Province of Valencia), in February; Alcoy (Alicante), in April; Villajoyosa

(Alicante), in July; Villena (Alicante), in September. *Fallas de Valencia* is one of the most spectacular shows in Spain. Don't miss it if you're a firework freak. Huge firework-filled statues are burned in the streets. Held in Valencia on Saint Joseph's night in March. Alicante has a similar show on Saint John's Eve. *Semana Santa*, Holy Week features vast Easter parades; best places to see them are Sevilla, Málaga, Valladolid, Granada. Also, during Holy Week, Passion Plays are held in various towns. Most outstanding in Esparraguera (Barcelona), Ulldecona (Tarragona), Moncada (Valencia). The Passion Plays are relics from the medieval theatre, as are certain other plays held during the year in Spain, namely the *Misterio de Elche*, in Elche (Alicante) in August, and the *Misterio de San Quillen y San Felicia* in Obanos (Navarra), in August. *Ferias:* all cities have their *ferias* (or fairs). Amongst the best: Sevilla's Spring Fair, in April, and Madrid's San Isidro in May. *Feria de Caballo*, the Horse Fair, is held in Jerez de la Frontera in May. *Corpus Cristi* in June, especially in Granada, Sevilla and Toledo. In Sitges, Barcelona, the roads are paved with magnificent flower carpets. *Romeria del Rocia* in Almont (Huelva) in June: the most famous *romeria* in Spain. But you need about a week spare and a horse to join in properly. *San Fermin*, in Pamplona, in July: the famed running of the bulls. (Be warned: statistics show that more foreigners than Spaniards get gored!) The *International Festival of Music and Dance*, at Granada, in July, is held in the fabulous Alhambra. You have to book well in advance. *Human Castles:* you have to see it to believe it. People on top of each other, six high; popular in the north. Try Villafrance de Panades (Barcelona) in August. *Batalla de las Flores* in Laredo (Santander) in August: parade during which those taking part and the spectators pelt each other with flowers. *Fiesta de la Vendimia:* the grape-harvest fair in Jerez de la Frontera in September.

★**Wine** Many, many villages in Spain make a small supply of local wine. So when roaming through the back areas, drop into local bars and ask for *vino del pueblo* (the wine of the village). Some of it is remarkably good. It's always cheap.

★**Cigarettes** They come as cheap as 12 pesetas for 20 and you can buy a first-class cigarette for 20 pesetas a pack. Worth stocking up to carry you through more expensive countries.

★**Piropos** If you're a lady-hitcher, don't be surprised if a Spaniard suddenly walks up and starts whispering passionate-sounding phrases to you. Keep your nose in the air and keep walking. It's purely the Latin manifestation of hairy-chestedness, like a harmless wolf-whistle in London or New York. The *piropo*, or compliment, is usually of a very personal nature and if you don't speak Spanish you're going to miss out on some wildly endearing pieces of Don Juan-ism, like: 'If only I was worthy to be the father of your children', or 'Your body is a flower to be plucked by the grateful'.

★**Boots** A superb buy in Spain is leather boots. Really good-quality ankle-length boots for around 1,200 pesetas and knee-boots for about 2,000 pesetas. Men's and women's.

★**Drugs** Don't be tempted to bring drugs into Spain from Morocco via Algeciras (or anywhere else). The Algeciras customs post caught 360 smugglers in 1977, bagging 2500 kilos of hash. They use specially trained dogs to sniff out the goodies. Even if you arrive in Algeciras from Ceuta, or in Malaga from Melilla you may still be searched by mainland customs. Ceuta and Melilla are Spanish territories on the Moroccan coastline, but people entering the mainland from these cities are subject to a second customs hassle.

★**Crossing to the Canary Islands** About 2,700 pesetas from Algeciras, or from about 2,200 pesetas from Cadiz. The seven main islands of the Canaries lie about a thousand miles from Spain's southern tip and just off the Saharan coast. (The nearest, Lanzarote, is only 70 miles from Africa.) They're blessed with year-round Spring-time temperatures and thus are popular with hitchers heading south to escape the annual northern freeze. There's no way of hitching there, unless you catch a yacht from Gibraltar or one of the harbours on the Costa del Sol, but regular ferry services run from Algeciras and Cadiz.

Here's a run-down on the islands, starting with the biggest:

Tenerife (area: 2,800 square miles pop 600,000).

Chief town **Santa Cruz de Tenerife** (pop 100,000) is one of the world's busiest shipping ports, but a surprisingly quiet and pleasant town to walk through. Apart from a relaxed colonial atmosphere it has nothing special to offer.

Puerto de la Cruz, 22 miles west across the island, is where the action is. A former fishing village turned high-rise resort, it's filled with bazaars, hotels, bars, restaurants and discos. Plenty of chances to meet the opposite sex. **Warning**! Meals and rooms are expensive here. This is Charterflightsville and priced accordingly. (Avoid the Tenerife wine, too. It's three times the price of mainland plonk and tastes worse.)

The **Botanical Gardens** just outside Puerto de la Cruz are worth a look.

Founded in 1788, they are famed for a collection of trees brought from all over the world. Don't miss the monkeys.

La Orotava, 4 miles inland, is a typical Canary town. Houses with traditional wooden balconies overlook the banana-filled valley below. 22 miles further inland, after crossing giant pine woods, you reach the foothills of **Mount Teide**. Standing at 12,000 feet, it's the highest mountain in Spain – mainland or islands. A cable car takes you to the peak. The views are worth the price of the ticket. (You can see several islands on a clear day.)

West of Puerto de la Cruz, the town of **Icod de los Vinos** boasts the world's oldest dragon tree. This monstrous sixty foot high shrub is said to be 3,000 years old.

Two of Tenerife's best beaches are at **Los Cristianos** fishing village and **Playa de las Americas**, a honky-tonk seaside resort. To reach them, hitch down the forty mile coastal highway from Santa Cruz.

Gran Canaria (area: 600 square miles, pop 650,000).

Capital **Las Palmas de Gran Canaria** (pop 275,000) is a raucous, bustling wide-open port, full of duty-free shops, bars, restaurants and dives. You name it, you can usually get it. Tourists are mainly Scandinavians. La Vegueta is the town's old quarter. Amongst its historical buildings is the Casa de Colon (Columbus' house, where the famous explorer lived during a stay on the island). Now it's a Fine Arts Museum and home of the island's historical archives. Nearby the Canary Museum has nine galleries devoted to the culture of the Guanches, Gran Canaria's original inhabitants. The Canary Village, in the beautiful Ciudad Jardin (Garden City) has a museum of local paintings, traditional Canary architecture and a folk-lore show. Worth a visit if you don't mind tripping over a few tourists. For cheap restaurants and rooms in Las Palmas, nose around behind the old fishing port and 'Muelle de la Luz' (literally, Jetty of Light). Swimmers should head for the terrific sandy beach of Las Canteras, shielded by an offshore reef. It's right in the town. (Good beaches down south are at **Maspalomas**, where sand dunes spread for miles inland, and neighbouring resort, **Playa del Ingles**.)

Caldera de Bandama is the island's biggest extinct volcano. It's nearly a mile across and tomatoes grow like weeds on the fertile valley floor. From the lookout point on top you can see Las Palmas in the distance.

Teror, the island's prettiest village, is a peaceful town in spite of its name. It's full of medieval houses lined with delicately-carved wooden balconies. On 8 September it celebrates Gran Canaria's greatest religious festival, when each village on the island brings a float to participate in a massive procession. It's all in honour of the patron saint, Our Lady of the Pines. Teror's fifteenth-century church stands on the spot where she is supposed to have appeared.

Lanzarote (area: 350 square miles, pop 40,000).

Here is a desolated volcanic landscape of craters, caverns and weird lava formations. The island's last eruption occurred in 1736 when molten lava trespassed into the sea, adding fifty per cent to the island's workable land.

Capital **Arrecife** (pop 20,000) is a simple port with little going for it, but you can find cheap restaurants and pensions. Watch out when the wind blows the wrong way from the fish-canning factory.

You can find further cheap accommodation in nearby **Puerto del Carmen**, a fishing village whose good beaches have turned it into the island's main tourist area.

Playa Blanca, down south, is an unspoilt little port with beach tavernas and a couple of bars. On clear days you can see both Fuerteventura Island, and the African coast 70 miles away. Quiet, white-sanded beaches offer ideal free accommodation.

For the full tourist bit in Lanzarote, ride a camel over orange-black dunes near **Fire Mountain** and feel the heat coming out of live volcanoes.

Up north try not to miss **Jameos del Agua**. It's a massive cave, complete with tiny lake, formed from a volcanic bubble. On Saturday night it doubles as a nightclub with a folklore show one end and a disco the other.

Interesting villages inland are **Haria**, with its palm oasis, and **Yaiza**, which must be the most immaculate 'pueblo' in Spain. Try the local green-white Malvasia wine – 15 per cent proof and truly volcanic.

Fuerteventura (area: 780 square miles, pop 20,000).

This looks like a giant chunk of the Sahara which landed in the sea. It has the odd boarding house and marvellous sandy beaches that seem to cover half the island. Capital **Betancuria** (pop 950) is a simple village that has seen few changes since Jean Bethancourt, a Norman adventurer, founded it in the fifteenth century.

La Palma (area: 280 square miles, pop 100,000).

This lush, pear-shaped island is famous for its cultivated craters. Capital, **Santa Cruz de la Palma** (pop 20,000) is quiet and quaint with several pensions and a seafront promenade lined with neat old houses.

La Cumbrecita, in the centre of La Palma, is one of the world's biggest craters. It's six miles across, and the valley floor is planted with sub-tropical vegetables and citrus fruits.

Gomera (area: 150 square miles, pop 40,000).

On this rugged island of fertile valleys and mountains, locals communicate with each other by a remarkable whistling language known as *silbo*.

Capital **San Sebastian de la Gomera** (pop 10,000) has a few pensions.
Hierro (area: 120 square miles, pop 12,000).

This wild island counts over a thousand volcanic mountains. It's the most westerly of the Canary islands. Capital **Valverde** (pop 6,000) is 2,000 feet above the tiny port of **La Estaca** where boats arrive from Tenerife.

★**Crossing to the Balearic Islands** From Valencia, Alicante or Barcelona to Palma – about 350 pesetas. Don't believe all that newspaper clap-trap about the **Balearics** being spoilt. Of course, they're popular. You only have to read travel brochures to see that. But there's a lot more to them then that cliché-ed world of concrete and 'fish 'n' chip' signs harped on by journalists who seldom stagger beyond their hotel bar.

The archipelago includes four islands which lie halfway between the Spanish Mediterranean coast and Algeria. Boats from Barcelona, Valencia and Alicante visit them all, except Formentera which you reach from Ibiza.

Mallorca (area: 1,350 square miles, pop 400,000).

Capital **Palma de Mallorca** (pop 250,000) crams in nightclubs, sophisticated shops, a big yacht harbour and fishing port, and an old Gothic quarter. A great city for walking. Don't miss the Gothic Cathedral, begun in 1230 and finished 300 years later. Four Mallorcan kings are buried here, and the treasury, with its gold plate and jewelled candelabras, is worth visiting. In nearby Terreno suburb see the well-preserved Moorish Castle of Bellver and the Pueblo Espanol next door (same as Barcelona's, only smaller). Plaza Gomila, below, is the Pigalle-like nightclub area. Good spot for meeting up with the opposite sex, though expensive. Rooms in any of the *fondas* behind Pio XII square at the top of the Borne (Palma's central boulevard) are around 150 pesetas a night. For eating out try the cheap but simple restaurants at the far end of the gaudy Apuntadores alley-way off the Borne.

Take the little train from the station in the Plaza Espana across the mountains to French-looking **Soller**. It's easier than hitching, and cheap. Notable hill villages nearby are **Deya,** for thirty years home of English author Robert Graves, and claimed by many to be the prettiest village in Spain; and **Valldemossa**, where Chopin passed a lousy winter with George Sand in the Carthusian Monastery. A mass of island caves (Drach, Arta, Campanet, Genova) are worth viewing. The best is **Drach**. But be warned: in summer up to 1,000 visitors at a time are strolling through. Good unspoilt beaches are **Alcudia** and **Cala Ratjada** in the north.

Minorca (area: 250 square miles, pop 45,000).

Nick-named the 'blue and white island', the most northerly Balearic island sports neat white villages and blue-watered coves. It also has green fields with cows, wet, windy winters and a few Georgian-fronted houses to remind you the British occupied it for fifty years.

Capital **Mahon** (pop 20,000) is a sleepy white-washed town huddled around the longest inlet in the Mediterranean. They say that 200 years ago Nelson dallied here with Lady Hamilton in Villa San Antonio (just across the inlet from the town), thereby scandalizing the local populace. By day Mahon is pleasant enough, but at night it's a crock. So after sundown try one of the lively open-air bars in the neighbouring harbour town of **Villa Carlos**. Someone's usually playing a guitar. Soloists are welcome – in any language.

Ciudadela, at the other end of the island, is a quiet Moorish town that suddenly goes crazy during the wild San Juan horse-riding *feria* on 24th June.

For archaeological buffs, the island is dotted with *taulas* and *talayots*, huge Stonehenge-type constructions that date back to the Bronze Age. They're the oldest traces of previous inhabitants to be found in any of the islands. There are a hundred different sites to visit. The most convenient is the taula at Trebalugar, just behind Villa Carlos. The beaches of **Arenal d'en Castell** (in the north), and **Santo Tomas** and **San Jaime** (in the south) provide some of the best swimming in the Balearics. Behind **Son Bou** beach are caves which were inhabited thousands of years ago.

Don't leave without trying the local gin, another legacy of the British. It's good value at 200 pesetas a bottle, and a dash of soda and lemon gives you the favourite Menorquin aperitive, *pallofe*.

Ibiza (area: 220 square miles, pop 40,000).

Capital **Ibiza Town** (pop 20,000) was once a haven for freaks. Now you mostly find put-ons who can safely play the bohemian because they have big bank accounts to back their independence. Still, there are plenty of good types around and in the cobbled Dalt Vila (old quarter) above the town strange dives are full of local artists and eccentrics. At the top of the Dalt Vila the fifteenth-century Gothic Cathedral has fine views of the bay and town. The Archaeological Museum opposite contains a unique collection of Punic relics excavated from Puig dels Molins, the nearby Phoenician burial ground. You can find low-budget restaurants and pensions behind the waterfront. (And a joint called Johann Sebastian Bar.)

Eight miles up the coast, **Santa Eulalia del Rio** is a relaxed town, popular with artists and writers.

On the other side of the island, ten miles from Ibiza Town, the one-time small fishing port of **San Antonio Abad** staggers under an avalanche of package tourists. But, amongst the sea of high-rises you can still find cheap bars and eating-spots (mainly at the back of the town). If you avoid July and August, boat trips to the half-dozen beaches outside San Antonio Bay are pleasant and cheap.

Formentera (area: 50 square miles, pop 3,500).

This tiny sickle-shaped island has white beaches and a bleached port, La Sabina, that looks as if it's a left-over from the old Spanish Sahara.

Tiny capital **San Francisco Javier** (pop 1,000) is a dusty one-horse town with an eighteenth-century church which used to have cannons on the roof to repel pirates. When I visited it in 1975 there was a boutique beside the police station called 'Fuzz'.

Es Pujols is the island's single diminutive resort. Its handful of apartments and restaurants are filled mainly by German tourists.

Just beyond it, the simple village of **San Fernando** provides the best value meals and rooms on the island, and is a good place to meet fellow-travellers.

The island is lined with unspoilt beaches which provide ideal free accommodation in summer. **Playa Mitjorn**, in the south, is the longest.

Madrid: where to sleep

Spain is one of the few countries where you can relax and let your hair down money-wise. It's amongst the even fewer countries – Portugal, Greece, Turkey, Morocco – where you are advised to keep away from student accommodation because it is generally more expensive than what you can find around the streets. You should always stay in a *pension* – never in anything calling itself a hotel – and in Madrid it is no great thing to find a *pension* for 150 pesetas. This is a good average price. Try in the Plaza Mayor area, in the little streets off Calle de Toledo.

Madrid: where to eat

Eat where you like. Just avoid anything with chrome or plastic trimmings. In the warren of streets between Plaza Mayor and Puerta del Sol you can find little bars which will serve small omelets for 50 pesetas and *cerveza de presion* (draught beer) for 20 pesetas a glass. Choose your place well and you can treat yourself to a good meal, wine included for 170 pesetas. Avoid the three-course Tourist Menus you will see advertised all over the place. Most of them offer a good deal but you can eat cheaper by just ordering yourself one big special course. Calle del Barco which is off Avenida José Antonio has half a dozen really cheap and good restaurants. Don't be frightened to drop in on some bars before you eat to have a few *vinos* and *tapas* (tiny appetizers) – they'll set you up well for your meal and usually won't cost you more than 15 or 20 pesetas a go. Spaniards, incidentally, don't eat their evening meal until 9 or 10 at night.

Madrid: what to see and do

THE PRADO One of the really great art galleries of the world. Unbelievable collection of Goya, just about everything that Velasquez ever put on canvas, rooms full of El Greco and four or five fantastic works by Bosch – and that's just a part of it. Admission charge, except on Saturday afternoon when it's free.

EL RASTRO This is the flea market along Ribera de Curtidores. Open every morning, but at its best on Sunday. Costs nothing and it's great fun. If you want to buy something, haggle like mad – but you'll be haggling against experts, because half of the stall-holders are gypsies.

THE PLAZA MAYOR One of the most beautiful squares in Europe and a good place from which to start exploring the 'old' Madrid. Don't eat or drink in the Plaza – too expensive. Move to the streets behind.

STAMP MARKET for philatelists who want to try and pick up a bargain, or people who want to watch some expert haggling. Plaza Mayor between 11 in the morning and 2 in the afternoon every Sunday.

BULLFIGHT TICKETS To buy a ticket (summer only) and to get a glimpse of the Madrid Hemingway wrote about in *The Undefeated*, go to Calle Victoria – a small street on your right as you walk up Carrera de San Jeronimo which leads out of the Puerta del Sol. Streets in this area, like Calle Echegaray, have great bars.

BULLFIGHT MUSEUM at the Las Ventas bullring. This shows the history of bull-fighting in paintings, engravings and models. Small admission fee. Open from 10.30 a.m. to 1 p.m. and from 3.30 to 6.30 p.m.

PALACIO REAL (The Royal Palace) at Plaza de Oriente. A huge and richly-decorated palace probably of interest to architectural fans. Stiff entrance fee of around 140 pesetas.

SESAMO A café at Principe 7 and a good place to meet people. After dinner (around 10 or 11) is the best time. You can get a smallish jug of *sangria* for about 110 pesetas and sit on it all night, even if you're sharing it between two.

Transport in Madrid

It's all cheap. The rock-bottom method of getting around is on the Metro. Anywhere to anywhere in the city will cost you about 8 pesetas. Next cheapest are the buses which carry you for 10 pesetas. If you're in a group, say four people, don't be scared of taxis. A long trip, say 4 or 5 kilometres, will only cost you around 100 pesetas. Trouble is that the vehicles are driven by hell-drivers.

Student discounts

Theoretically, in Spain, you should get reduced admission to various places like the Prado and the Alhambra. Practice and theory in Spain, however, are two different things. If you have a student card try your luck by flashing it everywhere. Details from:

TIVE,
José Ortega de Gasset 71, Madrid (Tel: 401 95 01).

Addresses

Main Post Office (for Poste Restante) at Plaza de Cibeles, Madrid.

American Express at Plaza de las Cortes 2, Madrid (Tel: 222 11 80).

TIVE at José Ortega de Gasset 71, Madrid (Tel: 401 95 01).

Viajeseu at Avenida José Antonio 615, Barcelona 7 (Tel: 231 34 62).

Tourist Information Office at Plaza Mayor 3 (Tel: 266 48 74).

US Embassy at Serrano 75, Madrid (Tel: 276 34 00).

British Embassy at Fernando el Santo 16 (Tel: 419 02 00).

Portugal

Population	9,000,000
Size	35,404 square miles
Capital	Lisbon, population 850,000
Government	Republic
Religion	Roman Catholic
Language	Portuguese

After Lisbon, **Porto** is the largest Portuguese city. It's the big wine centre of Portugal and the ideal place to spend a couple of days if you have a nose which enjoys tracking down the smell of the grape. Sitting on the River Douro, which carries barge-loads of produce down from the vineyards, its waterfront areas offer attractive sights and provide cheap living. There are plenty of architectural monuments to look over, including the beautiful Freixo Palace and the unusual Serra do Pilar Monastery.

South of Porto is **Coimbra** with a university founded in 1290, one of Europe's oldest. Because of the students you're likely to find the hitching a little better than usual. The Coimbra valley, which carries the Mondego River, is attractive and relaxing.

If you're interested in religion, or in the phenomenon of crowd psychology, and you are in Lisbon on May, June, July, August, or September 13th, head out to the village of **Fátima** (halfway between Coimbra and Lisbon) where, on May 13th, 1917, the Virgin Mary is said to have appeared to some shepherd children. On the dates mentioned above, pilgrims flock to Fátima to worship. It's all worth seeing. Whether you're religious or not you'll find some comment to make about the gross commercialism which has turned a sacred place into a gigantic supermarket where the purveyors of tin and plastic religious trivia turn a fast buck.

For something more down to earth, the huge beaches on the coastline between **Espinho** and **Viera de Leiria** are host to tiny fishing villages where big rowing boats manned by up to thirty men crash out over the surf each day to lay nets which are hauled in by oxen teams. Many of these villages are slowly but surely turning into beach resorts and within a decade they'll be unrecognizable. Better get to them now.

Two other places worth special mention are **Evora,** on the N114 about 150 kilometres east of Lisbon, which with its beautiful Roman ruins has been declared a 'museum city', and the area known as the **Costa do Sol,** west of Lisbon, which admittedly is a package-tour paradise, but which also, like Torremolinos in Spain, is the ideal place to meet up with someone of the opposite sex.

★**Bullfights** If you find the Spanish version of the bullfights bloody, you may prefer the Portuguese fights which come into the category of sport rather than ritual. The bull is never killed. All good, clean fun. Check at the tourist office for dates. Students can buy half-price tickets through SIAEIST, the student travel bureau.

★**Fiestas** Festivals and fairs in Portugal are great fun. You should check with Portuguese National Tourist Offices for exact dates, as they tend to change. Try some of the following: *Mardi Gras Carnivals* in Estoril-Cascais,

Torres Vedras, Loulé and Ovar during the four days up to Shrove Tuesday. *Holy Week* – Easter religious processions in Braga. *Festivals of the Popular Saints*, Lisbon, in June. *Festival of St John in Porto* features funfair, fireworks, handicrafts, regional cooking; in June. *Festival of the Red Waistcoats* at Vila Franca de Xira (Lisbon) with bullfights, amusements; in July. *International Music Festival* in Sintra, during second fortnight in August. *Fiesta of Our Lady of Nazaré* in Nazaré in September with fair and bullfights.

Lisbon: where to sleep

Portugal is not as cheap as Spain, but it tries hard. All round I'd say things are about 20 per cent more expensive. You can find a bed easily for 100 escudos, and I have heard of them for as low as 50 escudos. The best place to search for a *pensão* is in the nest of streets on the hill leading up to the Castle of St George, but on the *west* side. The southern side, the real Alfama, caters to the tourist types, and prices are correspondingly higher. The next best place is on the west side of the Rossio, the big main square, or failing that, in the area called Bairro Alto which is to the west of Rua da Misericórdia. All of these places are right in the main commercial area of town. Make sure you hire a bed only, and don't get quoted a price which includes all meals.

Here is a list of some of the really cheap places.

Pensão Chave de Ouro at Rua de Alegria 19, 1st floor (Tel: 32 47 49).

Pensão Glória at Rua D. Duarte 2, 1st floor (Tel: 86 36 30).

Pensão Imperial at Praça dos Restauradores 78, 4th floor (Tel: 32 01 66).

Pensão Madeirense at Rua da Glória 22, 1st floor (Tel: 32 58 59).

Pensão Luanda, Rua dos Anjos 77, 1st floor (Tel: 5 04 70).

Pensão Pérola da Baixa at Rua da Glória 10, 2nd floor (Tel: 36 28 75).

Pensão Santiago at Rua dos Douradores 222, 3rd floor (Tel: 32 78 53).

Pensão Norte at Rua dos Douradores 159, 2nd floor (Tel: 32 66 32).

Pensão-Restaurante Vinhais at Calçada do Garcia 6, 1st floor (Tel: 86 29 47).

Lisbon: where to eat

Pick your place carefully and you have a feast for 50 escudos. Happy hunting grounds for cheap meals are in the Rua das Portas de Santo Antão (parallel to the Avenida da Liberdade), the Rua da Madalena and in many of the small streets leading off those two.

Lisbon: what to see and do

CASTLE OF ST GEORGE Best place for an overall view of Lisbon and the harbour. Walk up through the Alfama for nothing or ride up on Bus 37 (from Praça do Rossio).

ALFAMA This is the oldest section of Lisbon, huddled on the hill crowned by the castle. It's a maze of narrow, winding streets and steps and scruffy kids being chased by their mothers. Nice place.

PRAÇA DO COMERCIO The big square down on the waterfront. Street vendors and fish-sellers work there most mornings.

NIGHTCLUBS Best districts for Portuguese style nightclubs are the Alfama and Bairro Alto districts. It's in those areas that you can find the *fado* singers. It'll cost you about 60–75 escudos if you play it on the cheap.

MOVIES Nearly always showing in original language with Portuguese sub-titles. Plenty of English language shows around, most quite recent. Seats are reasonably priced even in the city centre.

THE COACH MUSEUM A world-class collection of horse-drawn conveyances, both royal and otherwise. At Pr. Afonso de Albuquerque, Belém.

THE BELEM TOWER on the waterfront near the Coach Museum. A strange, ornamental sixteenth-century fortress jutting out into the River Tejo.

FLEA MARKET at Campo Santa Clara on Calçada de São Vicente. Open all day Tuesday and Saturday.

Transport in Lisbon
The subway is the quickest method of getting around Lisbon and the cheapest. A ticket to anywhere costs about 6 escudos. City buses are just as cheap. Taxis, as in Madrid, are the cheapest in Europe. If you're in a group they're the ideal way of moving around. An average city ride should only cost 30–40 escudos.

Student discounts
For information contact:
SIAEIST – Turismo Universitário,
Av. Rovisco Pais, Lisbon 1 (Tel: 77 18 84).

Addresses

Main Post Office (for Poste Restante) at Praça dos Restauradores,
Lisbon 2.

American Express at STAR, Avenida Sidónio Pais 4a, Lisbon
(Tel: 53 98 71).

Siaeist - Turismo Universitário at Avenida Rovisco Pais, Lisbon 1
(Tel: 77 18 84).

Tourist Office at Palacio Foz, Praça dos Restauradores, Lisbon 2
(Tel: 36 70 31).

US Embassy at Avenida Duque de Loulé 39, Lisbon 1 (Tel: 55 51 41).

British Embassy at Rua de São Domingos à Lapa 37, Lisbon 3
(Tel: 66 11 91).

Hitchers' tips and comments
I notice you hardly touch on the south of Portugal which I think is much
better than the north.

Faro isn't so good, full of rich Americans and not much to do. But
Albufeira was cheap and pleasant and there was plenty to do. Lots of
hitchers there.

Lagos, further west, is cheap and nice. Good seafood cafés there. One
place – I can't remember the name – served me more lobster, green salad,
rolls, butter and pate than I could eat, and I'm a pretty big guy (16 stone).

All in all, for the hitcher coming in down the south coast of Spain into
Portugal there's a lot of cheap, good fun and sightseeing to be had.
Glyn E. Hall, Holland Road, London

In South Portugal: Lagos is too full of tourists. Go west to Salema and
Burglau. Salema – beautiful and unspoilt. Get in with the fishermen – great
lads. We went to sea and then were given fish to sell ourselves!
Nicholas M. Steven, Sherborne, England

Greece

Population	8,500,000
Size	51,123 square miles
Capital	Athens, population 2,000,000
Government	Republic
Religion	Greek Orthodox
Language	Greek. Some French and English understood

If you enter Greece from Yugoslavia or Bulgaria, **Thessaloniki** will probably be your first stop. It is the country's second city (after Athens) and was founded in 315 BC on the site of an even older city – Thermai. As guardian of such a long history, you'd think the city would offer a rich selection of ruins to visit. Unfortunately, a devastating fire in 1917 burned out much of the city centre and, consequently, the choice is limited. But the old Turkish quarter in the upper part of the city survived and remains one of the most fascinating sections to wander through. To really appreciate the age of Thessaloniki you should visit the Archaeological Museum. Amongst its exhibits see the fantastic treasure of gold jewelry found in tombs as recently as 1961. Also worth a visit: the city's ancient churches, particularly the fifth-century Basilica of St Demetrius and the third-century church of St George.

About 150 kilometres south-east of Thessaloniki, on the tip of the eastern-most of the three peninsulas of Chalkidiki, is the strange place called **Mount Athos**. This is an autonomous region, in effect a state unto itself, and run by monks. There are twenty monasteries, many of them around 1,000 years old. Known as 'The Holy Mountain', Mt Athos cannot be visited unless you arrange for your embassy or consulate to get authorization on your behalf from the Greek Ministry of Foreign Affairs or from the Ministry for Northern Greece. According to a law made in 1060 by a monk called Constantine the Gladiator which is still in force, no woman is permitted to approach the monasteries. And that goes for all female creatures – dogs and cats included.

A hundred miles north-west of Athens is **Delphi**, situated at 2,000 feet on the slopes of Mount Parnassus. This is the place where the famous Oracle lived – he who was known as 'The Holy of Holies'. See the Temple of Apollo and plenty of other excavated ruins.

The plain of **Marathon** traditionally lies twenty-six miles and 385 yards from the centre of Athens. It was here that the decisive battle of 490 BC took place between the Athenians and the Persians. Outnumbered ten to one the Greeks nevertheless won and sent a messenger named Pheidippides to tell the people of Athens the news. The guy made it in record time, gave the message, and died on the spot. Exhausted. The Olympic Marathon honours the event. It's hardly worth hitching out to see the field – it's marked only by the grave of the Greeks who fell – but if you do, continue on an extra few kilometres to **Ramnous** where there are two temples, one of them to Nemesis, the Goddess of Divine Vengeance. (She still wreaks it – the road to Ramnous is rotten.)

Forty-five miles due south of Athens, on the tip of the peninsula and at **Sounion**, is the beautiful temple of Poseidon, one of the best sights in the country.

Corinth is one of a cluster of important sites on the Peloponnese Peninsula. Modern Corinth, a city of 16,000, is five miles from the ancient city which was once the largest and most powerful in Greece. It was razed by the Romans in 146 BC, then again by the Goths, and then hit by an earthquake in AD 521. Understandably there are plenty of ruins to see.

Fifty kilometres on from Corinth are the ruins of Mycenae, a city inhabited as far back as 3000 BC. It was the German business man/ archaeologist Heinrich Schliemann – the man ridiculed by popular opinion when he set out to find Troy – who excavated here and found skeletons of men and women adorned with gold masks and crowns. Schliemann believed them to be the bodies of Agamemnon and his companions, though this has yet to be proven. You can see the treasure he unearthed in the Mycenaean Room of the Archaeological Museum in Athens. At the site itself, you can see the Gate of the Lions, the Treasure of Atreus and the Royal Tombs. All in all Mycenae counts as one of the most exciting archaeological spots in Greece.

Farther south again and you come to **Epidaurus**, which in ancient times was a famous health centre – perhaps the first ever – and which was visited by ailing people from all over the civilized world. The main sight is the old theatre, the most perfect in Greece, which can seat 16,000 people and is still used each year at the annual Epidaurus Festival (July–mid August).

There's not much left of **Sparta**, the capital of Laconia, to tell you what the place once was. These days it's a deadly boring town of 11,000 with only a few identified ruins surviving from the days when it was the most powerful city in the world. (The Pass of Thermopylae where Leonidas and his handful of Spartans held the Persians at bay in 480 BC is just a few miles south of **Lamia**.) Seven kilometres west of Sparta, on one of the slopes of Mt Taygettus is the ruined city of **Mistra**, which dates from AD 1249. Even though by Greek standards the place is a 'modern' ruin, it's worth looking over because it's a treasure house of Byzantine art.

Whatever you do, try not to leave the Peloponnese without getting up to

Olympia, site of the ancient Olympic games, first held in 776 BC. (Not to be confused with Mt Olympus, south of Thessaloniki, and home of the ancient Greek Gods.) The Sacred Flame of the Olympics is still kindled at Olympia every four years and carried by relays of runners to whichever city is staging the spectacle. Plenty to see, including the Museum and the Stadium; best of all, though, is the rare beauty of the setting.

Hitching in Greece, on the main highways, is about the same as anywhere else, but if you get off the beaten track – easy to do in Greece – it can be very slow. If you're stuck on the way to some mountain village, don't hesitate to grab the local bus. It'll be cheap enough.

★**Trips to Crete and the Islands** The main tip is to always go 'Deck Class' which is the cheapest. The best place to find out about costs (and also to check if your student card will get you a fare reduction) is ISYTS at 11 Nikis Street, in Athens. This is a student outfit and not a regular travel bureau.

Crete (area: 3,245 square miles, pop 440,000).

Capital **Heraklion** (pop 80,000) is an untidy, bustling town founded by the Saracens in AD 823. Visit the daily market to buy cheap food. Low-budget pensions in town are near Daidolou Street. Don't miss the Archaeological Museum, which covers Crete's 4,000 year-old Minoan civilization in fascinating detail.

Three miles inland is **Knossos,** the ancient Minoan capital lovingly restored by British archaeologist, Sir Arthur Evans, in 1900. Among its best sights are the throne room (oldest in Europe) and the well-preserved central court. See the wall-paintings of bull-vaulting.

Rethymnon, 45 miles west of Heraklion, has a Turkish-Venetian waterfront, and a skyline of minarets and turrets proclaiming the town's Ottoman past. Low-priced spots are on Makedonia Street. If you're in town in July don't miss the wine festival in the municipal park.

Chania, 45 miles further west, has a crescent-shaped Venetian harbour promenade lined with tavernas and open-air restaurants.

Inland, the rugged Sfakia mountains form a natural stronghold which centuries of Venetian, Turkish and German invaders failed to crack. You understand why when you tackle the arduous mountain paths leading to the Sfakians' hospitable but fiercely independent villages. Try *raki*, the local firewater. It'll blow your head off.

An energetic five-hour walk there (locals do it in three!) is along the 12 mile **Samaria Gorge,** largest in Europe. Cliffs rise as high as 2,000 feet, while at its narrowest the gorge is only 16 feet across. In Spring, streams run along the valley bottom. Starting point is the inland village of **Omalos.**

At the end of the gorge you catch a boat round to the tiny fishing village of **Chora Sfakion**, where British troops made their escape from the island in 1941. From here you can hitch or bus your way back to Chania.

Phaestos, on a hill overlooking the Messara plain 40 miles south of Heraklion, houses the well-kept ruins of Crete's second largest Minoan city. Worth the trip for the evocative location.

Aghios Nikolaos, 40 miles east of the capital, is the island's top resort, an Aegean Saint Tropez with expensive bars and a selfconsciously attractive harbour setting. But a great place to meet people. Boats sometimes run from here in summer to the Cyclades islands.

Try not to miss the fertile inland Lassithi plain with its 10,000 windmills and **Cave of Dikte** where legend says Zeus was born.

The Greek Islands

Argo-Saronics These four small islands run closely parallel to the Greek Peloponnese mainland as it descends south from the Saronic into the Argive Gulf. But hitching is difficult in the Peloponnese because of lack of cars, so only try it if you have plenty of time to spare. All (except Spetsai) are easy to reach from Piraeus if you can only spare a day for island tripping. You need two days to enjoy Spetsai at leisure, due to the travelling time involved.

Aegina (area: 35 square miles, pop 12,000; 1½ hours from Piraeus).

Capital **Aegina Town** has plenty of cheap waterfront rooms and restaurants. But be warned: at weekends the place is packed with day-trippers from Athens.

Aghia Marina, 10 miles across the island, is a popular beach resort stacked with tavernas. A short walk up through orchards of pistachio trees brings you to the impressive Doric Temple of Aphaia, with its Parian marble sculptures and limestone columns, standing evocatively above the sea.

Poros (area: 25 square miles, pop 5,000; 2½ hours from Piraeus).

The island capital of **Poros** is a tumbling white port with lively harbourside cafes facing the Peloponnese town of Galatas only 400 yards away. Here the channel between island and Greek mainland is so narrow that it resembles a large river. The caique (boat) crossing only takes three minutes. Caiques also run regularly up the island coast to Monastiri, an 18th-century monastery.

Inland, among Poros' pinewoods, is the ruined Temple of Poseidon (the Greek God of the sea) where the Athenian orator Demosthenes poisoned himself.

Hydra (area: 21 square miles, pop 4,000; $3\frac{1}{2}$ hours from Piraeus).

Hydra Town boasts 18th-century Venetian houses (symbols of its seafaring past) and a waterfront array of fashionable boutiques and restaurants. Once a backwater for artists, it's now inundated by international trend-setters and hourly cruise ships. So avoid that incredibly expensive harbourside. Cheaper rooms and meals can be found at the back of town.

Because of the island's barren and mountainous terrain local transport is still by donkey. (The island also has *one* taxi.) Hike up to the hilltop monastery of **Aghia Tria**. Its views over the Peloponnese mainland and sea are out of this world.

Spetsai (area: 10 square miles, pop 5,000; 5 hours from Piraeus).

Spetsai Town is a stylish port popular with Athenians. The waterfront Dapia square is a stage set of bars and open-air restaurants. Ask at Takis Tourist Office near the jetty for cheap rooms in town.

Spetsai's so small you can walk round the pine-wooded coastline in six hours. Take a caique (very cheap) to **Anarghiri**, the island's best beach. As few cars are allowed on the island, main transport is by horse and buggy. (Warning: they are expensive.) Spetsai was the setting for John Fowles' book *The Magus*, wherein he called the island Phraxos.

Sporades

Our word ' sporadic' is taken from the Greek word used to describe these green isles which are strewn hap-hazardly offshore from Euboea, a large island attached by drawbridge to the eastern Greek mainland at Chalkis. Boats run to most of them from Kymi, Aghios Konstantinos and Volos.

Here's some basic information about the three largest:

Skiathos (area: 25 square miles, pop 5,000).

Capital **Skiathos Town** is a white, red-roofed port surrounded by pines. It's a favourite with writers and artists. Inland, the ruins of **Castro** are worth a visit. **Koukounaries**, fringed by olive groves, is the pick of the island's fine beaches.

Skopelos (area: 35 square miles, pop 5,000).

Skopelos Town, the capital, has a rising amphitheatre of multi-coloured houses, and low-priced, waterfront pensions. Two cliff-top churches guard the harbour entrance. Inland **Episkopi** boasts the medieval ruins of a bishop's palace. Several nearby seventh-century monasteries have been converted into hotels. Visit the southern village of **Agnonda** for the island's best beach.

Skyros (area: 75 square miles, pop 4,000).

You'll find rooms to let in the white, flat-topped houses which climb the precipitous slopes behind the capital of **Chora**. At the town's entrance stands a nude statue of British poet Rupert Brooke, who died here of fever during World War I. He's buried in an olive grove at Tri Boukes on the west coast, near the fishing village of **Linaria**.

Skyros' barren and isolated villages are depositaries of folk-arts like woodwork, weaving and embroidery. The coast offers miles of unspoilt beaches and dozens of caves ideal for underwater exploration. (Got a mask and snorkel in your pack ?)

Cyclades

These barren islands surround the holy island of Delos in the centre of Homer's 'wine-dark' Aegean Sea. Altogether 211 islands (yes, 211 !) form this group, though many are only uninhabited chunks of rock.

Boats regularly make the five-hour run from Piraeus to Mykonos. Connections to other islands from here are frequent and cheap. (**Warning!** Avoid August for two reasons: the *meltimi* wind can give you a rough ride, and room prices on the islands rocket.)

Mykonos (area: 30 square miles, pop 12,000).

Capital **Mykonos Town** (pop 5,000) is picture postcard Greece, all windmills and white cube houses set against the blue sea. The place brims with open-air cafés, crowded shopping stalls and lively tavernas, popular with tourists and locals alike. Seven of the island's 365 churches are situated in Paraportiani Square, and the little museum on the quay contains religiously significant tombs from Delos. Private houses and a youth hostel provide cheap lodgings, and outside of town there's a camping site. For good beaches try **Aghios Stephanos** and **Ornos**.

Visit Delos for the day. Four thousand years ago this was the religious centre of the Greek world. Now, the ten square miles of rock is inhabited only by a few goatherds and their animals. The archaeological site includes a museum, shrine and mosaic ruins. Most impressive remains include the Sanctuary of Apollo and the Terrace of Lions.

Santorin (area: 30 square miles, pop 10,000).

Thira is the capital and her brilliant white houses stand on an ash-grey pumice cliff, the outer rim of a vast volcano which disappeared in a cataclysmic explosion 4,000 years ago. You can walk up the 2 km zig-zag path to the town from the harbour, but it's easier to use the cheap donkey transport. Local houses have low-priced rooms to rent.

The island is dotted with small ruins: Minoan, Doric, Roman and Venetian. Best are the Minoan excavations near **Akrotiri** on the south coast. Inland, tomatoes and vines grow miraculously out of the multi-coloured rock landscape. Try the strong Santorin wine – famous since the Middle Ages.

Naxos (area: 180 square miles, pop 15,000).

The largest Cyclades island lives from agriculture, not tourism, and is full of vineyards, lush valleys and citrus orchards.

Capital **Naxos Town** offers cheap rooms, tavernas and a beautiful old Venetian quarter called the Castro.

Across the island the unspoilt village of Apollon lies beside a near deserted beach. If you want to see what real Greek island life is like, stay here in a private house. It's idyllic and easy on the pocket.

Ionian Islands

These six cypress-and-olive-green islands lie off the coast of North-West Greece. Boats run regularly to Corfu, the most important, from Brindisi in Southern Italy and Igoumenitsa on the Greek mainland.

Corfu (area: 225 square miles, pop 100,000).

Capital **Corfu Town** beautifully blends its past cultures. French colonnades overlook an English cricket pitch, and Venetian backstreets merge with a market wafting smells of oriental spices. You'll find cheap pensions near the Old Harbour. Worth a look is Mon Repos, the former Greek Royal Summer Residence where England's Prince Philip, Duke of Edinburgh, was born.

The fishing village of **Benitses**, 8 miles south, is popular with both expatriate artists and tourists. Lively tavernas line the waterfront, and in summer spontaneous street dancing often brings traffic to a standstill. At nearby **Gastouri** see Kaiser Wilhelm's monstrous Achilleion. Built in 1891 in mock Florentine style, it's a museum by day and a casino by night.

Paxos (area: 20 square miles, pop 1,500).

This is a mini-island of olive trees and coves only three hours by boat from Corfu Town. Prices in **Gaios** (pop 600) have boomed since the arrival of the yacht-set.

Cephallonia (area: 300 square miles, pop 70,000).

The modern port of Argostoli was totally rebuilt after an earthquake in 1953. Worth visiting on the island are the **Necropolis of Mazaracata**, with its 83 Mycenean tombs, and the fishing village of **Assos**. Inland are vast unspoilt pine forests, and mountains rising to 5,000 feet.

Zante (area: 180 square miles, pop 45,000).

Zante Town, once known as the 'Flower of the Levant', now nestles under a solitary ruined Venetian castle. The 1953 earthquake robbed the island of any architectural glory, but there are beautiful Italianate gardens and vineyards to visit. **Porta Roma** boasts one of the island's many fine beaches.

Levkas (area: 110 square miles, pop 30,000).

In August **Levkas Town** hosts an international Folklore Festival which gobbles up every free bed on the island. But it's worth visiting if you don't mind sleeping on the beach. See **Vliko's** beautiful bay, and the Temple of

Apollo in the south, where seventh-century BC poetess Sappho jumped to her death from the cliffs.

Ithaca (area: 40 square miles, pop 2,500).

This is Homer's 'precipitous isle', home of Ulysses.

Capital **Vathy** is a tiny modern port with an inlet and a beach. Above it stands the ruined medieval Parachorion. Mount Aetos' 2,600 year-old Alaleomenae castle offers incredible views of the island.

Dodecanese

Greece's most easterly islands, the Dodecanese, lie just a few miles off the Turkish mainland. The trans-Aegean boat trip from Piraeus to Rhodes takes 20 hours.

Of the group's twelve islands, try these three:

Rhodes (area: 550 square miles, pop 70,000).

Capital **Rhodes Town** (pop 35,000) is an international tourist town of bars, hotels and restaurants. The busy harbour is guarded by two statues of deer which mark the spots once straddled by the 100 foot high Colossus of Rhodes, one of the seven ancient wonders of the world, which was destroyed by earthquake in 227 BC. In the walled medieval quarter Turkish minarets and the Suleiman Mosque vie with the Christian-built Grand Masters' Palace and the Street of the Knights. Cheap rooms and restaurants are in Apellou Street. There's a youth hostel nearby.

Don't miss beautiful **Lindos**, 38 miles south, a white village of cobbled lanes overlooking a sandy bay. No cars are allowed here: only donkeys, which carry tourists up to the superb cliff-top acropolis behind the village. Avoid summer if you want a room. They're all booked by travel agencies.

Also worth a look are the third-century BC ruins of ancient **Kamiros** on the west coast, and the strange **Valley of the Butterflies,** where giant plane trees shade a gorge filled by millions of butterflies. Catch superb island views from **Mount Philerimos,** with its nearby Byzantine monastery.

Kos (area: 115 square miles, pop 15,000).

Mosques remind you of the Turkish heritage lurking in the modern port capital of **Kos**. (Look for cheap pensions near the harbour.) Hippocrates, the famous physician, was born here; outside town see the ruins of the fourth-century BC Asclepeion, sanctuary and site of his medical school.

Inland Kos is green farming country, full of citrus and vegetable orchards. The coast is lined with unspoilt sandy beaches, which solve accommodation problems.

Patmos (area: 15 square miles, pop 3,000).

Tiny capital **Skala** is a lively harbour village. See the medieval Chora (citadel) and fortified monastery where St John the Divine wrote his revelations. The ancient library and treasury, perching above the town, are worth the climb. Caiques run along the wild barren coast to beautiful coves and beaches.

★**Language** Greek is not the sort of language you conquer overnight. For most of us it's not the sort of language which is conquered at all. But a few odd words can be picked up without too much trouble. Try these:
Yes – *neh*   No – *oh-kee*
Please – *pah-rah-kah-lo*   Thanks – *ef-ha-ree-stoh*
Good day, good evening, goodnight and goodbye are all covered by – *yas-sou*.

★**The Evil Eye** The Greeks are still a little superstitious. The Greek Orthodox Church has a special prayer to ward off the evil eye and many people, women especially, carry special little blue stones to help them in their fight against evil. Shy girls secretly pin the stones to their bras – though God knows which evil eye *they* are trying to divert. You can buy these stones very cheaply. Nice souvenir.

Athens: where to sleep

Expect to pay between 170 and 200 drachmas, except in youth hostels which charge 85–100 drachmas. (It's much cheaper in the outer suburbs, but *all* the sights are in the centre which is where you've got to be.)

Youth Hostel at 57 Kypselis Street (Tel: 8225 860).

Residence Pagration at 75 Damareos Street, Pagrati (Tel: 751 95 30). Ask to sleep on the roof – it's even cheaper!

Hotel Carolina at 55 Kolo Kotroni Street (Tel: 322 08 37). Ask for dormitory.

Cleo's Guest House at 18 Apollonos Street (Tel: 323 56 40).

Hotel Orion at 105 E. Benaki Street (Tel: 362 84 41). Open January 1st to October 30th. Ask for dormitory.

Guest House Giorgos at 18 Eolou Street (Tel: 32 22 997).

Lord Byron Youth Hostel at 20 Kallipoleos Street (Tel: 76 64 889). (Fair way out of town.) Open April 1st to September 30th. Students only. Ask for dormitory.

YWCA (XEN) at 11 Amerikas Street (Tel: 62 42 91/4). Women only. Ask for dormitory.

YMCA (XAN) at 28 Omirou Street (Tel: 62 69 70). Men only.
Ask for dormitory.

Fantis House at 39 Nikis Street (Tel: 23 25 92).

For help with all student accommodation, drop into ISYTS at
11 Nikis Street. They know it all and probably won't insist that you
be a student (as long as you look like one) before helping you.

 Because of the quirks of the current in-power politicians in Greece,
this book does not recommend places for sleeping rough in Athens.
Check with local kindred souls before bunking out. Athens is one place
to keep right away from the cops. In fact, a note from the polite and very
efficient Greek Tourist Office informs me that: 'Greece has a Police Force
of a high standard. Camping . . . is not permitted other than on authorized
camp sites. Drugs, nude bathing/sunbathing and other well-known
infringements of the law are also not permitted.'

Athens: where to eat

Cheap eating in Athens presents no problem. 140–150 drachmas should
see you through a fairly big meal. Stick to the *tavernas* rather than
restaurants and keep away from where the tourists eat. If you think you
might be in a tourist place, take a quick look at the menu.
If it's in English, leave!

 Which leaves the problem of figuring out a Greek menu, which is no
easy task. The following are some standard dishes which are OK:
Dolmades is rice and minced meat wrapped in vine leaves.
A traditional dish.
Souvlaki is a shishkebab – spiced meat and vegetables on a skewer.
Buy them from street stalls for cheap eating.
Moussaka is a casserole of aubergines, meat and spices.
Kalamaraki is squid.
Retsina is the local wine which has a resin flavour.
Ouzo is a killer drink just right for setting you on your ear.
If you want to live it up with a big meal (got 280 drachmas?) try one of
these three:

Rouga at 7 Kapsali Street.

Saitis at 17 Kydathineon Street.

Fatsio at 5 Efroniou.

Athens: what to see and do

THE ACROPOLIS For many people this hill in Athens will be the climax of their European wanderings. It's beautiful. You can spend half a day up there without even knowing it. It costs about 50 drachmas, but half-price with student card and free on Thursdays and Sundays. What to see? *The Parthenon*, first of all. Then the *Acropolis Museum*, the *Temple of Athena Nike*, the *Erechtheum*, the *Propylaea*, the *Theatre of Dionysus*, the *Theatre of Herod Atticus*, etc.

THE AGORA to the west of the Acropolis. This was the old city centre. Don't miss the museum.

TEMPLE OF OLYMPIAN ZEUS on Leoforos Amalias. Also, nearby, the *Arch of Hadrian*.

NATIONAL ARCHAEOLOGICAL MUSEUM in Pattission Street. Entrance charge but free on Thursdays and Sundays. Closed Mondays. Very important museum of Greek sculpture and objects discovered during digs all over Greece.

SOUND AND LIGHT DISPLAY AT THE ACROPOLIS Costs about 60 drachmas. Tickets and information from 4 Stadiou Street.

MUSEUM OF POPULAR ART In Kydathenaion Street. If you're into the handcrafts scene, drop in here for some ideas. Good collection of handcrafts from all over the country, plus pottery, etc.

FLEA MARKET On Ifestou Street near Monastiraki Square. Best days, Saturday and Sunday. Good place to go to find items of equipment you want to replace. (Remember to bargain!) Also a big underground book market with secondhand books in most languages.

GREEK MUSIC AND BAR LIFE Go into the *boîtes* in the area known as Plaka which is just below the Acropolis. Try the following streets – Mnisikleos, Erechteos, and Tholou. This is where you can hear the *bouzouki* music and watch the *sirtaki* danced. And good luck to you; the *retsina* and *ouzo* will kill you!

MOVIES Most Athens cinemas show up-to-date films in original language versions with Greek subtitles. Prices are OK.

DISCOS Try *Dolce Vita* at Adrianov 97, *Mekka* at Flessa 9 and at the same address, but upstairs, the *Karyatis*.

Transport in Athens

At 9 or 10 drachmas a long ride, subway and buses are the best way to get around. If operating in a group, you can save money by taking a taxi. They're cheap.

Student discounts

Large reduction on entrances to museums, galleries and archaeological sites; also fare reductions on inter-island ferries. For information contact:

ISYTS,
11 Nikis Street (2nd floor), Athens 118 (Tel: 322 12 67 and 323 37 67).

Addresses

Main Post Office at 100 Eolou Street, Athens.

American Express at 17 Venizelou, Athens
(Tel: 323 47 81).

ISYTS (for students) at 11 Nikis Street (2nd floor), Athens 118
(Tel: 322 12 67 and 323 37 67).

National Tourist Information Office at 2 Amerikis Street, Athens
(Tel: 322 31 11/9) and at Syntagma Square, Athens (Tel: 322 25 45).

US Embassy at Vassilissis Sophias Boulevard 91, Athens (Tel: 71 29 51).

British Embassy at Ploutarchou 1, Athens 139 (Tel: 73 62 11).

Hitchers' tips and comments

In Thessaloniki the gardens on the waterfront are good for kipping, but watch your gear.
M. Pickersgill, South Africa

The rundown on Greece doesn't cover the route Thessaloniki-Istanbul. Hitchers hitting this trail should stop off at Kavala, it's a beautiful place, the sort worth a promise for a return trip one day.

Athens train station is OK to bed down for a night or two, cops wake you about 7 a.m. but no pressure to move on. Dunno what it's like from Piraeus to the Greek Islands but from Volos to the three eastern islands (Skopelos, Skiathos and Skyros) make sure you take the *same* boat back as you went out on. The situ is that they promote one boat company out to the islands, and once there another company covers the advert boards for the run back. Those that aren't informed (and deciphering a Greek boat ticket is like deciphering a Greek anything else) get it all explained on the way back, stating that you've got to pay again, with no refund on the first ticket. I noticed a lot of travellers were getting caught out this way – me included!
Marcel Thomas, Horndean, England

8 Scandinavia and Finland

For the hitcher from Australia or North America, the big wastelands of Norway and Sweden will spur a memory of the endless, brooding countryside typical of their homelands. Think of Nevada or the Nullarbor and take away the heat but keep the distance. The sort of distance where you can drive all night and by dusk of the next day be only halfway to where you're heading. The scenery is different, vastly so, but the distances hold the same mood because Norway and Sweden are the big lands. Malmo to Kiruna, for instance, is about 2,000 kilometres.

The physical beauty of Norway, Sweden, and Finland is legendary (Denmark is flat, not very interesting visually) and the beauty of the female inhabitants of the four countries has entered the spectrum of legend. It's all true. The fjords and mountains and tundra plains are exciting. The women are unbelievable.

But apart from such physical aspects, Scandinavia is exciting sociologically. It is in these countries that the finer ideas of socialism have been put into practice. Poverty is practically unknown, education is an experimental science, medicine is available to all, prison reform is a reality, the arts are encouraged by the governments, and the housing problem – in places like Oslo – is treated as a problem. Taxation, of course, pays for all this and it's high, but the money seems to be put to fair use.

Scandinavia seems to have reached the level of balanced affluence craved by the rest of the world. Its citizens nevertheless are the first to point out the many failings of their governments. They gripe and groan until you nearly believe they are getting a bad deal. Well, a bad deal is a relative thing, I suppose, and perhaps the Scandinavians aren't getting all that they should. But you only need look around some place like Helsinki's Tapiola Garden City or a couple of Denmark's experimental schools or consider that neutral Sweden hasn't been involved in a war since 1814 to know that whatever the failings of the governments, their achievements are not only many, but bright.

The common complaint you hear from students in Scandinavia is that for all their worldly goods and social benefits, the bulk of people are bored. This seems to be true. The Scandinavian middle classes are amongst the most affluent in the world, but also the most complacent.

It's an axiom of human existence that if you give a man something he

has fought for most of his life the odds are he won't know what the hell to do with the *rest* of his life. He has nothing left to fight for. The problem is not what do you do with a car, a house, a washing-machine, a television and a stereo, but what *else* do you do? Physical accruements solve physical problems and add a bonus of comfort and convenience. They offer freedom from drudgery – but freedom to do what? The answer should be that after the body is cared for, man must attend his mind. But man doesn't. Man turns to television for six hours a night and indulges himself to the point of zombie-ism in what J. B. Priestley has termed the 'secondary gratifications'. Sadly, to most men, the primary gratifications, those that the mind can offer, are unreachable, for as surely as a man must learn to use his hands and be in the habit of using them, so he must also learn to use his mind and be in the habit of using that, too.

But this is not only Scandinavia's problem. It is becoming the major problem confronting the entire Western world. Perhaps Scandinavia may be the first to find the answer to it.

Sweden, any conversational bore will tell you, has the highest suicide rate in the world. Not true. For instance, in 1961, Sweden's suicide rate per 100,000 persons was 16·9. Austria's was 21·9, Czechoslovakia's 20·6, West Germany's 18·7, Hungary's 25·4, Japan's 19·6 and Switzerland's 18·2. The rumour started, believe it or not, when, to quote from Erwin Stengel's book, *Suicide and Attempted Suicide*, 'President Eisenhower singled out the Swedish suicide rate as a warning of what happened to a country with a leftish government. He must have been unacquainted with the even higher suicide rate of some other countries whose political complexion was more to his liking.'

Other 'facts' which really break Scandinavians up include the popular belief that Nordic ladies lay at the drop of an appropriate word. The rest of the world's attitude to Scandinavian sexual *mores* is really remarkable. Men's magazines from Tokyo to San Francisco tell you that people are practically fornicating in the gutter and then throw it in your face that the whole thing has come about through enlightenment.

Well, even if the outlook is a sight more optimistic for the vagabond male than it is in, say, Spain, the emancipated Northerners certainly don't throw themselves into the nearest set of hairy arms which comes their way. They're not *that* enlightened. They seem to be pretty honest about sex, but because they're honest doesn't mean they're easy. Scandinavian girls are just like any others – only they're more beautiful, which makes guys try harder – which naturally results in a higher rate of success. Which may have been what started the story,

Scandinavian humour is something which takes a little getting used to. It's just a trifle droll. The classic story concerns the American hitcher with his national flag on his pack who had been walking along a back road in Denmark for hours without even sighting a car. Finally one came and he frantically gave it the old international. The young driver slowed down and rolled to a stop 200 yards beyond the American and then hung out the window and waved him forward. The Yank, dragging his heavy pack after him, ran stumbling down the side of the road. As he reached the car the driver yelled, '*Get out of Vietnam, mother-fuckers!*' and took off with a maniacal laugh in a stone-spitting churn of rubber.

A somewhat gentler story concerns my wife and me when we pitched our tent amongst some trees half a mile from the youth hostel on the outskirts of Halsingborg – we were nearly broke and couldn't afford the price of a bed. We thought we were in the wide open spaces, but morning dawned brightly with a knock on the door. I struggled out of my bag and untied the tent flap. A smiling policeman bid us good morning in perfect English and then bemusedly inquired if we would normally pitch a tent in, say, the middle of Hyde Park, London. I told him, normally not. He suggested we vacate the Halsingborg public park immediately.

All in all, the Scandinavians seem fairly easy to get along with. The older generations have that perpetual hint of suspicion on their face that you find on the faces of older generations the world over when they're confronted by a beard and a dirty pair of boots, but they're OK and react well when you're in company with them. The Finns seem, if anything, more withdrawn than their Scandinavian neighbours. This might have something to do with their extremely complicated history. Forty-two lost wars with the Russians have left them with plenty to be moody about.

The students of Scandinavia are *really* the citizens of tomorrow – especially the travelling types. Danes, particularly, have filtered into every corner of Europe and North Africa. The Danish universities must have more members on the road, either hitching, or bounding around in Citroën DCV2s than they have in their lecture halls. They're a great bunch.

Finally, with cigarettes in Scandinavia approaching the price of gold, make sure you take in enough to keep you going. If you're staying for a while it might be best to take rolling tobacco which can be picked up cheaply in Belgium or Luxembourg. If you do that, don't forget cigarette papers – they can cost a fortune in Norway!

Denmark

Population	5,000,000
Size	16,615 square miles
Capital	Copenhagen, population 1,400,000
Government	Constitutional Monarchy
Religion	The state religion is Lutheran
Language	Danish. English and German widely understood and spoken

You can enter Denmark through Germany, by the E3 Flensburg–Kolding
highway and then cross over to the main island of Sjelland by the
Knudshoved–Halsskov ferry (approximate cost: 25 kroner), or by going up
to Fehmarn Island in Germany and crossing on the Puttgarden–Rødbyhavn
route (approximate cost: 37 kroner). Both ferries cross a minimum of
twenty times daily in both directions.

Be warned that when you get off at Rødbyhavn there is no traffic except
what comes off the ferry with you. If you miss a ride, you must wait
an hour for the next ferry to dock. Often you *do* have to wait because
the Rødbyhavn immigration officials are notoriously rough on hitchers.
If you're loaded you're all right, if you're not you have to talk fast.
They're extremely concerned about the amount of cash you have in the
pocket. If you're expecting to pick up funds in Copenhagen, try and carry
some documentary proof of the fact. Once I was going through with only
£5 and had to strike up with nearly an hour-long Academy performance
before I got the magic stamp.

Once through Danish customs and immigration you're right for the rest
of Scandinavia. You're unlucky to get picked up at the Norwegian or
Swedish points of entry – they're often not even manned – though you
might have a performance with the Finns.

Hitching in Denmark, as with all of Scandinavia, seems OK. After two
visits, I can't complain. One of the beauties of travelling in these countries
is that you're very unlucky – except in Finland – if you don't get at least
half of your rides with people who speak English. Consequently you can
pick up a lot of information in a very short time.

Principal cities after Copenhagen are Aarhus, Aalborg and Odense.

One of the things worth seeing at **Aarhus** is its 'Old Town' museum,
which is a collection of some 50 houses dating as far back as 400 years and
transplanted from all over Denmark into the one area. The city's Prehistoric
Museum is the most recent resting place of the Grauballe man. He lay in
a bog for 1,600 years and remains in an excellent state of preservation.

Aalborg, the chief city of North Jutland, is a gourmet's paradise.

This city of 120,000 boasts something like 170 restaurants. It's worth picking one for a splurge meal! For those interested in Vikings, the remains of a Viking village and a 600-grave cemetery can be seen at **Nørresundby** just outside Aalborg. The site of the village is known as **Lindholm Høje**. If you're American and passing through Aalborg on July 4th, head on out to Rebild National Park, 30 kilometres south of the city. Each year since 1912 they have held huge Independence Day celebrations there.

Although primarily visited by tourists to see the monuments and museum connected with Hans Christian Andersen (1805–75), **Odense** has plenty more to offer. It's one of the oldest towns in Denmark. St Canute's Cathedral – King Canute was killed in Odense 900 years ago – is one of the most important Gothic buildings in the country. The Funen Village, two kilometres from the centre of town, is a museum of peasant-culture and an operating farm. At **Ladby**, 20 kilometres north-east of Odense, you can descend into an underground mound and see a tenth-century Viking Ship. The 72-foot ship was the coffin of a Viking chief who was buried with his weapons and jewellery, four hunting-dogs, and eleven horses.

Hillerød, some 40 kilometres north of Copenhagen, is famous for its Frederiksborg Castle. Built, originally, between 1602–20 in Dutch Renaissance style, much of it was destroyed by fire in 1859. A fair lump of the money used for its restoration came from Carl Jacobsen, the famous Carlsberg brewer.

Castle fiends will also want to see Kronborg Castle at **Elsinore**, 30 kilometres north-east of Hillerød. It is the setting of Shakespeare's *Hamlet*. Unfortunately, there is a confusion of dates. Hamlet was a twelfth-century gentleman and Kronborg is a sixteenth-century castle. Nevertheless, worth seeing, especially as the castle contains the Danish Museum of Trade and Shipping.

Ten kilometres west of **Roskilde** is an Archaeological Experimental Centre which is working on the reconstruction of an Iron Age village – not just the house, but the crafts and farming techniques as well.

Finally, for summer-wanderers of both sexes who are yearning for the opposite sex, the beach resorts of Northern Jutland might provide the answer. Towns like **Skagen**, **Lønstrup** and **Løkken** (the largest resort) are where the summertime action is; but remember that they're tourist towns and expensive (though beach-sleeping is obviously 'in') and that they're inundated by suburbia on the loose.

Copenhagen: where to sleep

With hotels taking just about a minimum of 65 kroner for a single room, student accommodation is all that's left for the hitch-hiker. But even these can take a fee of up to 35 kroner, so you see that things can be pretty rough.

The following list of student hostels starts with the least expensive and works up. The cheapest you can expect is around 25 kroner.

Bellahøj Vandrehjem at Herbergvejen 8, Brønshøj (Tel: 28 97 15). Closed December 21st to January 6th. Otherwise open all year. Membership card needed.

Active University at 40 Olfert Fischers Gade (Tel: 11 91 91). Open all year.

Thomas P. Hejle's Ungdomshus at Nørre Voldgade 23 (Tel: 15 69 30). Open May 1st to September 1st.

Brønshøj-Husum Ungdomshus at Frederikssundsvej 159, Brønshøj (Tel: 28 84 98). Open June 16th to September 15th.

Vesterbro Ungdomsgaard at Absalonsgade 8 (Tel: 31 20 70). Open May 5th to September 1st.

One of the big disadvantages of student accommodation is that many of the places insist on a curfew (of course, they *might* let you stay out late to go to the movies if you ask *nicely*), but with the high prices in Scandinavia you have to put up with such institutional-type carryings-on or lump it. If you're in Copenhagen and considering lumping it, I wish you and your wallet the best of luck and suggest you find your way to the street called Istedgade. There are quite a few reasonably-priced hotels there around the 60 kroner mark. If you're with someone and can make up a double or a triple, you'll probably save 5 or 6 kroner each.
Here are two worth a try:

Hotel Absalon at Helgolandsgade 19 (Tel: 24 22 11).

Hotel Selandia at Helgolandsgade 12 (Tel: 31 46 10).

You'll find lots of friendly ladies around this area, but even the most uninspiring conversation starts at around 100 kroner.

If you can't find anything still, and you're looking fairly clean, you can drop into the **Copenhagen Tourist Association** office at the Central Railway Station, Kiosk P, and they might be able to find you lodgings in a private house. But the Association charges a 10 kroner fee for this service.
The rate goes from 50–65 for a single and from 75–100 for a double room.
Failing all that, head out to Langelinie and sack out on the grass.

Find a quiet spot and play it cool. Needless to say, sleeping in Langelinie is absolutely and completely forbidden.

For all sorts of info about Copenhagen contact Use It, at Magstræde 14 (Tel: (01) 15 65 18). Ask for the excellent *Playtime* magazine which is free, and contains a useful city map plus pages of facts about accommodation, food, entertainments, etc in the capital. At the Use It office you can check the board for offers and messages, get free use of a locker (for a 10 kroner returnable deposit) and even arrange a ride. Use It also allow you to use their address as a Poste Restante address. Here it is again:

USE IT, Magstraede 14, 1204 Copenhagen.

Copenhagen: where to eat

Eating out anywhere in Scandinavia can be an expensive proposition, but the list which follows will allow you to have a meal for around 18–25 kroner if you watch the menu carefully and eat a lot of *smørrebrød*, the tasty open-cut sandwiches. For breakfast, try Danish pastry at about 2 kroner apiece. For midday snacks you can't beat the *pølser*, Danish hot-dogs sold at street-corner stands for 4 kroner each.

In fact, remember that *pølser* can save your life in Copenhagen. It's pretty hard to eat more than four of them which means that if you pick a cheap stand you can stuff yourself for only 16 kroner. There is a student restaurant at 52 Købmagergade, Copenhagen K, open from 9 a.m. to 5 p.m. (closed in July). You must have a student card. Here is a list of reasonably priced restaurants:

Skipper Klement, 18, Laederstraede

Spisehuset, 14, Magstræde

Universiteskafeen, 2, Fiolstræde

Chinese Cafeteria, 30, Dronningens Tværgade and 51, Nørrebrogade

Magasin (department store), 13, Kongens Nytorv.

In high-priced Scandinavia remember that Chinese restaurants are amongst the best deals you can find – rice is cheap and fills you up quickly.

Two other good places are the **Vista Self-Service Restaurant** upstairs at Vesterbrogade 40 and **Cafe Sorgenfri** at Brolaeggerstræde 11.

Copenhagen: what to see and do

TIVOLI GARDENS The fun-park to end all fun-parks. Plenty to do for nothing once you get in, but there is an entrance fee. Saturday is more expensive than other days. Open from May 1st to September 17th. Plenty of opportunity to meet the opposite sex.

BREWERIES The two great Danish breweries, *Carlsberg* at Ny Carlsbergvej 140 and *Tuborg* at Strandvejen 54, offer a tour of their premises and plenty of free beer at the end of the walkabout. Visit *Carlsberg* at 9 a.m., 11 a.m. or 2.30 p.m. weekdays and *Tuborg* between 8.30 a.m. and 2.30 p.m. weekdays.

LIBERTY MUSEUM OF DENMARK (also called the Danish Resistance Museum). Fascinating collection of objects used by the Danes in their underground fight against the German occupation forces during the Second World War. On Esplanaden. No admission fee.

LANGELINIE A pleasant walk – if you like that sort of thing – along the favourite promenade in Copenhagen. High spot for those over forty is the famous *Little Mermaid* sitting on her rock. Those under forty – like Copenhagen students – have a bad habit of knocking off her head or painting her a variety of colours. But she's OK. Good sleeping-out area.

FIOLSTRAEDE This, apart from being a pleasant street, is where the university is. Good place to meet up with students or get information about whatever is worrying you.

PORNOGRAPHY Free attraction and worth half an hour of anyone's time. Just about any bookshop or news-stall. Most fascinating display of gymnastics you ever did see. Particularly try Istedgade.

THE GLYPTOTEKET MUSEUM This houses the national art collection. Free on Sundays and Wednesdays. Some good works by Degas, Renoir, Manet, and Cézanne, and also Rodin's 'The Citizens of Calais'. The museum was founded last century by Carl Jacobsen who also founded the Carlsberg breweries. At Dantes Plads.

THE ROUND TOWER at Købmagergade. Costs to get in but it gives you a good view of Copenhagen from the top. There are no steps, but a spiral ramp all the way up. Legend tells that Peter the Giant galloped up to the top on his horse followed by his queen in a carriage.

CIRCUS STARTIME World-famous circus and well worth seeing. Bit of a hit to get in. Cheapest seat over 18 kroner. Open April 1st to end of October.

BAKKEN AMUSEMENT PARK Not as flamboyant as Tivoli, but free admission and plenty of chance to meet the opposite sex. Open April through August. Twenty-minute train ride from Central Station to Klampenborg Station, so probably cheaper to go to Tivoli, anyway.

BELLEVUE A beach between Copenhagen and Helsingør. It's also known as *Fluepapiret* which means 'fly-paper', meaning it has a great attraction to bikinied blondes which in turn means it's an attraction to bearded Danes. Draw your own conclusions – and the best of luck.

LOUISIANA This is Denmark's museum of contemporary art. It's on the coast at **Humlebaek**, about 40 kilometres out of Copenhagen and beyond Bellevue. Probably worth the trip for art-freaks and architecture students.

CINEMA Movies in Copenhagen are usually shown in the original language with Danish sub-titles. All the latest American and British movies are showing. Prices reasonable. Much cheaper in the suburbs, of course.

NYHAVN This seaman's quarter is worth a couple of hours one night. Maybe they'll hit your pocket if you step inside for a drink (you can usually spot the clip-joints), but it's a trip just digging the characters – tourists included – in the streets.

NIGHTLIFE *Tequila Bar* at 29 Longangsstræde and *Pilegarden* at 44 Pilestræde seem like two OK places to listen to music and meet people. For discotheques try *Golden Club* at 4 Løvstræde, or *Bonaparte* at 15 Gothersgade. Neither require membership. For live music, try *Hand I Hanke* at 20 Griffenfeldtsgade (for folk), *Daddy's Dance Hall* at 9 Axeltorv (for beat), or *De tre Musketerer* at 25 Nikolaj Plads (for jazz).

Transport in Copenhagen
Best way of getting around Copenhagen is on the bus system. Tickets are interchangeable and can be used on as many buses as you like within one hour. Cheapest way to buy them is eight at a time for 14 kroner. Otherwise they are 2.50 kroner each. If you're broke and want to go somewhere, stand at the appropriate bus stop and watch people getting off. If they throw away their ticket, grab it. There might be a few minutes left to run on it in which case you can jump aboard for free. Conversely if you're finished with a ticket which has time left on it, pass it to any waiting types who look like they could use it.

If you're staying in town for some time and are feeling energetic, a cheap way of getting around is by bicycle. About the cheapest place to rent from is *Københavns Cyklebørs* at the corner of Gothersgade and Nansengade, where the rate is 15 kroner a day. You have to leave a deposit of 60 kroner.

Student discounts

Half-price on admission to museums and art galleries for card holders.
Also possible to buy certain goods on discount. Check with

DANISH INTERNATIONAL STUDENT COMMITTEE,
Skindergade 28,
Copenhagen K (Tel: 11 00 44).

Addresses

Main Post Office (for Poste Restante) at Vesterbro, Tietgensgade 35–39,
Copenhagen.

American Express at H C Andersens Boulevard 12, Copenhagen
(Tel: 12 23 01).

Danish International Student Committee at Skindergade 28, Copenhagen
(Tel: 11 00 44).

Scandinavian Student Travel Service at Skindergade 28, Copenhagen
(Tel: 11 00 44).

Danish Tourist Board at Banegårdspladsen 2, Copenhagen
(Tel: 11 14 15).

US Embassy at Dag Hammarskjöldsallé 24, Copenhagen
(Tel: 12 31 44).

British Embassy at Kastelsvej 36–40, Copenhagen (Tel: 14 46 00).

Hitchers' tips and comments

First of all I am finding your guide very helpful in many respects. But I find
it annoying and insulting while reading along about the beauty of some
country to run into where-to-get-a-lay tips for males. In short, next time
re-title your book 'Hitch-hiker's Guide for Men', or leave out the sexist
remarks.
Simcha Deitch, Toronto, Canada
What can I say? K.W.

Sweden

Population	8,143,000
Size	173,665 square miles

Capital	Stockholm, population 1,350,000
Government	Constitutional Monarchy
Religion	Lutheran
Language	Swedish. English widely understood and spoken
	Some German and French

Presuming that you'll be crossing into Sweden from Denmark you have several ferry crossings to choose from. Amongst them:

1 Copenhagen to Landskrona, costing about 8 Swedish kroner.

2 Copenhagen to Malmo, costing about 11 Swedish kroner.

3 Helsingør to Helsingborg, costing about 6 Swedish kroner.

If you're entering Sweden from Norway, the two fastest routes are the E18 if you're heading for Stockholm, or the E6 if you're going to Göteborg and the south for a crossing into Denmark.

Göteborg, along with Kiruna, Visby, Kalmar and Ystad (and Stockholm, of course) can give you a pretty fair picture of Sweden. But remember that Sweden is a summertime place if you want to do it on the cheap. With the high cost of hotels in Scandinavia, sleeping out when you're on the road is just about mandatory unless you're loaded, and you can't sleep out in the Scandinavian winter! The Swedish law, *Allemans Rätt*, or Everyman's Right, allows you to camp out anywhere, except public parks (see Introduction to this chapter) or in someone's front garden, as long as you don't cross ploughed fields, leave rubbish lying about, or light fires where they can be dangerous.

Göteborg is a city of 449,000. Things worth seeing include the Guldhedens Vattentorn, the 400-foot water tower, the Røhss Museum of Arts and Crafts which will give you a run-down on the best of Swedish design, the Maritime Museum, the Archaeological Museum (featuring finds back to 2000 BC), and the Military Museum in Kronan Fortress. The best museum in this city of museums, though, is the Göteborg Art Gallery which features dozens of good pictures by people like Pissarro, Rousseau, Matisse, Picasso, Van Gogh, and Braque. Also sculptures by such greats as Rodin and Moore, and a superb representative collection of Scandinavian painters. For stage buffs there is even a Theatre Museum – something you don't find in many cities.

At **Boras**, 70 kilometres east of Göteborg on Route 40, is the Freedom Zoo in Boras Park, something really worth seeing if you're one of those people who likes looking at animals but hates the conventional method of caging them. These beasts – elephants, giraffes, rhinos, and all the rest – roam in wide open spaces.

If you're heading south to Ystad, you might want to drop into **Varberg**,

80 kilometres from Göteborg, where, in the Varberg fortress you can see the remains of Bocksten Man, another gentleman, this time medieval, who was recently hauled from a bog. He was preserved so well that his clothing is claimed as the only complete set of medieval clothes in existence.

Ystad, right on the southern tip of Sweden, in the province of Skane, is interesting because of its Middle Age aspect. Ancient winding streets, half-timbered houses, and old churches dot the town, while in the surrounding countryside, you find castles, manor houses, and also a medieval monastery.

Visby, on the **Island of Gotland,** is another leftover from the old Sweden. Unfortunately, it costs a packet to get there. The trip from Oskarshamn or Vastervik (about four hours) costs better than 75 kroner each way. (Flash your student card for a reduction.) Known as the City of Ruins and Roses, Visby, population 16,000, was once an extremely important seaport, but after being captured in the 1300s it drifted out of history and towards oblivion. It remains today the only walled city in Northern Europe. To see? Everything. Just walk around – the Maiden's Tower, where a girl was entombed alive for helping an enemy king, Gallow Hill, the ancient Powder Tower. Catch 22 . . . you'll get your money's worth if you've got some money.

Kalmar, 80 kilometres south of Oskarshamn and on the Route 15 east coast road up to Stockholm, is a worthwhile place. A city of 52,000, it is the sister city of Wilmington, Delaware. This international handshake salutes the first Swedish immigrants to America who came from Kalmar and went to Wilmington in the 1600s. The main sight is Kalmar Castle and its museum.

If you can't afford the Gotland Island trip, you may like to compensate with a trip to Oland Island, which is a fantastic area for amateur archaeologists interested in the Iron Age. A fair percentage of the Swedes in America, incidentally, must have Olander ancestors, because about 25 per cent of the island population emigrated. You cross the island via Europe's longest bridge – nearly four miles long.

Kalmar is in the middle of an area containing about 40 of Sweden's famed glass factories. For a free visit to the best-known glass factory in the world, visit **Orrefors,** which is easy to hitch to, being 45 kilometres west of Kalmar on Highway 31. The factory is open all year and conducted tours are available Monday to Friday at 8.00 a.m. to 10.30 a.m. and 11.30 a.m. to 3.30 p.m.

Kiruna, in Northern Lapland, is the big trip. It is 1,350 kilometres north of Stockholm and 150 kilometres into the Arctic Circle. From Stockholm you have a choice of routes: the east coast E4 up to Lulea and then a swing inland on Highway 97, connecting with the 98 outside Gällivare; or the E4 up to Sundsvall and a swing west along the E75 to Osterund, followed by a straight northern route to Kiruna along road numbers 88, 343, 97 and 98. If you're working against a time limit, then you're better off on the eastern sea-road to Lulea. The inland route takes you through a cross-section of Swedish geography – really great country – but the population is spread thin and so are the cars.

Although it hosts only 31,000 citizens, Kiruna is the world's largest city in area, containing within its distended limits, plains, lakes, Lapp camps, 30,000 reindeer, and two mountains of iron totalling some 2 billion tons of ore.

The town itself is not wildly interesting, but it's a good stopping place after the long haul from Stockholm, and it's the ideal place to watch the Midnight Sun between May 31st and July 14th. For those six weeks there is continual daylight and you can enjoy the unique experience of watching the sun beginning to rise again without first sliding below the horizon. Mosquitoes, incidentally, are really bad in mid-July.

★Canoeing If you're in the forest areas of Dalsland and Värmland (north of Göteborg), you might want to try a two- or three-day canoe trip. Check at lakeside towns. At **Dals Langed**, just off Highway 172, a canoe costs about 25 kroner a day. A rich hitcher's sport, but great fun!

★Prospecting For semi-precious crystals and stones and alluvial gold, the Kopparberg district of Orebro county is the place. (Orebro is 200 kilometres west of Stockholm.) Check for precise details from the tourist office in Stockholm or Orebro. I've never done it myself, but have heard of people making the odd pound. Don't count on it!

Stockholm: where to sleep

Sweden is the most expensive of all Scandinavian countries and along with Switzerland the most expensive in Europe. Single hotel rooms for 45 kroner are cheap. Once again it's the hostels and dormitories which save the day. The following list starts at the cheapest, which are still exorbitantly expensive and works up . . . and up.

Hotel Frescati at Professorsslingan 13–15 (Tel: 15 79 96).
Open 1st June until 31st August.

Af Chapman at Skeppsholmen (Tel: 10 37 15). This is the famous floating youth hostel, the **Af Chapman** being an ex-Swedish Navy training vessel. Open mid-March until October 31st.

209 Sweden

YH Lilla Wärten, Södra Hamnvägen 40 (Tel: 67 87 00). Open January 7th to December 20th.

Jerum Student and Youth Hostel, at Studentbacken 21 (Tel: 63 53 80). Open June 1st to August 31st. Price about 28 kroner a night.

Kfum Hostal at Mariagränd 3 (Tel: 43 46 00).

For help in finding a room to suit your pocket consult *Hotellcentralen* at the Central Rail Station. They probably won't be too interested in booking you into a dormitory, but they'll be polite enough to give you the information you need. If they do place you somewhere they'll charge you a booking fee of about 10 kroner for hotels and 3 kroner for youth hostels, so you'd better decide if you'll get your money's worth before you let them do the work.

Camping grounds are good in Stockholm. The **Sätra** grounds (Tel: 08 97 70 71) are fairly close to town and can be reached on the Number 15 tram. All mod-cons, clean, and reasonably priced at about 15 kroner per tent.

For sleeping rough, try around Kaknäs Tower (take Bus 69). Sleeping out should present no problems – as long as it's warm enough – because just about all of the many islands upon which Stockholm is built are bordered with trees and parks.

Stockholm: where to eat

Be warned . . . buy at the supermarket, eat at student restaurants, department-store cafeterias, or at self-service places. Establishments listed here will fill you up for between 15 and 20 kroner.

Restaurang Domus at Körsbärsvägen 1 (Tel: 34 90 85). Open all year round from 11 a.m. to 8 p.m.

Michelangelo Pizza House at Vasterlanggaten (old town).

Any of the **ICA Ringbaren** places are OK. Some addresses are:

Tegelbacken 2,	Birger Jarlsgatan 16,
Sergelgatan 22,	Sergels Torg 6,
Drottninggatan 27,	Kungsträdgarden.
Mäster Samuelsgatan 42,	

Look for the **EPA** and **TEMPO** department stores. Their cafeterias serve breakfast and lunch.

Cafe Roda Rummet at 21 Barnhusgatan.

Cafeteria at 5 Skeppsbron. It's opposite the Af Chapman, but on the other side of the river, right near the ferries for Finland.

Kate's Bar at 23 Gamla Brogatan will allow you to eat well for 14 kroner. (Right opposite is *Impo*, a place with camping gear and clothes.)

The Cafeteria by the main entrance to Stockholm's railway station is cheap enough. (Corner of Vasgatan and Klarabergsgatan.)

The Restaurant at the railway station offers an *all-you-can-eat* breakfast for about 12 kroner between 6.30 a.m. and 10 a.m. (Sundays from 8 a.m. to 11 a.m.) Fill up and palm a few morsels into the pocket. You should get enough to take you through most of the day if you're cool about it.

Stockholm: what to see and do

GRÖNA LUND'S TIVOLI on Djurgaarden. Entrance charge. Super amusement park, not as pretty as the Copenhagen Tivoli, but OK if you like that sort of thing. Mainly of interest because there are plenty of friendly people of the right age floating around and because on the grounds are two clubs. The *Dance In* is more expensive than the *Dance Out*, but there's a better class of people. All in all, not very exciting, but it might amuse a sad hour. Open April through September.

CLUBS *Bobbadilla* at Svartmannagatan 27 is more highly priced but OK – and good for meeting people. Also try the pubs. They only serve beer, and close at midnight, but you can have some fun. *Magnus Ladulas* at Osterlanggatan 26 and *Engelen* at Kornhamnstorg 59B are both in the old town and are OK. And if you need something late at night (newspapers, hamburgers, etc) try the *Drugstore*, an all-night joint at Kungsgatan 9.

THE WASA on Djurgaarden. This warship which sank moments after being launched in 1628, was rediscovered in 1956 and lifted from the seabed in 1961. The story of the recovery is told in a film shown at the museum. One of the best examples in the world of an ancient sailing vessel. Admission charge.

SKANSEN Also at Djurgaarden. Open all year round. An open-air museum with examples of farms, town sections, etc from all over Sweden. Mostly eighteenth century.

THE NATIONAL MUSEUM OF ART on Södra Blasieholmshamnen. Fairly good collection. Admission charge during week, but free on Tuesdays.

MUSEUM OF MODERN ART on Skeppsholmen. Reasonable collection of modern European masters and good collections of Swedish stuff. Open every day. Entrance charge.

MILLESGARDEN on the island of Lidingö. Home and works of the famous sculptor Carl Milles. Admission charge.

SAUNA BATH Saunas are usually fairly expensive. This one, *Vanadisbadet* at Vanadislunden is cheap and good. Used to cost 5 kroner. Worth trying.

BLUE MOVIES If you want to see one – it'll cost you 20–25 kroner – go to the street called Klara Norra Kyrkog. There are quite a few porn-shops and blue cinemas there. (Make sure you don't cop an American-made show. The product isn't up to standard.)

Transport in Stockholm

The best deal in town is the *Turistkort* (Tourist Card) which allows visitors to wander for three days on buses and trains of Stockholm. At 34 kroner, the cost is high, but when you consider that the round trip to Drottningholm Castle costs about 7 kroner, you understand that you can make the card pay. Also, the cost includes entry tickets to Skansen and the TV tower and allows you on ferry boats as well. You can buy a one-day card for 14 kroner. Buy them at the Swedish Tourist Centre, the 'Pressbyran' kiosks, or at stations.

Student discounts

For information, contact:
Travel Department, Sveriges Förenade Studentkarer, Drottninggatan 89, Stockholm VA (Tel: 34 01 80).

Addresses

Main Post Office (for Poste Restante) at Vasagatan 28–34, Stockholm.

American Express at Birger Jarlsgatan 32, Stockholm (Tel: 23 34 20).

Student Reception Office in Sweden House at Hamngatan 27, Stockholm (Tel: 22 32 80). Summer only.

Sveriges Forenade Studentkarer (Student Travel Department) at Drottninggatan 89, Stockholm (Tel: 34 01 80).

Swedish Tourist Centre in Sweden House at Hamngatan 27, Stockholm (Tel: 22 32 80).

US Embassy at Strandvägen 101, Stockholm (Tel: 63 05 20).

British Embassy at Skarpögatan 6, Stockholm (Tel: 67 01 40).

Hitchers' tips and comments
Cigarette papers are horrendously expensive in Sweden (2000% tax) whereas in Norway they are relatively cheap. I rolled my cigarettes around Sweden using pages torn from the AA Camping Guide. It was disgusting. Get cigarette papers duty-free (along with duty free salami, about £1 per kilo) on the boat from Denmark.
Simon Calder, Coventry, England

The phenomenal cost of travelling in the Nordic countries is no secret. While in Stockholm, I discovered that by trying to pay for a ticket with a 100 kroner note, explaining in my best English that it was all I had, the result was a free ride every time. For two weeks I rode the tunnel Bana saving the price of a cup of coffee with every ride.
Bruce Alan Whitham, Newcastle, Canada

Norway

Population	4,000,000
Size	125,181 square miles
Capital	Oslo, population 465,000
Government	Constitutional Monarchy
Religion	Lutheran
Language	Norwegian. English widely understood and spoken. Some French and German

The cheapest way of getting to Norway is through Sweden (see Swedish section for ferry fares from Denmark) and then hitching along the E6 to the Norwegian/Swedish border. If you have more money and/or less time, two other ways of getting there are:

1 Copenhagen to Oslo ferry. Sixteen-hour journey, costing from 250 Danish kroners.

2 Frederikshavn (Jutland) to Larvik ferry. Six-hour journey, costing 185 Norwegian kroners.

Top towns in Norway, after Oslo, are Bergen, Stavanger, and Trondheim. **Stavanger,** some 584 kilometres from Oslo, is Norway's fourth city and one of the best from the point of view of seeing what the old Norway was like. The wooden houses in Old Stavanger and the narrow, winding, cobbled streets are a sight for eyes glazed by the dazzle of metal and plastic. Two sights in one are the cathedral at the market-place. The market swings every day, except Sunday, until 2 or 3 in the afternoon. The cathedral, a twelfth-century structure, is an outstanding example of Middle-Age architecture in Norway. For a cheap sightseeing trip, jump bus Number 8 at St Olavsgarden. It covers most parts of Stavanger. For a good look at the fjords, particularly if you're not heading up farther north, try the Stavanger to Sand ferry. It's a 3–4 hour trip which costs around 65 kroner, but you see some fantastic sights. Highly recommended. After heading out of Sand, and if you're going to Bergen, it's necessary to take another ferry, this time across the Hardanger Fjord. (Kinsarvik to Kvanndal is one way, costing 15 kroner and taking about an hour.) If in that area try and see the huge Folgefonn Glacier and the Laatefoss Waterfall near **Odda**.

Don't miss **Bergen**'s colourful harbour. It's a pleasure just to walk in the area. Right on the waterfront is the Fish Market – a sight and a smell in itself – while on your right as you face the water is the beautiful street called Bryggen, a row of timbered houses built in 1702 to recreate a slice of medieval Bergen after a fire destroyed much of the city. Also on Bryggen is the Hanseatic Museum which is devoted to life as the German merchants who traded in Bergen centuries ago lived it. The Rasmus Meyer Collection is worth seeing because it contains many of Edvard Munch's works, while for a display of a different sort, try the Fishery Museum, which gives a run-down on Norway's most famous industry. Both are at the Permanenten on Olav Kyrresgate. For getting around the city, the Tourist Information Office, and most hotels, sell a special tourist ticket which allows unlimited bus and tram-car travel for 48 hours within the city limits. If you can afford it and want to see a great view over this Viking city with its seven hills, you should invest a few kroner and take the funicular up the 1,050 feet of Mount Fløien. Along the waterfront you'll find dozens of fjord boat trips advertised and costing anywhere from 20 to 200 kroner. All are good because the scenery around Bergen is spectacular. It's just a matter of figuring if you want to pay out – and if so, how much. Not far from Bergen is **Troldhaugen** (Troll's Hill) which was the home of Edvard Grieg.

If you're heading farther north, **Alesund** is Norway's greatest fishing town and its large fleet, which operates from Baffin Bay, heads out after seals as well as smaller fry. There might be the possibility of odd-jobs in Alesund.

Trondheim, Norway's second largest city and the principal city to the north, was founded nearly a thousand years ago. A pleasant place with an

ancient cathedral and a very interesting Museum of Music History,
it has been known as the 'Royal Town' since the days when Norway's
monarchs were crowned there. When the Norwegian Royal Family visit
Trondheim these days they stay at Siftsgarden which is claimed to be the
largest wooden building in Europe.

Near the city is the village of **Grong** which sits on the Namsen River,
just one of Norway's 200 salmon-filled streams. Hitching fishermen may
be interested in knowing that there are a quarter of a million lakes
in Norway, most of which play host to trout. Fishing licences cost money
but if you can figure a way of rigging some light tackle you should be able
to haul a cheap meal out of most stretches of water in the backwoods
without much trouble. (Fishing with a licence does not mean that fish bite
better.)

Once above Trondheim, you're heading for the Arctic Circle. **Bodø** is
the most popular place for viewing the Midnight Sun (June 5th to July 9th
and *no* sun from December 19th to January 9th) and there's usually plenty
of traffic to that point. After Bodø the roads can be lonely and the people
scarce. Most of the time you have no proof you're on a civilized planet.
Once in Finnmark you're in an area bigger than Denmark but inhabited
by only 75,000 people. It's wild and it's beautiful and it's lots of other
appropriate clichés – but don't find yourself twenty miles from the nearest
town at night at the wrong time of year. You might get a cold.

On the way up to the North Cape, **Tromsø** is worth stopping at
if only to see its fabulous Arctic Church. (The wreck of the German
battleship, *Tirpitz*, which was bombed there by the RAF during the
Second World War can no longer be seen.) The Tromsø Museum will give
you an idea of how people – particularly the Lapps – have managed to live
in the Arctic Circle.

After **Steinkjer**, the road, National Highway 6, is mostly gravel, but as
you get farther and farther north you'll notice more and more tourist
facilities because the North Cape is slowly becoming 'the place' to have
been. Finally, when you reach **Honningsvaag** (ferry from Käfjord –
14 kroner), you've made the northernmost village in the world! Forty
kilometres farther on is the barren North Cape – the end of Europe –
a rocky plateau on a latitude of 70° 10′ 21″N which rises 1,000 feet
straight out of the Arctic Ocean.

Oslo: where to sleep

Oslo doesn't come as expensive as Copenhagen or Stockholm, but it tries
hard. One of the cheapest places around is the International Youth Hostel

(Haraldsheim) which charges 50 kroner for bed and breakfast! After that, expect to pay 50–60 kroner. This list of hostels and dormitories starts with the least expensive:

Haraldsheim Youth Hostel at Haraldsheimvn 4, Oslo 5 (Tel: 21 83 59). Open all year round. Must be member of YHA.

Bjerke Youth Hostel at Bjerke Studentheim, Trondheim 271, Oslo 5. Open 20th June to 18th August. Booking address: Boks 41, Grefsen, Oslo 4. Overnight charge 30 kroner.

Baptistsamufunnets Skoler at Drammensveien 406 (Tel: 53 38 53). Open from June 1st to August 31st.

If you don't want student accommodation, you must be prepared to fork out – but there are a few reasonably priced places:

For 7 kroner the *Innkvartering* desk (the Hotel Finding Service) at East Station will help you locate a hotel room to suit your budget or get you into a room in a private house. If you're staying in Oslo for more than a few days – especially in summer when hotels are often full – the investment could well save you money.

If you want to sleep for nothing, you have several choices (providing it's summer). There's the 75-acre Frogner Park in Western Oslo which should provide nesting holes for the sore of pocket without too much trouble; there are several smaller parks, for instance on Akersbakken; there's the cemetery at Ullevalsveien (you have to get over the wall) and on the Bygdøy peninsula there are larger parklands. (BUT I've had a letter from the Norwegian Tourist Office in London which passes on to me information given them by authorities in Oslo who seem to have read this book: 'We will not – repeat not – condone sleeping in the parks or have this even suggested. Loiterers will, in fact, be removed by the police.')

Oslo: where to eat

Norwegians have the habit of eating only two meals a day. A big breakfast and a big dinner – with maybe a snack somewhere along the line. As with most places in Scandinavia, expect to pay out between 30 and 45 kroner for a meal.

Aulakjelleren and **Frokostkjelleren**. Student cafeterias in the university buildings at Karl Johansgate. Very cheap. They don't ask for student cards. You should fill up for 25 kroner.

Restaurant Frederikke at Universitetssentret in the suburbs of Blindern (Tel: 46 68 80). Open all year.

Stratos at Youngstorget 2.

Den Runde Tonne at Ploensgaten (off Youngstorget).
A good chain group are **Kaffistovas** with branches at:

Karl Johansgate 13,   Storgaten 28,
Rosenkrantzgate 8,   Kristian Augustsgate 14.

Helserestauranten Bios at Kronprinsensgaten 5. Good prices and 20 per cent discount if you flash a student's ID card.

Wimpy Bars (same as in London!). Neutral food, cheap prices. Several around Oslo, including one at Akersgate 8 and another at Stortingsgaten 20.

Christiania Dampkjokken at Torggt. 8.

Expressen Cafeteria at Fred. Olsensgt. 11.

Frogner Baths Cafeteria at Middlethungst. 28.

Gamle Radhus Cafeteria at N. Slottsgt. 1.

Oslo: what to see and do

EDVARD MUNCH MUSEUM Admission free. At Tøyengate 53.
Munch (1863–1944) is considered a leading European contemporary painter. The work is interesting, giving a clue to the psyche of the Northerner. The man had a phenomenal output, creating over 1,000 paintings and 4,000 drawings. The museum exhibits about 300 paintings, plus sketches and some sculpture.

THE VIGELAND SCULPTURES Admission free. At Frogner Park.
Gustav Vigeland, another great Norwegian artist, was financed by the city of Oslo to create the 150 pieces of work on display in this park.
The work took him thirty years.

NATIONAL THEATRE Behind the theatre used to be a good meeting place for kindred spirits. Probably still a little action around there.

AKERHUS CASTLE Small admission charge. Open April to October.
Used to be the strongest castle in Scandinavia. Used as office space by the Germans during the war.

KON-TIKI MUSEUM Admission charge. In the Bygdøy area. This houses the balsa raft in which Thor Heyerdahl and his crew sailed 4,300 miles across the Pacific in 1947. Apart from proving his theory that pre-Inca Indians might have travelled the same way to reach Polynesia, Heyerdahl made around a million pounds out of the adventure and had his book, *Kon-Tiki*, translated into more than 80 languages.

THE VIKING SHIPS Admission charge. At Huk Aveny 35 in the Bygdøy area (within walking distance of the *Kon-Tiki*). You can see three Viking ships in fair state of preservation, along with a display of artifacts found with them. One ship is 1,100 years old.

HOLMENKOLLEN SKI JUMP The oldest in the world and the site of Olympic competitions. Thirty minutes or so by train. A very interesting Ski Museum (for snow-sport fans) is situated inside the jump tower. Admission charge to the museum.

FRAM MUSEUM This museum, built in the style of an ancient Norwegian boat-house, houses the polar exploration vessel *Fram*. It was this boat which carried Amundsen on his dash to the South Pole. The museum is in Bygodøynes. You reach it by taking a ferry from Pier 3 or Bus 30 from the National Theatre.

NORWEGIAN FOLK MUSEUM at Museumsveien 10, Bygdøy. (Bus 30 or Pier 3) Over 150 wooden buildings have been dismantled and shifted from their original sites and taken to Bygdøy where they have been re-erected to form a nearly complete collection of Norwegian rural architecture. All are complete with their original furnishings. All that – and more – is in the outdoor section of the museum. Indoors you'll find over 100,000 exhibits including playwright Henrik Ibsen's study and a section on the culture of Lapland.

TOWN HALL Town halls aren't usually recommended in this book. But have a look at this one! It's as much a gallery of contemporary Norwegian art as a red-tape machine.

CLUB 7 at Munkedamsveiun 15. Plenty of action, lights, and sound, but not up to the standard of London or New York clubs. Costs about 18 kroner weekdays and 30 kroner Fridays and Saturdays entrance fee. Another OK place is *Kroa* at Stortgaten 22. Folk-singing, jazz, student hangout.

Transport in Oslo
The tram and bus system in the city charges 3.50 kroner a ride. It's cheaper to buy a tikkekort for 35 kroner which gives you eleven rides on either tram or bus.

Student discounts
For details contact:

THE UNIVERSITIES TRAVEL BUREAU,
Universitetssentret, Blindern, Oslo 3 (Tel: 46 68 80).

Addresses

Main Post Office (for Poste Restante) at Dronningensgate 15, Oslo.

American Express at Karl Johansgate 33, Oslo (Tel: 20 50 50).

Studentenes Reisekontor at Universitetssentret, Blindern, Oslo 3
(Tel: 46 68 80).

Studentenes Reisekontor at Parkveien 1, Bergen (Tel: 33 191).

Tourist Information Centre at Munkedamsveien 15, Oslo 2 (Tel: 42 71 70).

US Embassy at Drammensveien 18, Oslo (Tel: 56 68 80).

British Embassy at Ths Heftysegt 8, Oslo 2 (Tel: 56 38 90).

Hitchers' tips and comments
If you're out of money in Oslo, don't sleep in the parks or at Bygdøy.
Take the tram to Frognerseteren or a bus (No 41) to Sorkedalen and walk
ten minutes into the woods.
Johs. Anken, Oslo, Norway

Finland

Population   4,733,000
Size   130,085 square miles
Capital   Helsinki, population 525,000
Government Republic
Religion   Evangelical Lutheran and Greek Orthodox
Language   Finnish and Swedish are the official languages.
               Some English spoken

Getting to Finland can be an expensive proposition. You have to spend
a lot of days on the road and enter at the Swedish-Finnish border at Tornio
on the E4 highway (fine if you're travelling south after the Kiruna trip)
or pay a fair wallop on the ferry boats.

Four of the ferry points are:

1 Stockholm to Helsinki, costing about 90 marks and lasting around 15 hours. Daily.

2 Stockholm to Turku, costing about 68 marks and lasting about 9 hours. Daily.

3 Kapellskar to Naantall, costing about 50 marks and lasting about 8 hours. Daily.

4 Umea to Sundsvall and Vassa (if you're a long way up north in Sweden), costing about 45 marks and lasting about 4 hours.

Turku, a ferry port, is Finland's second city, with 165,000 people. It is also the oldest city in the country and the former capital. (Abo is its Swedish name, as Helsingfors is the Swedish name of Helsinki.) Resurrection Chapel is considered a masterpiece of Modern Finnish architecture, while for something a little older, the Cathedral and Turku Castle date from the twelfth century. Music fans will be interested in the Sibelius Museum, while sport nuts might want to see the Turku Sports Park running track, reputed to be the fastest in the world and on which Olympian Paavo Nurmi set many of his world records. Of more general interest is Scandinavia's biggest open-air market-place at the old trade hall in the city.

Tampere, 180 kilometres north-west of Helsinki, is about the same size as Turku. It is known as the 'City of Sapphire Lakes'. Twenty-two lakes are within its city limits, as are the Tammerkoski Rapids. At Pyynikki, the National Park, is the famous summer theatre, which was the first in the world to operate with a revolving auditorium. Watching a production as you move around the stage is quite something. For details of plays check with the tourist office – but it's generally expensive – 15–25 marks a ticket. The university, a nice piece of architecture, is the best place to meet up with people. For a speed trip (gentle type) and a glimpse of one of the fastest games in the world, drop in on an ice-hockey match at the new stadium.

For those in Finland only briefly, Helsinki, Turku and Tampere are probably the best bets for a quick look around. For those with time and money and who are heading north into Lapland, **Kuopio** (population 72,000) is a good stopping place. This city four hundred kilometres north of Helsinki is the centre of lake shipping. (In Finland there are 60,000 lakes, comprising 9 per cent of the country's total area and resulting in another 30 per cent being marshland.) The big thing at Kuopio is to climb the 700-foot Puijo Hill and the 225-foot tower on top of it for one of the best

views in Scandinavia. From the top you can gaze over 18,000 square miles
of the lake country! If you're in the Market Square try the *kalakukkos*,
hard-crusted fish pasties native to the province.

Vaasa, on the west coast, where many cross to from Umea in Sweden, is
a pleasant city of 55,000. There are actually two towns, Old Vaasa and New
Vaasa. The Old was destroyed by fire in 1852 and is now a place of ruins
and monuments. Worth visiting is the fishing village of **Björkö**, 10 kilometres
north of Vaasa.

If you've crossed the Swedish/Finnish border up north, the first town
you'll come to is **Tornio**. It's an island, accessible only by bridges and a
good town to meet people. Population 20,000. Try and get out to the
salmon weir at **Kiviranta**.

Just a few miles below the Arctic Circle and 850 kilometres from
Helsinki is the capital of Finnish Lapland. **Rovaniemi** was completely
destroyed during the Second World War but has been rebuilt and is now
three times as large with 30,000 inhabitants. There are only a few thousand
Lapps left in Lapland, but many of them work around Rovaniemi. Here
you can learn about Lapp hand-crafts and their nomadic life-style. If
you're up there before or after summer when the snow is down, try the
Pohtimolampi Sports and Excursion Centre (28 kilometres out plus a
3-kilometre walk) where they run the only reindeer-driving school in the
world. For the Midnight Sun you have to go farther north. Try **Sodankylä**.

Beyond Rovaniemi is a strange wilderness of frozen lakes, rivers,
and tundra plains – and very few people.

★**Language** *Minä rakastan sinua! Ymmärrätteko? Minä rakastan sinua!*
It doesn't matter how sincere you are, you won't get away with it. It means,
'I love you! Do you understand? I love you!' Try English or French, or
even Swahili. It's easier. The language is of Finno-Ugrian origins, related
to Hungarian and Estonian. (Wouldn't hurt to try *kiltos*, meaning thank
you.)

★**Pori Jazz Festival** Third week in July at Pori, a coastal town in
West Finland. Finnish and international names. Details from:
Pori Jazz Festival, Luvianpuistokatu 20, 28100 Pori 10.

★**Reindeer Joring** Exclusively a Lapland sport. You get in a *pulkka* –
a one-seated chariot fitted with skis – have a quiet word with your
power-source, which is a frisky reindeer, hang on tight and wish
yourself *bon voyage*.

★**Trips to Russia** See **The Communist Countries**.

Helsinki: where to sleep

Helsinki just doesn't have hitchers at heart. The average year-round temperature of 41 degrees (low 20s most of the winter, though it averages around 70 in July) makes it hard to sleep out and hotel prices are astronomical, with low-priced singles around 50 marks. However, there are a few hostels and dormitories which offer singles around 35–40 marks and those are listed below:

Youth Hostel Stadionin Maja at Pohj. Stadionintie 3B (Tel: 496 071). Showers, self-service kitchen, or breakfast served. Between 19 and 35 marks per person. Open all year.

Hotelli Satakuntatalo at Lapinrinne 1A (Tel: 647 311). Open June 1st to August 31st (ask for dormitory).

Hotel Otaniemi at Otaniemi (Tel: 460 211). Open June 1st to August 31st.

The official room-finding service at Central Station is called *Hotellikeskus* (Tel: 11 133). They attempt to find hotels or rooms in private houses at a price which fits your pocket.

For sleeping out (and God help you) try Hietaranta Beach, Sibelius Park or find a place in the parks around Olympia Stadium.

Camping Rastila, about 7 kilometres east of Helsinki (Tel: 316 551). Open May 15th to September 15th. Camping fees around 5–8 marks per person, per day. Cooking facilities, cafeteria, supermarket and sauna.

Helsinki: where to eat

With dinner in the student hostel costing the best part of 13 marks you get the idea that it's best to head for the supermarket. (And even that's not cheap!) Meal prices in the places listed below will come out between 15 and 21 marks.

Hotelli Satakuntatalo at Lapinrinne 1A (Tel: 647 311). Open all the year. Lunch served between 11 a.m. and 2 p.m. and dinner from 5 p.m. to 8 p.m.

Marian Grill at Kapteeninkatu 7.

HOK 1 at Mannerheimintie 55. (Any place belonging to the HOK chain gives a good meal for around 13 marks.)

Other chain groups which don't entirely bust the budget are *Colombia*, *Nissen*, *Elanto*, *Fazer*, and *Primula*. Try:

Elanto 8 at Mannerheimintie 68.

Nissen at Mannerheimintie 3.

Colombia at Keskuskatu 3.

Helsinki: what to see and do

FINNISH DESIGN CENTRE Kasarmikatu 19. Free. Displays the best in crafts and design in the country. Particularly interesting are the fabric designs.

ATENEUM ART GALLERY Kaivokatu 2. Fair collection of European masters, but fine collection of Finnish art from the last few centuries.

TAPIOLA GARDEN CITY This is one of the best designed living centres in Scandinavia. It shows you what suburbia can be like when someone puts their mind to creating a liveable-in situation. Miles better than anything you'll see in England or America. Take Bus 4 or 5 from the Bus Station, or walk – but it's six miles from the centre of Helsinki.

SAUNA BATH The cheapest in town seems to be at Olympia Stadium at Elaintarha. (Tram 3T or 3B from Central Station.) Costs about 7 marks. Also a swimming pool at the Stadium and in summer it's as good a place as any to meet people.

HÄMIS near the Bus Station. Dance Hall. There's an admission charge, but there's plenty of ladies looking for escorts and plenty of gentlemen wishing to escort them. In what's generally a sad-time night-time town, Hämis at least tries for the action.

LINNANMÄKI Fun fair. Admission charge. Open May to mid-September. Get there on street-cars 7 or 8. For a little movement, try the *Ronda*, the discotheque in the middle of the park. (Extra admission, but it may be worth it if you're looking for something.)

NATIONAL MUSEUM Mannerheimintie 34. It contains three sections. Prehistoric, historic, and ethnographic. It's also free on Tuesdays if you're looking for somewhere dry and warm.

Transport in Helsinki

The Helsinki bus and tram system is the way to get around. Cheapest way of doing it is to take advantage of the special offer of 24 hours of unlimited travel for less than 15 marks. You can buy tickets aboard the vehicle. It'll pay off if you want to do a quick flash around the city.

Student discounts

Various museums, art collections, and theatres offer discounts to card holders. For full information check with:

STUDENT SERVICE FINLAND (FSTS),
Kampinkatu 4B, 00100 Helsinki 10 (Tel: 648 434).

Addresses

Main Post Office (for Poste Restante) at Mannerheimintie 11, 00100 Helsinki 10.

American Express at TRAVEK Travel Bureau, Eteläranta 16, 00130 Helsinki 13 (Tel. 171 900).

Student Service Finland (FSTS) at:
Kampinkatu 4B, 00100 Helsinki 10 (Tel: 90 648 434).
Kauppakatu 12, 40100 Jyräskylä 10 (Tel: 941 17507).
Hallituskatu 33, 90100 Oulu 10 (Tel: 981 211 858).
Tuomiokirkonkatu 36, 33100 Tampere 10. (Tel: 931 309 95).
Hämeenkatu 14, 20500 Turku 50 (Tel: 921 337 033).

Helsinki City Tourist Office at Pohjoisesplandi 19, 00100 Helsinki 10 (Tel: 169 3757 and 174 088).

Finnish Travel Association at Mikonkatu 25, 00100 Helsinki 10 (Tel: 170 868).

US Embassy at Itäinen Puistotie 14A, 00140 Helsinki 14 (Tel: 171 931).

British Embassy at Uudenmaankatu 16–20, Helsinki 12 (Tel: 125 74).

Hitchers' tips and comments

If you're really hungry and down and out, go for the dried kippers which you can buy in supermarkets very cheaply. You can eat them straight away because they're precooked. Very nutritious.

If you want to spend a while in Lapland, walking around (the only real way to see it), buy a map or two in Rovaniemi to show you the many little country huts. Only the scale maps show them, but you need scale maps for walking anyway. The cost of the map is cancelled out by the fact it shows you where to get free accommodation and basic facilities, in return for which you are only asked to chop firewood and leave the place clean. If you've got good boots and gear you can have a real 'back to nature' trip inside the Arctic Circle.

Duncan S. Grey, Durham City, England

Helsinki's night life centres on bars, where the Finns are friendliest. The best is 'Pub Baari' on Leppasuonkatu, which has about the loosest crowd of young Finns there every night. Great meeting place. Around the corner is Helsinki's only all-night snack bar (open till 6 a.m.) where you can buy a large plate of meatballs, chips and a cup of coffee for about 6 marks. One of the best deals in highly priced Scandinavia.

Joachim Fechter, Berlin, Germany

9 The Communist countries

Hitching in the Communist countries presents a whole lot of problems which many people would rather avoid. To start with, you usually need visas to enter and with many of the countries that visa can be expensive, there being a basic rate to pay per day you remain in the country.

Because of the hassle involved, it is advisable to check out visa requirements *before* you start on your trip, otherwise you might find yourself turned back from a border because you don't have the necessary documentation.

The last few years have seen travel restrictions in these areas eased considerably and the coming years will probably see things getting easier still.

The following is a very brief run-down:

Albania

From a hitch-hiking point of view forget all about it. The Albanians aren't interested at this stage. If you want to pay a visit – and from all reports it's a fascinating place – you'll have to join up with a guided tour. Make enquiries at travel agencies.

Bulgaria

Population	9,000,000
Size	42,800 square miles
Capital	Sofia, population 900,000
Government	Socialist People's Republic
Religion	Eastern Orthodox mostly
Language	Bulgarian. Russian widely spoken. Some German, French and English understood

There's no problem entering Bulgaria. You don't need a visa if you are staying more than 48 hours and less than 2 months. If you're heading straight through the country in less than 48 hours then you have to buy a transit visa. You can buy them at any Bulgarian Embassy or Consulate or at border crossing points (but check this in case things change after we go to press). Transit visas currently cost around 3 leva if you buy them at Embassies or Consulates, about 9 leva if you buy them at the border.

Hitching is permitted in Bulgaria, but the authorities get uptight about people camping out. The law is that you can only sack out in camping grounds (which are very cheap). If you do decide to sleep out, don't light a fire.

Important cities are **Plovdiv, Nessebur, Varna** and **Sofia.**

In five-thousand-year-old Sofia visit the Alexander Nevsky Cathedral and go down into the crypt to see the fabulous collection of old icons. Just as interesting, particularly if you're on your way to Turkey, are visits to some of Sofia's mosques. Try the Bouyuk Mosque. See also the great Archaeological Museum on Stamboluski Boulevard with its incredible Vulchi Trun treasure.

Accommodation is expensive, so check with the tourist office for the latest on youth lodgings.

Addresses

Orbita, Bureau for International Youth Tourism at 76 Anton Ivanov Boulevard, Sofia.

Balkantourist, State Tourist Office at 37 Dondukov Boulevard, Sofia.

US Embassy at 1 Alexander Stamboluski Boulevard, Sofia.
(Tel: 88 48 01).

British Embassy at Boulevard Marshall Tolbukhin 65–67, Sofia
(Tel: 88 53 61).

Czechoslovakia

Population	14,000,000
Size	49,000 square miles
Capital	Prague, population 1,400,000
Government	Socialist Federal Republic
Religion	Both Catholic and Protestant
Language	There are two official languages: Czech (spoken in Bohemia and Moravia) and Slovak (spoken in Slovakia). Some English and German understood

To enter Czechoslovakia you must have a visa. The cost depends on your nationality (for instance, £3 for British subjects, £4 for Americans). You don't have to obtain your visa in your country of origin. You can get it at any Czechoslovak Embassy or Consulate in any country. But remember, *you cannot get it at the Czechoslovak border*.

Hitching is tolerated throughout the country. You're also allowed to sleep in the open, but you are not permitted to light a camp fire outside of a camping ground. If you do and you're caught you can be hit with a heavy fine.

All foreign tourists over the age of 15 are obliged to exchange $10 per day into local currency.

Important cities are **Brno, Bratislava** and **Prague**.

In Prague visit Hradčany Castle. From there you get a good view over the city. Architecture freaks will be particularly interested in the castle because it incorporates examples of just about every architectural style the city has ever known. Wander through the Old Town down to Old Town Square which is a good place to meet people. Have a look at the fabulous City Hall clock which gives a great, free clockwork show (what else!) on the hour. Museums worth seeing include The National Gallery of Modern Art, the National Gallery and the Museum of Asian, African and American cultures.

Hotels can be expensive. For up-to-date information on youth lodgings contact the State Tourist Office either in Prague or in your home country.

Addresses

CKM, Travel Bureau of the Czechoslovak Youth and Student Travel at Zitna 12, Prague.

Cedok, State Tourist Office at Na Příkopě 18, Prague.

Prague Information Office at Na Příkopě 20, Prague.

US Embassy at Trziste 15, Prague (Tel: 53 66 41).

British Embassy at Thunovska 14, Prague I (Tel: 53 33 47).

East Germany

It is possible to hitch from West Germany through the East to West Berlin but this must be done with one ride which you pick up at the border. Full details of this in the section on *West Germany*. My letters to the East Germans requesting information about their country and any regulations which may be in force about hitch-hiking were not answered. I don't think they like the idea.

Hungary

Population	10,500,000
Size	35,900 square miles
Capital	Budapest, population 2,000,000
Government	Socialist People's Republic
Religion	Mostly Roman Catholic and Protestant.
Language	Hungarian. Some English understood in tourist areas

There's no problem entering Hungary, but the trip can be a bit expensive. You need a visa which you can buy usually within a day or two from any Hungarian Embassy or Consulate. (You can also get a visa at points of entry.) If you're just passing through Hungary you need a transit visa which is valid for a 48-hour stay. To get the transit visa you have to show that you have relevant entry visas for the countries you are about to visit which border Hungary.

Hitching is officially not permitted in Hungary, but there's plenty of it and you'd be very unlucky to be stopped.

Good places to visit are the **Lake Balaton** area, **Miskolc** and **Budapest.**

In Budapest see the Royal Castle, the ancient Church of Matthias, the Fisherman's Bastion and the Gellert Hill Citadel. Try the Museum of Fine Arts, the Hungarian National Museum and the Hungarian Folkloric Centre. Consider, as you walk around, that more than 30,000 buildings were wrecked in Budapest during its vicious World War II siege, and the work which has gone into restoration.

There are quite a few reasonably priced beds in the city. For details check with the tourist office.

Addresses

Express Youth and Student Travel Bureau, Szabadsagter 16, Budapest.

Tourist Information Service at Rákóczi 52, Budapest.

US Embassy at V. Szabadsag Ter 12, Budapest (Tel: 32 93 75).

British Embassy at Harmincad Utca 6, Budapest (Tel: 18 28 80).

Poland

Population	34,000,000
Size	121,000 square miles
Capital	Warsaw, population 1,300,000

Government Independent People's Republic
Religion Roman Catholic
Language Polish. A little German and English understood

To enter Poland you need a valid passport and a tourist visa which costs around 120 zloty. If you're just passing through you have to buy a transit visa worth around 150 zloty which is valid for 3 days. To get the transit visa you have to show that you have any necessary entry visas for the neighbouring country. In addition you have to change a certain amount of money for each day of your stay in Poland. The amount depends on your nationality. For instance an American has to change about £5·50 per day, an Englishman £4 per day. However, people who will be camping and can show that they belong to a camping club, and people with student cards, can change less. Write to the nearest Polish Consulate or Embassy for up-to-date info on visas and compulsory exchange.

As for hitch-hiking, it seems that the Poles are definitely on your side. The situation is best explained by Jerzy Gajewski from Krakow who sent in the following letter for the information of all hitchers who want to hit Poland:

'*In Poland there are special hitch-hiking booklets with coupons to pay drivers. You buy them at the Polish Tourist Association shop for 40 zloty or in the sportsclubs or tourist offices. You go 2,000 kilometres on the book and then buy a new one. The book is valid for one year.*

When the holiday season is over the drivers send the coupons to Warsaw to the Auto-Stop Committee. Those who send the biggest numbers are awarded prizes. This idea was started thirteen years ago and has proved a great success.' Jerzy adds: '*Right now I want to thank all the European drivers who took my friends and me in their cars.*'

Theoretically then, there'll be cars pranging into each other in their attempts to get to you first. Wouldn't you like to believe it . . .

Important cities to visit are **Gdansk**, **Krakow** (the only major Polish city not destroyed in the second war) and, of course, **Warsaw**.

Warsaw was wrecked in the war, but you'd never know it as you wander around today. Many of the 'old' buildings you see have only been built since the war – based on the original plans which somehow survived the holocaust. See the lovely, restored streets of the Old Town, see the Historical Museum and National Museum. If you're a music buff you'll want to drop in on the Chopin Museum. Visit Castle Square and the Royal Castle. Have a look at the Heroes of the Warsaw Ghetto Monument – and contemplate what happened.

Even student accommodation is expensive in Warsaw. Get the latest info from student organizations and tourist offices.

Addresses

Polish Association of Youth Hostels at Chocimska 28, Warsaw.

Almatur (Travel and Tourism office of the Polish Students Association) at Ordynacka 9 and Krakowskie Przedmiescie 24, Warsaw.

Polish Tourist Association at Swietokrzyska 36, Warsaw.

US Embassy at Al. Ujazdowskie 29/31, Warsaw (Tel: 28 30 41).

British Embassy at Aleja Roz 1, Warsaw (Tel: 28 10 01).

Rumania

Population	21,000,000
Size	91,700 square miles
Capital	Bucharest, population 1,500,000
Government	Socialist People's Republic
Religion	Mainly Rumanian Orthodox
Language	Rumanian, with English and French understood in tourist areas

Rumania is easy to enter, but you must buy a tourist visa (check in London for current prices), and you must change $10 for each day you are in the country with a minimum of 3 days. Further, you cannot change back the money you have changed.

Hitching is permitted throughout the country, but the comment was added by the official I spoke with that: 'The population is not very familiar with this custom, so things might be a little slow.'

Important cities to visit are **Deva** (sample the brandy!), **Brasov, Cluj** and **Bucharest**.

In Bucharest try and visit the Folk Art Museum and the Village Museum with its collection of genuine peasant houses which have been brought from all over the country and reconstructed. Stroll down the Calea Victoria, one of the main streets, for a taste of modern Bucharest, and for a more relaxed walk go into the marvellous Cismigiu Gardens where you'll have a good chance to meet up with students and other travellers.

Addresses

National Tourism Office at 7 Boulevard Magheru, Bucharest.

BTT Youth Tourist Office at Onestix 4–6, Bucharest.

American Embassy at Strada Tudor Argezhi 9, Bucharest (Tel: 12 40 40).

British Embassy at Strada Jules Michelet 22–24, Bucharest (Tel: 11 16 34).

Russia

Population	242,000,000
Size	8,700,000 square miles
Capital	Moscow, population 7,200,000
Government	Union of Socialist Republics
Religion	Officially atheist. Varying degrees of toleration towards Russian Orthodox, Catholic, Protestant and Jewish congregations
Language	Russian is the official and great unifying language, but there are more than 100 dialects used throughout the country Some English, German and French understood in larger cities

Everyone I have ever met who has visited Russia has told me that the country is great and that the people are fantastic and that they want to go again. But when I've asked about the procedure for entering the country they've clammed up, not through a lack of willingness to answer my question, but through pure confusion.

This is a quotation from a pamphlet issued by the Russian Tourist Organization, INTOURIST, which describes how people based in Britain get themselves a Russian Tourist Visa:
'Tourist, Transit and Business Visas are obtainable through travel agencies. Applications must be supported by:

1 a valid passport;
2 a completed visa application form.
Note: In Section 1 of the visa application form, the SURNAME should be underlined.

In Section 6 ALL towns to be visited in the USSR should be entered together with dates of entry and exit, and purpose of journey.

3 three recent passport size photographs (approximately $1\frac{3}{4} \times 1\frac{1}{2}$ inches or $4 \cdot 5 \times 4$ cms) on a white background.

All documents and passport(s) must be submitted through a travel agency *not later than seven days* before date of entry into the USSR. In June, July,

232 The Communist countries

August and September, it is advisable to apply for visas as early as possible to avoid delay. *No charge is made for visas.*

If tourists wish, they may apply for a Soviet visa in person. In this case, in addition to the documents mentioned above, they should give the Soviet Consulate in London (5 Kensington Palace Gardens, London W8, Tel: 229 3215/6, open Monday to Friday, 10 a.m. to 12.30 p.m.) a voucher from a travel agency with the number of INTOURIST (Moscow) confirmation on it.'

Got it? Right. Believing that some brave souls might still want to hitch-hike – presuming they think they can guarantee the dates of entry and exit to the towns they wish to visit – I wrote to INTOURIST asking if hitching was permitted in Russia. The answer didn't say yes or no, but went as follows, 'with reference to your letter . . . we would like to advise you that taking into consideration the distances in the USSR we do not encourage tourists to travel on a hitch-hiking basis.'

A later letter, which I wrote to INTOURIST asking about hitching, student hostels, etc, was answered like this: 'I am afraid that hitch-hiking is not permitted at all in the Soviet Union. Tourists must travel by air, rail or car. There are no hostels available to foreign tourists – they are accommodated in hotels, motels or camp sites. Camp sites are available to tourists travelling by car only, as they are often at some distance from railway stations, etc. There are no student concessions.'

An address to contact which may be able to offer you more hope than I can is:

Soviet Youth Travel Bureau 'SPUTNIK',
4 Lebyazhy Pereulok,
Moscow, USSR.

For anyone thinking of making a quick jaunt into Russia from Finland (there are plenty of tours at a variety of prices), the following are a selection of addresses to contact:

FINLAND STUDENT SERVICE,
Kampinkatu 4B, Helsinki 10.

FINNISH TRAVEL ASSOCIATION,
Mikonkatu 25, 00100 Helsinki 10.

FINLAND STEAMSHIP COMPANY,
E. Ranta 8, Helsinki.

It's a pity that things are so difficult in Russia. It's the largest country in the world (more than twice the size of the USA) and has some fantastic cities and sights. Perhaps things will get easier soon.

Addresses (in case you make it)

Soviet Youth Travel Bureau (Sputnik) at 4 Lebyazhy Pereulok, Moscow.

InTourist Travel Office at 16 Marx Prospekt, Moscow.

US Embassy at Ulitsa Chaykovskovo 19–23, Moscow (Tel: 252 00 11).

British Embassy at Naberezhnaya Morisa Toreza 14, Moscow (Tel: 231 95 55).

Yugoslavia

Population	21,000,000
Size	98,766 square miles
Capital	Belgrade, population 1,200,000
Government	Socialist Republic
Religion	Greek Orthodox, Muslim, Catholic, Protestant

No trouble entering Yugoslavia. A valid passport gets you a visa at your point of entry which will do you for 30 days. Check that things haven't changed before you head out.

Hitching is permitted and an accepted mode of transport amongst young Yugoslavs. Things get awfully tough, though, when you get into the outback, mountainous country. Officially you are only supposed to camp in camp grounds, but you'd be unlucky to get picked up. If you do camp out, best not light a fire.

The most important cities and towns outside of **Belgrade** are **Zagreb, Sarajevo, Ljubljana, Skopje, Split, Mostar** and **Dubrovnik.**

In Belgrade just wander around and enjoy what I think is one of the better planned city centres in Europe. Visit the gardens and fortifications of Kalemegdan and see the confluence of the Sava and Danube rivers from high up in the park. While you're up there have a look at the dramatically presented War Museum which tells the history of Yugoslavia through its centuries of invasion and battle. See also the Cathedral with its icons, the National Museum, and the Fresco Gallery with its fine collection of frescoes taken from ancient monasteries. In the evening wander down the street called Skadarlija, centre of what was once the old Bohemian part of Belgrade. It's a nice place to spend an hour and a good place to meet people, but be warned that restaurant prices there can be high.

Nearly all Yugoslav cities have youth hostels; and it's worth knowing that you can arrange accommodation in private homes.

Student Identity Card holders can get 25 per cent reductions on boat and train fares throughout the country. Check with the youth travel office (address below) for details.

Addresses

YÚS (For Youth Travel) at Mose Pijade 12, Belgrade.

Tourist Information Office at main railway station or in the Terazije Square pedestrian underground passage.

US Embassy at Kneza Milosa 50, Belgrade (Tel: 64 56 55).

British Embassy at 46 Ulica Generala Zdanova, Belgrade (Tel: 64 50 55).

★**Photography** Remember, in the Communist countries, to keep your camera pointed right away from military installations or anything which could be interpreted as such.

★**Drugs** If they catch you in the Communist countries it's goodbye world for a long, long time.

Hitchers' tips and comments

I find in most Communist countries you can only change back 50 per cent of the money you originally exchanged and only then with bank slips in hand to prove you changed the money in the first place. (Got that?) Best to change in small amounts so you don't get stuck with pockets full of East German marks, etc.

Jimmy Freedman, San Francisco, USA

With reference to the Yugoslav coast route. I suggest people *don't* take it unless they have stacks of time. It's really fantastic scenery, especially toward the south, but it took me *three weeks* of hell-for-leather hitching (I left a stack of leather behind, especially on the 69 km Lenj to Karlobag walk without a lift. My shoulder strap gave out and I had to use my tension strap as a replacement. Now my hip bones are a couple of centimetres narrower). I'm not unique. I've heard similar reports from other travellers.

M. Pickersgill, South Africa

Note *Several readers have written in to say that the Poles are interested in buying cheap pocket calculators. One guy claims he sold a calculator for 3,000 Zlotys which cost only 30 DM in West Germany – 500 per cent profit! Anyone got any more hints along these lines? K.W.*

10 Morocco and Northern Africa

Morocco

Population 15,000,000
Size 174,471 square miles
Capital Rabat, population 360,000
Government Constitutional Monarchy
Religion Moslem
Language Arabic. Spanish and French also official languages.
Some English and German spoken in tourist centres

Cheapest way to Africa is from Algeciras, in Spain, to Ceuta, which is the tiny Spanish colony just across from Gibraltar. Cost of this hour-long ferry ride is less than 250 pesetas. The Algeciras–Tangier ferry is three times more expensive.

Tetouan, just a few miles from Ceuta, is becoming a favourite stopping place for hitchers on their way south. At the moment it's not particularly tourist-minded and is a good place to enjoy your first glimpse of a Moroccan city. Plenty of mosques, a fairly good market section, and OK people.

Tangier, 45 miles away, is an out-and-out tourist town and every Arab in it is chasing the fast buck. Nevertheless it's worth a day and if you go down into the *medina*, go to the Petit Socco (the small square) where you can sit in the cafés and talk with Arab students and other hitchers.

Ketama, up in the Rif Mountains, is promoted by the Moroccan tourist office as the ideal area for nature-lovers. So it is. But it's also where a great proportion of Morocco's grass is grown – priced around £30 a kilo if you're a clever enough haggler (considerably cheaper than the 20p a gramme asked in the city areas). But to anybody thinking of buying a kilo, this book warns you strongly about the dangers of exporting the stuff. The Spanish officials at Algeciras do spot-checks on every boatload of tourists arriving. They do a lot of their checking on hitch-hikers. The ones they catch out get locked away for a few years.

Fez is an indispensable stop. One of the four Imperial Cities – the other three are Marrakesh, Rabat, and Meknes – it is actually three cities in one. The old city, Fes El Bali, is the one to head for. Here is one of the best market areas you'll find anywhere in the world; a tiny winding street some three kilometres long which probably hasn't changed much since the city was founded in AD 808. Scores of side streets lead off it creating such a maze that you can get lost by turning two corners. Deep in the *medina* you'll see people working at trades with implements as old as time; men hand-beating copper pots, sewing fine embroidery to kaftans, turning wood on string lathes worked with the toes, workers splattered with dazzling colours from the dye pots. Lots to see. Don't miss Fez!

Meknes, 60 kilometres west of Fez, although interesting, is a let-down. After Fez anywhere with the exception of Marrakesh is an anti-climax. But just north of the city are the ruins of the old Roman town of **Volubilis**.

Rabat is the capital of Morocco and has a fair amount to offer the wanderer. Linked by a bridge over the Bou Regreg to its sister city of **Sale** (once a pirate port), it has a good market area. See also the famous Tower of Hassan which was to have been part of the largest mosque in Islam, but was never finished, and the Mechouar, the Royal Palace.

Casablanca, like staid old Tangier, is no longer as rough as it was in the '30s and '40s when they made the great Humph Bogart movie. Nowadays it's a big bustling modern city and the main commercial centre in Morocco. But the old *medina* area is still intact and a delight to wander through.

Ask most people which is their favourite city in Morocco and you'll find it's a toss-up between Fez and **Marrakesh**. Marrakesh, called the 'pink city' because of the light which reflects from its ochre walls, has one great attraction which keeps visitors amused day after day and which has kept the Arabs amused for centuries. It's Djemma el Fna – the Place of the Dead – the great market-place which in the mornings handles most of the city's trading and where in the late afternoon jugglers, acrobats, snakecharmers, and storytellers come to entertain the crowds. See also the Koutoubia Mosque, with its 221-foot-high minaret and, just north of Djemma el Fna, the *medina* area which is nearly as good as the one in Fez.

Goulimime, way, way down south of Marrakesh, is where you see the famous Blue Men – desert nomads who have permanently blue-stained skin as a result of dye running from the robes they wear.

Beyond Goulimime the roads get very rough and if you're hitching on for any great distance (and the distances between towns can be very great) try and get aboard a truck. They go longer.

Hitching in Morocco is OK – particularly if you're a man and woman travelling together. The Arabs – a happy, easy-to-get-on-with bunch at any time – are very much taken by Western ladies, especially if they have long, blonde hair.

For people who want to head east across towards Egypt, the coastal road is good most of the way.

★**Haggling** It can't be stressed too much that a price asked in Morocco is merely a manner of beginning a discussion as to the true value of the object. That goes for beds too. In the *souks* (the markets) the general rule for bargaining is to offer slightly less than one half of what the seller is asking and then act like crazy until you've agreed to pay slightly over half, and even that will be too much. If you don't get a 30–40 per cent reduction, you can be sure that you're *really* being done! One of the best haggling techniques is to enter a shop in league with someone else. One of you expresses interest in the article, the other is non-committal. As the bargaining progresses the non-committal one becomes more and more bored, insisting it's time to go. At crucial moments during the bargaining the one who's doing the buying pretends that he has to go to keep his friend happy. This act, if well performed, gets the price down with a speed which is in exact proportion to the amount of concern felt by the seller that he may lose his sale altogether.

Morocco: where to sleep

Sleeping in Morocco presents no problems. In many cities you can have a really good bed with room service and the works for 15 dirhams. Cheap and dirty places, of which there are plenty, rarely charge more than 6 dirhams – and even this is an arguable matter. I have heard of beds going for two dirhams – but they're not for me. I've stayed in plenty of 6 dirham hotels and although sometimes they're fine, mostly they stink. Out on the roads, in the smaller towns like Ouezanne and Tetouan, you can find clean, first-class accommodation for 10 dirhams a head, while in the same places the cheap accommodation is *really* cheap! Prices in Marrakesh and Fez are going up as fast as tourists begin to discover Morocco and to counter this about the only hint that can be offered is to keep away from the tourist areas of the *casbahs* because hotels there are quite often *more* expensive than in European quarters.

Morocco: where to eat

How cheaply you can eat depends upon how strong your stomach is. Eat in the *casbah* where it is cheaper, of course, but you should take a little care in choosing your café. Go into something which doesn't look *too* filthy. Plenty of guys you meet in Morocco will tell you that *they're* never sick, but they might neglect to say that they've been living there for six months and that their stomachs are used to whatever it is stomachs get used to. Odds are that whatever you eat you're going to get a touch of diarrhoea, especially if you have a pampered American or English belly. Moroccan hygiene and European hygiene are two different things.

Prices are cheap. 6 or 7 dirhams should get you a good plateful of *cous-cous* with bread and a Coke to wash it down. Out on the streets the little *shishkebab* braziers sell one or two kebabs with bread for a dirham. If you're really broke, buy a couple of those and get yourself some fruit from the market and you can eat for around 3 or 4 dirhams.

In the big cities the water is generally OK to drink, but out on the road, in the small villages, you can't be so sure.

Transport in Morocco

In Moroccan cities, don't worry about jumping a bus. They're cheap! If you decide to take inter-city transport, buses are cheaper than trains, but as with everything else in Morocco it's hard to establish the correct price. I once checked around Tangier to find how much a bus ticket was to Fez. I asked at three different places; the tourist office, the bus-station, and at the bus itself. Each price quoted was different. I ended up hitching. If you do take a bus, try and get one of the 'peasant' buses. They're loaded with chickens, goats, and God-knows-what – and the Arabs are great travelling companions!

Addresses

Main Post Office (for Poste Restante) at Poste Principale, Rabat.

American Express, 26 Boulevard Mohammed El Hansali, Casablanca (Tel: 636 61). 10 Avenue du Prince Moulay Abdallah, Tangier (Tel: 382 46). 173 Avenue Mohammad V, Marrakesh (Tel: 302 83).

Student Union of Morocco at 55 rue Zayanes, Agdal, Rabat.

Moroccan Tourist Agency at 22 avenue d'Alger, PO Box 19, Rabat (Tel: 21252/53/54).

US Embassy at 2 Avenue de Marrakesh, Rabat (Tel: 303 61).

British Embassy at 28 bis Avenue Allah Ben Abdallah, Rabat (Tel: 314 03).

Because of tense political situations in some parts of North Africa, particularly Egypt, it is advisable to be well informed before you enter those areas. Also, in Egypt, Algeria, and Libya, don't even pretend to point your camera at anything which looks vaguely military.

Hitchers' tips and comments

The Marrakesh souk boys go insane over European gear like jackets, desert boots and printed T-shirts. I traded a pair of beat-up DBs for some shin-high embroidered Berber boots and I saw better deals than that.
Frank Scahill, Punchbowl, Australia

Take an extra watch or two if you're heading for Morocco, especially the very cheap but flashy kind you can pick up in the UK. It's a good investment. Just walk around with the watch you want to sell on your wrist. Eventually you'll be approached by a buyer who, after a lot of haggling, will give you double what you paid.

Watch out for thieves in Morocco. Once a Moccy's set his sights on your wallet or something, he'll sit up all night, if need be, to pinch it. Lots of tales of people having sleeping bags delicately cut open during the night and all possessions taken from inside. It's a way of life.
Clive Gill, Birchington, England

Algeria

Population	13,000,000
Size	919,590 square miles
Capital	Algiers, population 950,000
Government	Independent Republic under one-party military presidency
Religion	Moslem
Language	Arabic, with French widely spoken

Algiers is the capital of the country. See the old *casbah* area, the Mosque of Sidi Abd er Rahmane, the National Museum of Fine Arts with its collection of works by Arab artists, and the Moslem Cemetery of the Marabout.

Anyone feeling like a 1,250-mile trip into the desert might like to head to **Tamanrasset** which is due south of Algiers and the capital of the Taureg nomads. For just a whiff of the sand and of an oasis town, try **Laghouat**, 260 miles south of Algiers and on fairly good roads all the way.

Constantine is probably the most striking city in Algeria – it's surrounded by a 500-foot-deep gorge. See the 600-foot-high Sidi M'Cid suspension bridge, one of the highest in the world, and the Palace of El Hadj Ahmed. Go into the Place de la Breche in the centre to test the pulse of the city.

Addresses

US Embassy at Villa Mektoub, 4 Chemin Cheikh Bachir Brahimi, Algiers (Tel: 60 14 25 through 29 or 60 36 70 through 72).

British Embassy at Residence Cassiopee, Bâtiment B, 7 Chemin des Glycines, Algiers (Tel: 60 56 01).

Hitchers' tips and comments

Here's a bit of info about Algeria, which isn't as simple as it looks on the map. First of all, crossing the border from Morocco is very dodgy, for two reasons: the Algerians are in the middle of a political war with Morocco, hence they're wary of anyone coming across the border, and as they don't allow Moroccans to cross (and vice versa) there's not an awful lot of traffic; secondly, and rather more seriously, the Algerians will quite simply turn back *anyone* who tries to cross the border on foot, or who has a rucksack, or who seems to be hitching. We saw two guys (who looked perfectly straight) get turned back and heard stories of many, many more. The solution is fairly simple, however. In Oujda, the last Moroccan town, buy a large travel bag for about 15 dirhams in the market, and put all the contents of the rucksack inside. You'll just have to carry the frame loose. Then get a bus to the border (or hitch) and ask people at the customs post if they are willing to take you across. Pack all your luggage into their car and try to go through the border as though you're travelling with them, and don't make the slightest mention of hitching.

Once in Algeria, there are several things to note. First, the Moroccan attitude to tourists of I'm-going-to-do-you-if-I-can disappears completely, and everyone is willing to help, even offering us beds in their homes when we had nowhere to sleep. We were a bit wary at first but after a few days realized they meant it.
Andy Mitchell, Edinburgh, Scotland

Tunisia

Population	4,800,000
Size	63,380 square miles
Capital	Tunis, population 700,000
Government	Independent State under one-party presidential regime
Religion	Moslem
Language	Arabic, with French widely spoken

There are ferry connections from Naples to Tunis at £40 for a single third-class fare and from Palermo to Tunis at £30 for a single third-class fare. Also from Marseilles for £35.

Tunis, the capital, is a city of 750,000. Visit any of the old areas for the real thing – though the tourists are ruining the place now. Visit the Zeitouna Mosque and the Palace of Dar el Bey. For historians, just a few miles from the centre of Tunis are the ruins of **Carthage** which was defeated and destroyed by the Romans in 146 BC.

Sousse is fast becoming a tourist town, but is attractive nevertheless. See the catacombs where 15,000 second- and third-century Christians are buried. A couple of miles south is the fortified town of **Monastir** with its renovated Ribat fortress, while south again at **El Djem**, sitting alone on a plain, is the Colosseum of El Djem, the largest Roman building in North Africa.

Djerba is Homer's 'island of the Lotus eaters'. At the beautiful capital of **Houmt Souk**, you can see sponge-divers plunging 50 feet deep, using rock ballast.

Kairouan, 60 kilometres inland from Sousse, is known as 'the mother of cities' and 'Kairouan the holy' for it is the sacred city of Tunisia and amongst its 89 mosques is the Great Mosque of Sidi Okba, the fourth most important in all of Islam. See also the Bir Barouta Well, the waters of which are said to meet and mingle with the waters of the holy well of Zemzem in Mecca, and the *souks*, especially those of the carpet-makers.

In **Dougga**, set in wild moorland to the west of Kairouan, wander through ruins of almost complete Greek and Roman towns.

At **Matmata**, on the edge of the Sahara, three-quarters of the 9,000 population live in caves. Locals are delighted to show you through their troglodyte homes.

Addresses

US Embassy at 144 Avenue de la Liberté, Tunis (Tel: 282 566 or 282 549 or 258 559).

British Embassy at 5 Place de la Victoire, Tunis (Tel: 245 100).

★A cheap way of getting around is to share seats in a *louage*. This is a sort of long-distance taxi that can be flagged down like a bus as long as there's a spare seat going. They go all over the country and each town and village has its main *louage* stop. Passengers share costs. (Similar to the *dolmus* in Istanbul.)

Libya

Population	2,000,000
Size	679,358 square miles
Capital	Tripoli (population 350,000) and Benghazi (population 200,000) are co-capitals
Government	Proclaimed as the Libyan Arab Republic
Religion	Moslem
Language	Arabic, Italian widely understood

Tripoli ('the shores of Tripoli' is relevant to the US Marines' action against the Libyan Pirates) is a city of 350,000 people. Several good mosques to see, several interesting museums, plus the Arch of Marcus Aurelius which dates from AD 163. See the castle and the market of Suk-el-Mushir.

Close by (60 miles east along the coast road) you come to the ancient Roman city of **Leptis Magna,** one of the least visited but best preserved Roman cities in existence.

A couple of hundred miles inland, through a stark desert landscape, you come to the oasis city of **Ghadames,** which sits right at the point where the territories of Tunis, Algeria, and Libya converge. This is a Taureg city, focal point of desert caravans, and one of the most fascinating in Africa. Strongly recommended to anyone searching for *real* Arab flavour.

As a startling contrast, **Benghazi,** which was savagely mauled in the Second World War, is a city of wide streets and with a completely modern aspect. Any students of the military (are there any left?) might like to visit the battlefields in the area surrounding the city or drop in on **Tobruk,** near the Egyptian border, and which was the scene of a siege and terrible fighting during the desert war. In Benghazi itself, however, you can see the Royal Palace and the Cathedral and search out shops which sell the famous Benghazi rugs.

Addresses

US Embassy at Garden City, Shari 'al Nsr, Tripoli (Tel: 34 021 or 320 26).
British Embassy at 30 Trig Alfatah, Tripoli (Tel: 31 191).

Egypt

Population	33,000,000
Size	386,660 square miles (including Sinai Peninsula)
Capital	Cairo, population 4,500,000
Government	Independent State under one-party presidential regime
Religion	Moslem
Language	Arabic, with English widely understood

Cairo is the big focal point of any Egyptian trip. This city of 5,000,000 was founded in the tenth century, but **Giza**, just a few miles out, is considerably older and the site of the famed Pyramids and the Sphinx. The Pyramid of Cheops is the largest of the three at Giza, standing 446 feet tall and having a base of 740 feet on each side. It covers 12 acres and contains more than 2 million blocks of stone, each weighing around $2\frac{1}{2}$ tons. Visit the Tomb of Cheops, right in the centre of the mammoth. The Sphinx, near the Pyramids, was built at about the same time – 2700 BC. See, in Cairo itself, the Alabaster Mosque which has one of the most startling interiors you'll find in any religious building anywhere. Also in the Citadel area you can see a City of the Dead, a cemetery built like a miniature town. The Egyptian Antiquities Museum has the best collection of its type in the world, including the fantastic treasure removed from the tomb of Tutankhamun.

Alexandria, which was founded in 331 BC by Alexander the Great, was once the centre of both Greek and Egyptian culture. These days it's a busy port city. See Pompey's Pillar, the Catacombs of Kom Al-Shoqafa (only rediscovered seventy-five years ago), the Greco-Roman Museum and the Ras-at-Tin Palace. West of Alexandria are the battlefields of **Alamein** and east, **Rashid**, where the famous Rosetta Stone which gave scholars the clue to translating hieroglyphics was discovered in 1799.

The **Nile** trip is one of the most exciting you can undertake. There is plenty of traffic all the way down to **Luxor** and there's also the possibility of hitching rides on river transport. In and around Luxor, a town of 5,000 people near the site of ancient **Thebes**, you can see a fantastic collection of buildings dating back to 1500 BC, many of them still in first-class condition even down to the paint on their walls. See the Valley of the Kings and the Valley of the Queens, the Karnak Temples, the Temple of Luxor, the Tombs of the Nobles, and the Funerary Temples of the Kings.

The beautiful *Abu Simbel Temple*, which was built by Rameses II 3,000 years ago is situated 160 miles south of **Aswan** which is 150 miles south of Luxor. The 400,000-ton temple has been cut into sections and relocated 200 feet up a mountainside to save it from being submerged in the Nile as a result of dam works. The area is not easily reached by hitching.

Addresses

US Embassy at 5 Sharia Latin America, Cairo (Tel: 28 219).

British Embassy at Kasr El Doubara, Garden City, Cairo (Tel: 20 850).

11 Turkey and the Middle East

Turkey

Population	37,925,000
Size	301,381 square miles
Capital	Ankara, population 1,200,000
Government	Republic
Religion	Moslem
Language	Turkish. Some English and French understood in large cities

When you cross the Bosporus at Istanbul you've reached Asia. More than that, you are entering the area which archaeologists are now considering as the cradle of civilization, for in 1960, at **Hacilar** in the south-west of Turkey, a village was discovered which dates back to 6000 BC.

In a country where there is so much to see merely by wandering from any town to any town, the outstanding cities, after Istanbul, must be Izmir, Ankara, and Konya. The two indispensable historical sites to visit are Troy and Ephesus.

Troy (or Truva) is just a few miles south of **Canakkale** and a dream for any student of history. Discovered in the nineteenth century by Heinrich Schliemann who used the writings of Homer in his efforts to locate it. Troy was previously considered only a legend. Excavations have now shown that no less than nine successive settlements were made on the site, the oldest dating back 5,000 years, the most recent to 280 BC. Homer's Troy was on the seventh level – around 1200 BC.

Izmir, about a day's hitching from Troy and situated beautifully on the Aegean Sea, is known as 'the Garden of the Gods'. Dating from eleven centuries before Christ, its history has been so rough that there are not as many ancient remains to be explored as you might think. It was destroyed in 600 BC and some time later rebuilt by Alexander the Great, then in AD 178 was destroyed by an earthquake and rebuilt by Marcus Aurelius. Then it was bashed around by the Crusaders, and after that by internal strife and then finally, between 1919 and 1922, it was occupied by the Greeks and once more badly damaged. Ataturk, the greatest man in modern Turkish history and first President of the Republic, took it from the Greeks in 1922 and reconstructed it. Things to see include Ataturk's house, the Agora (the ancient Roman market-place), the Kadifekale Castle from which you have a tremendous view over the city, and the Caravanserais, the ancient inns where the caravans from the east rested during their journeys.

Three kilometres from **Seljuk** (where you can see the tomb of the Apostle John) are the ruins of **Ephesus**. Dating from 2,000 BC, successive generations of Greeks, Romans, and Turks have all left memories of their stay. See the Arcadian Street, more than a quarter of a mile long, once the main street in the old city. See the Stadium where the gladiators fought, see the Gymnasiums, the Odean, the Agora and the gigantic theatre which can hold 24,500 people. Have a look at the Cave of the Seven Sleepers where, legend tells, şeven Christians and their dogs slept for 200 years and then awoke. And seven kilometres away, on Mount Aladag, see the House of the Virgin Mary where Mary is said to have lived after the death of Christ. The water which runs beneath the house is supposed to have healing properties and in 1963 the Pope declared the house a place of pilgrimage.

At **Bodrum** you can see the Castle with its tremendous collection of artifacts raised from the ocean bed. Bodrum was once the home of King Mausolus and here stood his famed Mausoleum, one of the Seven Wonders of the World before it was destroyed in an earthquake. (A second Wonder of the World stood near Ephesus. It was the Temple of Artemis which was four times bigger than the Parthenon. Now only a few columns stand. A third Wonder stood on the Greek island of Rhodes – just a couple of hours by sea from Marmaris – the Colossos of Rhodes.)

Marmaris, a semi-tourist town, makes a pleasant stop for a day. Beautiful beaches to swim from and sleep on and ancient rock tombs to visit.

Fethiye, yet another town so ancient that its origins are buried in legend, has rock tombs much more spectacular than those at Marmaris.

All along the Mediterranean coast lie dozens of villages and towns worth visiting, but it's when you start heading inland along the E24 that you end up in the *really* strange places – places where you may even get rocks thrown at you because you look different. The rock throwing is mostly an attention-getting device (though not always) and if you keep cool and play it by ear you won't have much trouble.

Good cities to visit in this area of south-east Anatolia include **Urfa**, one of the oldest cities in the world, with its fantastic fortress and pools of mysterious Holy water; **Mardin** (near the Syrian border) with its ancient monastery and nearby ruins of **Hasankeyf**, capital of the ancient kingdom

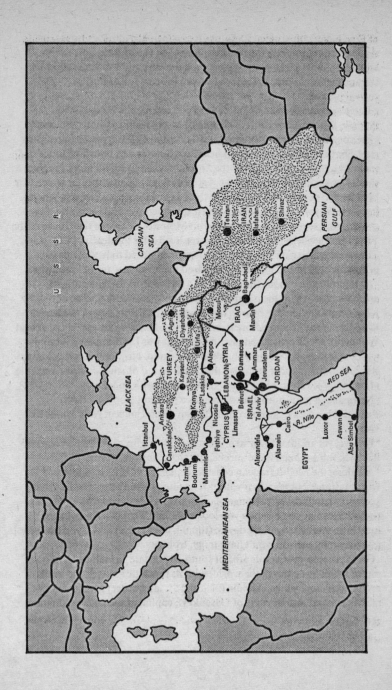

of Eyyub, and **Diyarbakir** where the beautiful walls of the old city intrude amongst the more modern buildings and where you can see the Ulu Mosque, considered one of the greatest in Islam.

Up in East Anatolia, if you have the money and the time to go so far, you might want to visit **Agri**, the site of Mount Agri, or Ararat where, according to ancient writings, Noah's Ark is said to rest. And if you get that far, just 100 kilometres away are the borders of Russia and Iran.

Heading west again, back to something which you'll recognize as civilization, you can travel through **Malatya** (merely 3,500 years old) on your way to **Kayseri**, known as the 'City of Mausoleums'. Plenty to see in the way of mosques and monuments and a nice town to wander in.

Konya, south-west on Highway 73, is a city with its origins in prehistoric times. St Paul visited three times, making it an important centre for Christianity. Tremendous choice of sights to visit.

Ankara, 200 kilometres north of Konya on the E5, is a city of more than a million people and the capital of Turkey. The exact age of the city is not known though it probably dates from the third century BC. Amongst the many things to be seen are the Ankara Citadel, the Temple of Augustus, the Haci Bayram Mosque and the Anit-Kabar which is the Mausoleum of Ataturk. Also have a look at the Hittite Archaeological Museum, perhaps the best in the country.

Hitching in Turkey, though not as fast as in some countries, is not all that bad, though the farther east you go the less cars there are. But don't worry you'll get used to waiting. Anywhere off the main roads can be very slow, but with buses as cheap as they are you can't drop much money by buying a ticket.

★**Camel wrestling** For one of the oddest sights you're likely to see anywhere, try and find yourself a real, live, genuine camel-wrestling match. Mostly found in the Aegean region. You might try the town of Denizli, which is on the E24 when you turn in from the coast. Around this area you can also find *cock-fighting*.

★**Greasy wrestling** Those interested in watching the strong-arms indulging in the famous Turkish wrestling in which contestants are covered from head to foot with oil should stop off at Edirne, just over the Bulgarian border. It is one of the main centres for the sport.

★**Language** Not an easy one. But try these few words:
Yes – *Ev-et*   No – *Yok*
Please – *Luf-ten*   Thanks – *Tes-ek-er-ed-erim*

★**Hitching** Sometimes in the more rural areas of Turkey you are expected to pay if you hitch. This idea of playing taxi seems to particularly appeal to Turkish truckies. So be careful, and if it happens haggle like hell!

★**For lady hitchers only** Sounds crazy to say it, but lots of ladies don't seem to realize that what gives in Europe or the States just ain't on when you're in the east. For instance, going bra-less under garments like light cotton Afghan shirts. In Istanbul you'll barely (so to speak) get away with it. Further east you could be heading for trouble. Men and women are pretty well closeted from each other in less sophisticated areas of Asia and the sight of blatant, bouncing boobies can be enough to make a local consider you a walking invitation.

Istanbul: where to sleep

You have to try hard to spend more than 24 or 30 lira for a bed in Istanbul. The cheapest areas are found on the European side of the city, up around *Sultanahmet*, which is the oldest section. The *Eminonu* section, behind the railway station, is also a good bet for centrally located and dirt-cheap hotels. Don't pay the first price on any room offered to you – bargain hard and you'll save about 10 per cent. Prices in better-class places are controlled by the government.

Istanbul: where to eat

Eat anywhere. 16 lira should give you a *big* meal! *Eminonu* is a good area for cheap cafés and restaurants. There's nothing more to be said on the matter – Turkey provides the cheapest eating in Europe.

For a nice breakfast, wander down to the stalls at the Galata Bridge and have a freshly caught fish which will be grilled while you wait.

As to what you'll be eating in the cheap restaurants, don't worry too much. Make appropriate sign language and the waiter will take you into the kitchen so you can see what's cooking.

LAHMASIN is like a pizza.

KOFTE is a meatball dish.

BALIK is fish.

HELVA is a sweet.

SISKEBAB is a shishkebab.

KAHVE is coffee.

Istanbul: what to see and do

THE MOSQUES There are over twenty mosques in Istanbul, and if you have never visited one it's worth going. The main ones are the *Sultanahmet Mosque* (known as the Blue Mosque) and *Saint Sophia* and *Suleymaniye*.

DOLMABAHCE PALACE Built in 1854 it is a fine example of Turkish architecture mixed with European. The famous TOPKAPI PALACE is considered one of the great buildings of the world. It was started in the fourth century and continually added to until the nineteenth. It contains fabulous collections of jewels and porcelain.

KAPALI CARSI (The Covered or Grand Bazaar) is the world's most famous market. Once you could really pick up a bargain. These days you have to be a little more careful. But look carefully and haggle hard. You might do OK.

MISIR CARSISI is the Spice Bazaar, also known as the Egyptian Bazaar. It's covered, like the Grand Bazaar, though not nearly as big. But the best attraction is not the bazaar itself but the streets all around which are packed out with sellers flogging everything you can think of. I like it better than the Grand Bazaar – one reason being that there are very few tourists in the area (unlike the Grand Bazaar which is crawling with them); thus you can find a much better deal if you need to buy something. I've said it a couple of times already in this chapter but I'm saying it again: *bargain* for *everything*. *Never* accept the first price. Example: I found a little metal ikon I really wanted. The junk seller who had it asked me 180 lira. I talked with him for fifteen minutes and offered him 20. He laughed and said he'd consider 150. I rolled around on the ground a bit and came up to 40. Then I couldn't budge him, so I left and came back an hour later. A bit more talking and he was down to 140 and I was up to 60. To cut it short, two visits and a lot of mirth later we agreed at 100. I'm sure, even so, a better bargainer would have got it for 75, but it was a lovely piece and I didn't want to risk losing it. But here's the sequel: next day in the Grand Bazaar I found another ikon exactly the same. Asking price? 700 liras!

THE MUSEUM OF TURKISH AND ISLAMIC ART in the Suleymaniye Mosque building. See the incredible carpet collections. Also a beautiful collection of ancient books and manuscripts.

THE ARCHAEOLOGY MUSEUM is worth a visit to see the relics of ancient Troy and the tomb of Alexander the Great.

BOAT TRIP ON THE BOSPORUS Don't take any of the advertised tours.
Go down to the Galata Bridge and pick your own tour on a regular ferry
route. Plenty of trips to choose from and one lasting a couple of hours
will cost you 10 or 12 lira return. Try the run to **Sariyer** which takes you by
the old fortress of Rumelihisar and, opposite it on your right, the smaller
fortress of Anadoluhisar. Ferry riding the Bosporus makes for one of the
cheapest and most pleasant outings anywhere in Europe (or Asia, because
the boats stop on the Asian side, too).

SULTANAHMET SQUARE Most hitchers and van travellers eventually
find themselves in Sultanahmet. It's the great stopping place for people
heading east and those coming from the east. This is where you can get
route information for the big India trip, or pick up a van ride to Kabul
for around £25–£30. From Sultanahmet you can join an economy bus
heading back to London for only £25. In Sultanahmet you can put up
a notice in the *Puddin Shop* or in *Yeners* (Yener calls himself The King of
the Hippies) if you need to sell something to raise a bit of cash. But in
Sultanahmet you can also get yourself in one hell of a lot of trouble.
It's a weird place. It's just a stone's throw from the Blue Mosque and the
Saint Sophia Mosque and thus one of the most heavily populated tourist
sites in Europe. But it's also one of the roughest joints in Europe. It makes
Soho look like a Sunday-school. If someone asks if you want to buy dope
tell him to get screwed, if he asks you to change money tell him to get
screwed. If you do either of those things with someone who hasn't been
vouched for as 100 per cent straight you're running an odds-on chance of
doing business with a police informer – who'll be getting a nice little
rake-off for dropping you in the shit. (The 'shit' in Turkey meaning about
six years.) Otherwise an OK place. Cheap food, cheap rooms, cheap travel,
lots of people and lots of information.

MOVIES Films are shown in original language with Turkish subtitles.
Tickets are cheap. Student cards get you a 50 per cent discount at
afternoon shows.

Warning! It's not only dope-peddlers, black-marketeers and police who
cause you trouble in Sultanahmet Square. Keep an eye on some of your
fellow-hitchers, too. Some of the freaks passing through are nasties.
They keep alive by stealing anything from anyone stupid enough
to leave stuff unguarded.

Transport in Istanbul
It's all cheap. Cheapest are the buses. Then comes the *dolmus* which can

only be described as a communal taxi. It usually costs about 25 per cent more than the bus fare and runs on routes roughly the same as the bus. What you get for your 25 per cent extra is a quicker trip and much more comfort. Some of the *dolmus* cars have the word painted on them, but most look exactly like a taxi. Therefore you should always check before you get in whether it's a *dolmus* or a taxi. A taxi will cost you ten times the fare! If you *do* have to take a taxi, remember the old rule. Bargain! (Yes, even for taxis! They all have meters but they are never switched on.) Something under half the price you're quoted will be about right. If you feel like taking a trip out of the city, don't worry about the price of trains. They're dirt cheap.

Student discounts
Cut prices on most transport between cities, cut prices on ferry boats. Reduction at certain cinemas and theatres. (Theory and practice are two different things in Turkey – but try your luck anyway.) For information:

TMTF,
Babiali Caddesi 40, Cagaloglu-Istanbul (Tel: 22 93 16).

Addresses

Main Post Office (for Poste Restante) at Büyük Postane, Istanbul.

American Express at Hilton Hotel, Istanbul (Tel: 48 39 05).

National Students Federation of Turkey, Travel Department (TMTF) at Babiali Caddesi 37, Cagaloglu-Istanbul (Tel: 22 93 16).

Tourist Office at Galata Yolcu Salonu, Galata (maritime station), Istanbul (Tel: 49 57 76).

US Embassy at 147 Mesrutiyet Caddesi, Istanbul (Tel: 45 32 20).

British Embassy at Tepebasi, Beyogw, Istanbul (Tel: 44 75 40).

Hitchers' tips and comments
In Turkey, as you cross the border you are allowed to buy duty-free cigarettes and booze in special shops. These can be resold in the Grand Bazaar at almost double price. Some currencies can be changed on the black market at a rate of almost 25 per cent better than the quoted rate. To do the deal all you have to do is walk along one of the main streets looking like a tourist and you will be approached. Make sure you ask

double what you are offered before dropping down about a third more than you were offered because all Turks like to bargain.
Phillip Bennett, London W.1

When I was in Istanbul the black market was hardly worth playing. Perhaps I was hitting bum information. But I want to make a point here I've hammered before. If you want to play the black market don't play it with someone who approaches you! Play it with someone you approach. That lessens the odds of that someone being a police informer (though it doesn't guarantee the fact!) This approach to the black market, or to buy anything else which is slightly illegal, is particularly important in Turkey and Morocco. See my comments about Sultanahmet Square. K.W.

Warning about Sultanahmet Square well taken. Also, I suggest a very strong warning to female hitchers in that country! Young English chap told me recently the cops cleaned out an entire fleabag near Sultanahmet Square and locked them all up for a week. No charges. No explanations. And many other such tales, especially against those unwise enough to camp in the open.
Unsigned, South Kensington, London

The stories keep coming through about Istanbul. Dirty noses are getting wiped out every day. Remember, if you get arrested anywhere for anything, it's the duty of your local consul to help you – that is, if he knows you've been arrested. Most countries will inform your consul if you're in a local prison, but some of the outback places don't bother. All you can do – if they won't let you near a phone – is to play it very cool and try and get a message out. While we're on the subject – if a cop at a station or a guard in a prison starts provoking you or roughing you up, don't fight back. If you do, that's the only excuse they need to bring the heavies and draw the truncheons. Just keep smiling and if you can't do that try and keep your head and balls protected. K.W.

When entering Turkey your driver will get a special stamp in his passport which shows he brought in a car. Make sure you don't get the same stamp! If you do, you won't be able to leave because customs officials will think you've sold an imported car in Turkey.
Peter Nash, Chelmsford, England

Istanbul. Point taken about Sultanahmet. For those wanting to sell duty-free stuff in the Grand Bazaar, Dunhills and whisky are the best sellers (100–150% profit).
Marcel Thomas, Horndean, England

Cyprus

Population	669,000
Size	3,572 square miles
Capital	Nicosia; population 120,000
Government	Republic
Religion	Greek Orthodox
Language	Greek and Turkish, with English widely used

The approximate cost of a one-way ticket to the island of Cyprus from Marmaris in Turkey is around £30, including port taxes. That is the summer rate. Winter rates are cheaper. People holding student cards are entitled to a reduction on most lines.

Nicosia, with a population of 120,000, is the capital of the island. See the excavated treasure in the Cyprus Museum and, in the fine old section, visit the former Cathedral of Santa Sophia, now the Selimiye Mosque.

Famagusta has a population of 38,000 and is the island's main port. Visit the old city and see the huge citadel identified with Othello's tower in Shakespeare's play.

Limassol is the second city of the island and although most of the old town is gone there is just enough left to give a whiff of what it must have been like. In the castle, Richard the Lion Heart married Berengaria, and it was the same castle which was the Headquarters of the Knights Templar and the Knights of St John.

Larnaca is said to have been founded by the grandson of Noah and has many religious associations, including the tomb of Lazarus who, according to legend, came to Cyprus after having been resurrected by Christ. Three miles outside Larnaca there is a very important monument of the Islamic world – the shrine of Hala Sultan who was a female relative of the prophet Mohammed.

Kyrenia is a small and very attractive seaside town with a beautiful old harbour fringed with cafés. It also boasts three castles. **St Hilarion**, which stands high above the city, is really spectacular and worth climbing up to see.

A really worthwhile expedition is to the ruined Gothic abbey of **Bellapais**, 3½ miles from Kyrenia and open, in summer, from 7 a.m. to 6 p.m.; in winter, from 8 a.m. to 5 p.m.

Addresses

US Embassy at Therissos Street and Dositheos Street, Nicosia (Tel: 65 151).

British Embassy at British High Commission, Alexander Pallis Street, PO Box 1978, Nicosia (Tel: 731 31).

Because of the continually tense political situation in the Middle East, it is necessary, if you are contemplating a trip to the area, to keep yourself well informed on what is happening. The best way to do this is through your embassy or consulate. Visas are needed in many countries.

Following is a brief summary of what there is to see in the Middle East countries.

Syria

Population	6,650,000
Size	71,498 square miles
Capital	Damascus, population 850,000
Government	Republic
Religion	Moslem
Language	Arabic

Damascus, (population of over half a million) which dates back to 4000 BC, is the oldest continually inhabited city in the world. Its Grand Bazaar is one of the great visits in the Middle East. See also the Omayad Mosque with the tomb of St John the Baptist, the Azem Palace, the National Museum and the tomb of Saladin.

In **Aleppo,** second city of Syria, see the bazaars, the Museum of Aleppo and the Great Mosque. And see the ruined Convent of Simeon. There, fifteen centuries ago, St Simeon lived on the top of a pillar for twenty-seven years.

Palmyra, was once the most important city in Syria, is now only a village. But there is much to be seen, including the ancient cemeteries with their weird decorations, and the Citadel of the Ma'anites.

Krak des Chevaliers – the Castle of the Knights – is the best preserved Crusader Castle in the Middle East. It saw tremendous battles before the Arabs took it in 1271. Complete with moat, dungeons, drawbridge and all the rest, it's worth going out of your way to see. Situated several miles off the main *Tartus* to *Homs* Highway – but vehicles can reach it.

Latakia is a very ancient city which is now Syria's main port. Many ruins to see, including a Roman Triumphal Arch. North of the city is **Ras Shamra** where important excavations are being made.

Addresses

US Embassy at Chare (*Ave*), Mansour, Abu Rummanih, Damascus (Tel: 32 555).

British Embassy at Quarter Malki 11, Mohammed Kurd Ali St Imm Kotob, Damascus (Tel: 332 561).

Iran

Population	31,500,000
Size	636,300 square miles
Capital	Teheran, population 3,000,000
Government	Monarchy
Religion	Moslem
Language	Persian

Teheran, with a population of 3,000,000 and at an altitude of 4,000 feet, is the capital of Iran. See the bazaars and the museums. Visit the Mesjedeh Sepahsalar mosque, the only one still in use which non-Moslems may visit. See the Crown Jewels collection, including the largest uncut diamond in the world and the famous Peacock Throne. Just outside of town, visit the ancient city of **Rai,** once the capital of Iran.

Isfahan is the home of the Mosque of Madreseh, the Palace of the Shahs and another good bazaar area.

Shiraz is known as 'the city of roses, nightingales and poets' and is just 40 miles south-west of **Persepolis,** which is the ruined capital of ancient Persia. Here you can see the tombs of Darius and Xerxes and the ruins of fantastic palaces. One of the big archaeological sites of the world.

Addresses

US Embassy at 260 Avenue Takti Jamshid, Teheran (Tel: 824 001).
British Embassy at Avenue Ferdowsi, Teheran (Tel: 450 11).

Iraq

Population	10,000,000
Size	167,925 square miles
Capital	Baghdad, population 2,000,000
Government	Republic
Religion	Moslem
Language	Arabic

Baghdad is your genuine Arabian Nights city. See (from the outside unless you're a Moslem) the Kadhimain Mosque with its pure gold domes, the Abbassid Palace with its tremendous collection relating to the history of Islam, and visit the carpet market in the Covered Bazaar.

Babylon, ancient capital of the Babylonian Empire and site of the Hanging Gardens of Babylon, one of the Seven Wonders of the World, is 55 miles south of Baghdad. See Nebuchadnezzar's Procession Street, the Lion of Babylon and the throne room.

Mosul once had a much better known name – **Nineveh**. It sits on the west side of the Tigris River and has a million inhabitants. The ruins of Nineveh, which was destroyed in 612 BC, are on the east bank.

Addresses

US Embassy at Nidhal St, Baghdad (Tel: 961 38).

British Embassy at Sharia Salah ud-Din, Karkh, Baghdad (Tel: 321 21).

Lebanon

Population	3,100,000
Size	4,000 square miles
Capital	Beirut, population 1,000,000
Government	Republic
Religion	Half Moslem, half Christian
Language	Arabic, but English widely spoken

Warning! Check things out carefully before trying to enter the Lebanon. As we go to press, it's a dangerous place.

The Lebanon can be reached from Istanbul by sea, for about £36.

Beirut with a population of 1,000,000 is the capital, and can be very expensive if you're not careful. Things to see include the Al-Khodr Mosque where it is said St George slew the dragon, the National Museum and the Pigeon Grotto. To meet people, try the American University, the largest American educational complex outside the States. People from all over the world study there.

Baalbek, 35 miles north-east of Beirut, was the Heliopolis of the Greeks and Romans. Many of the ruins are equal to anything you can see in Rome. The Temple of Bacchus, built around AD 150, is outstanding.

Byblos is another ancient town, one so important to archaeologists that they have been excavating there since 1921, discovering successive layers of settlement dating back 7,000 years. Plenty to see if you like examining rocks and ruins.

Addresses

US Embassy at Corniche at Rue Aiv Mreisseh, Beirut (Tel: 361 800).
British Embassy at Avenue de Paris, Ras Beirut, Beirut (Tel: 22 15 50).

Israel

Population	3,200,000
Size	7,993 square miles
Capital	Jerusalem. The diplomatic capital is Tel Aviv population 400,000
Government	Republic
Religion	Jewish
Language	Hebrew, with English widely spoken

Israel can be reached by sea from Istanbul and from Marmaris.

Jerusalem, with its 400,000 inhabitants is the religious centre of Israel, and the events of its 4,000-year-long history have caused it to become a Holy City for Jews, Moslems and Christians. In the Old City you can see the Church of the Holy Sepulchre which has been built on the traditional site of Christ's crucifixion; the Garden of Gethsemane where Judas betrayed Christ; the mosque of the Dome of the Rock, an important Islamic shrine; and the Wailing Wall which featured so prominently in the 1967 war. In the New City you can visit Mount Zion, the holy hill where King David is buried and where it is said Christ celebrated the Last Supper; the Israel Museum where you can see the Dead Sea Scrolls; and the Mea Shearim Quarter, a world of its own where Orthodox Jews live exactly according to the laws of their religion.

Beersheba, the principal city in the Negev Desert, is a good place to see Bedouins. Every Thursday morning they hold a market.

Masada is best reached from Beersheba. This great rock which rises 1,700 feet above the western shores of the Dead Sea was the site of Herod's Palace and where the Zealots made their last stand against the Romans in AD 73. When the Romans finally took the fortress they found every man, woman, and child dead. They had killed themselves rather than go into slavery.

Tel-Aviv-Jaffa combined, make Israel's largest city. Jaffa, where Jonah is said to have been spewed out by the whale, was founded in 1500 BC. Adjoining Tel-Aviv was founded in 1909. See the bazaars in the old city and the fine modern museums and galleries in the new.

For details of working on *kibbutzim*, see the chapter *Working in Europe*.

Addresses

Main Post Office (for Poste Restante), Tel-Aviv-Yafo Post Office, 8 Heharash, Tel-Aviv.

American Express c/o Meditrad Ltd, 16 Ben Yehuda Street, Tel-Aviv (Tel: 546 54)

Israel Students' Tourist Association at 2 Pinsker Street, POB 4451, Tel-Aviv (Tel: 59 613).

Israel Students' Tourist Association at 8 Shmuel Hanagid Street, Jerusalem (Tel: 28 298).

Israel Information Office at 7 Rehov Mendele, Tel-Aviv (Tel: 22 32 66).

US Embassy at 71 Hayarkon Street, Tel-Aviv (Tel: 54 338).

British Embassy at 192 Rehov Hayarkon, Tel-Aviv (Tel: 24 91 71).

Hitchers' tips and comments

Warning! People are coming to Israel without a return ticket and with prices high and jobs hard to find they're getting stuck here. Also it seems that the British Embassy isn't feeling so charitable nowadays as it happens every summer.
Chris Clarke, London

First a word of warning to anyone who wants to work in a Kibbutz. Beware of some of the agencies who promise to fix everything up for you. If you're unlucky you may meet a shady operator who screws as much as he can out of you and when you arrive in Israel nobody wants to know about you.

Hitching seems to be slow in Israel unless you happen to be a soldier. There's an unwritten law giving them priority, and there are always hordes of them grabbing the best positions. I got stuck halfway between Tel-Aviv and Haifa and ended up getting the bus which was relatively inexpensive and preferable to standing in the sun all day.
Hugh Dunne, Dublin, Ireland

Jordan

Population	2,600,000
Size	37,738 square miles
Capital	Amman, population 400,000
Government	Monarchy
Religion	Moslem
Language	Arabic

Amman is the capital. See the Roman Theatre which seats 6,000 spectators, go up to the Citadel to see the ruined Temple of Hercules, see the Jordan Archaeological Museum and see the Circassian Guards outside the Basman Palace.

Jerash, just 20 miles north of Amman, has been called the Pompeii of the Middle East. Founded around 330 BC by Alexander the Great, it reached prominence in Roman times. Then, slowly, the sand piled up and it was all but forgotten until the 1920s when archaeologists went to work on the site. Plenty to see, including three theatres, two baths, innumerable churches and the remains of the huge Temple of Artemis.

Petra, halfway between Amman and Aqaba, a weird sight, and for 500 years – between the twelfth century and 1812 when it was accidentally rediscovered – it was a true lost city. 'Rose-red Petra' (and it really is) was founded in 300 BC by the Nabataean Arabs who took 500 years to carve it out of the solid rock of the mountains. After you've seen Petra you won't regret the desert journey you had to make to get there.

Addresses

US Embassy at Jebel Amman, Amman (Tel: 44 371).

British Embassy at Third Circle, Jebel Amman, Amman (Tel: 412 61).

12 Working in Europe

Members of EEC countries (i.e. Belgium, France, West Germany, Italy,
The Netherlands, Luxembourg, Denmark, Ireland and the United
Kingdom) can work in other EEC countries without a work permit except
in areas of public administration, but, otherwise, permits are usually
required for aliens. For example, a French girl trying to get employment
in Denmark would not need a work permit, but she must still obtain a
stamp on her passport from Danish immigration authorities establishing
actual residence in Denmark. If she wanted employment in a country
outside the EEC she would probably need a work permit. For all that
it should be noted that the theory and the practice of a national of an EEC
country working in another EEC country are two different things.
The tendency seems to be for employers to favour their countrymen.
Theoretically you may have equal rights to the job, but when it comes to
the practicalities of the situation you run up against a couple of barriers,
the most obvious one being the language problem.

A non-EEC member will almost certainly require a work permit
anywhere in Europe. Sometimes this permit has to be obtained by the
visitor before he enters the country in question, other times it must be
obtained by the visitor's employer after he has found a job. The rules and
regulations are generally so wound up in red tape, and change so often,
that the only sure way of finding out complete details on the subject, as they
apply at any particular time, is to write to the nearest tourist agency in
your own country or the country in which you hope to work.

Presuming that most English-speaking people would be seeking a job in
England, the following addresses are offered. These tourist agencies will
give you the information you need or put you in touch with the people
who have the information.

Americans should write to the British Travel Offices at:
680 Fifth Avenue, New York, NY 10019

John Hancock Center, Suite 2450, 875 N. Michigan Avenue,
Chicago IL 60611

612 South Flower Street, Los Angeles, Calif 90017.

Canadians should write to:
151 Bloor Street W, Suite 460, Toronto, Ontario, M5S IT3.
602 West Hastings Street, Vancouver 2, BC.

Australians should write to:
171 Clarence Street, Sydney, NSW 2000.

New Zealanders to:
Box 3655, 97 Tarank Street, Wellington.

And South Africans to:
Union-Castle Building, 36 Loveday Street, PO Box 6256, Johannesburg.
Union-Castle Building, 1st Floor, 51–55 St George's Street, Cape Town.

Every day people arrive at English points of entry, hoping to find work but
without enough money in their pockets to support themselves. Many of
those people, unless they have a work permit in their hands, are sent right
back from where they came. These work permits are getting harder and
harder to find and generally are only available to people who can fill jobs
which British workers can't. If you do get one it applies only to one specific
job.
  Check it all out before you leave home!
  As for other countries, the position, as at the time of writing, is roughly
this:

Warning! Beware of job-finding firms, particularly those which
guarantee you work in the world's most exotic corners after they've
received your £10 registration fee. Obviously not all – or even most –
job-finding firms are crooked, but during the last couple of years there have
been reports of fly-by-night operators who advertise heavily for a week,
rake in the loot and are never heard of again.

Austria

You must have a work permit to work. If you manage to contract for a
job before entering the country your employer is supposed to apply for a
work permit for you and then mail it to you. You then take it to the
Austrian Embassy in your area who will arrange a visa. If you find a job
while passing through Austria then you have to front up to the local
authorities and make application for a work permit from them. You don't

need a permit to work as an *au pair*. There's often work available in hotels and in ski-resorts. For fuller information students should contact:

Okista (Austrian Committee for International Educational Exchange), Türkenstrasse 4, 1090 Vienna, Austria.

Belgium

Work permits are needed for non-EEC members. However, unlike Austria where you are permitted to enter the country, seek a job and then apply for a permit, in Belgium you must have the job *before* you enter the country. Your employer will have applied for your permit and sent it to you and you will present it when you enter Belgium. For non-EEC members, work is hard to find.

Denmark

Work permits are no longer issued to nationals of non-EEC countries, except for a few marginal cases. EEC people can stay three months to look for a job after having first applied to local police for procedure for obtaining a residence permit. Students can try writing to:
Danish International Students Committee,
36 Skindergade, 1159 Copenhagen K, Denmark.

Finland

Work permits are needed before entering the country. Jobs are limited. For students, however, there is a fair chance of *au pair* work and also of entering the 'Family Scheme' programme where you live with a family, help with their daily work and also tutor them in the English language. For the latter there is free board and pocket money. Contact:

International Trainee Exchanges of the Ministry of Labour,
Kalevankatu 16,
PL 524, 00101,
Helsinki 10,
Finland.

France

Work permits are needed for non-EEC members. You can take it as a basic rule that non-students *and* students must have a work permit before they enter France. However, occasionally this rule is relaxed and students (*only* students) are permitted to enter the country, seek employment and after having found it make application to the local Department of Work for a work permit. When you make this application you will need the following documents: (1) valid passport; (2) student identification card; (3) a letter from your university or college establishing your *full-time* student status; (4) a letter from your proposed employer which will state his intention to employ you; (5) (if you are a minor) a written permission from your parents allowing you to enter France and work, witnessed by a member of a French Consulate or French Embassy. Jobs are not easy to find but there is some work available. For information about *au pair* work, farm work and grape picking try:

Vacation Work International,
9 Park End Street,
Oxford OX1 1HJ,
England.

West Germany

Work permits are needed for non-EEC members. You may find jobs available on factory assembly lines, on building projects, in the hotel and catering trades . . . in short, in unskilled areas. If you are bilingual you may find office work, but this is rarer. *Au pair* work is available. To find work you should get in touch with:

Zentralstelle für Arbeitsvermittlung
Feuerbachstrasse 42
0-6000 Frankfurt am Main, Germany

This is a government labour agency through which trades and businesses channel staff requests. The agency can put you in touch with possible employers. It will also give you full information on applying for a work permit.

Greece

Practically impossible to get a job unless it is with a foreign firm. That firm will apply for your work permit, which you must have. Information from any Greek National Tourist Office or, in Greece, from:
Ministry of Labour, 45 Piraeus Street, Athens.

Ireland

Work permit needed for non-EEC members, and if you enter the country with the stated intention of working, it must be shown at the border. You are supposed to arrange the job and have your employer apply for the permit.

Israel

As we go to press work permits must be obtained by your prospective employer before you enter the country, but you should contact the nearest Israel Tourist Office to make sure this remains true. The main work for young people is available on *kibbutzim*, for which you receive completely free board and replacements of worn-out clothing, etc, and, sometimes pocket money. For full information you should write to one of the three main *kibbutzim* organizations, which are:

Ichur Harvuzet, 132 Hayarkon Street, Tel-Aviv, Israel.
Hakibutz Hameuchad, 27 Suten Street, Tel-Aviv, Israel.
Hashomer Hatzair, 4 Itamar Ben Ani, Tel-Aviv, Israel.
Or try Israel Student Tourist Association,
109 Ben Yehuda Street, Tel-Aviv, Israel.

Italy

Work permits not needed for EEC members. For others it is very difficult and you almost certainly can't take a job which could be satisfactorily filled by an Italian citizen. If you manage to find something your employer will have to get you a permit before you actually start working. For *au pairs* things are brighter. One address to inquire from about *au pair* work is:

Au Pairs – Italy,
46 The Rise,
Sevenoaks,
Kent TN13 1RJ.

Luxembourg

Work permits not needed by EEC members. Others may search for a job but before beginning work must have their employer apply for their permit.

Netherlands

Work permits not needed by EEC members. For others it is difficult.
Also, you must have your work permit in hand as you enter the country.
Not much work available, though some *au pair*. Students might manage
to find something temporary by contacting:
Studenten Werkbureau Amsterdam,
Koniginneweg 184a, Amsterdam.

Norway

Although some work is available in the fish processing and hotel and
catering industries, the law requires you to have a work permit in hand
before you arrive in Norway. After finding a job and making application
for a permit to your nearest Norwegian Embassy you may face a wait
as long as three months before you get the piece of paper. Embassies can't
find a job for you but they may be able to supply addresses of companies
looking for staff.
   Students interested in working on Norwegian farms and receiving room
board and pocket money, should contact:
Norwegian Committee for International Information and Youth Work,
Akersgata, 57, Oslo 1, Norway.

Portugal

Not a great deal of work about and, because of the low wage scale, if you
do find something you can't earn enough to get ahead. The method of
getting a work permit and a visa to go with it is complicated and must
be applied for by the prospective employer.

Spain

Spain currently suffers a chronic unemployment problem, thus, for
foreigners there's little work around outside of the tourist industry.
However, it may be possible to find a job in resort areas. If you do, your
employer should make application for your permit on your behalf. Legally
you should have the permit before you actually begin working.
   Students requiring information on vacation work should write to:
Spanish Union of Students, Bolsa Universitaria de Trabajo,
Glorieta de Quevedo 8, Madrid 8.

Sweden

To work in Sweden you must have a permit, and get it before entering the country. To do so, you must have documented proof that you have a job and that you have somewhere to live.

For information write to:

International Association for the Exchange of Students for Technical Experience,
Imperial College, London SW7.
or
Arbetsmarknadsstyrelsen,
Fack, S-17199 Solna, Sweden.

Switzerland

Not much work available for foreigners and documentation must be arranged in advance. Even *au pairs* require work permits.

For good information about working in Europe you should buy the annual, *Directory of Summer Jobs Abroad*, published by Vacation-Work, 9 Park End Street, Oxford. This excellent book gives up-to-date work permit and visa information plus long lists of companies and organizations seeking staff.

For people who want good, steady (rather than casual) work outside of the British Isles, the best thing to do is to check through the classified advertisements in London newspapers like the *Observer* and *The Times* or an international paper like the Paris edition of the *Herald Tribune*.

If you are in a particular country and in need of a job, one trick is to check out the local English language papers. They flourish where there are big tourist populations. For instance in Spain, there are at least five, all of which carry classified advertisements, some of which offer work. They are *Lookout Magazine* which covers the Costa del Sol, *Guidepost* which concerns itself with the north and a rather strange little daily paper called the *Iberian Sun* which is available in most large cities. The *Costa Blanca News* covers the Costa Blanca and The *Majorca Daily Bulletin* covers the Baleares.

The type of work offered by advertisements in these papers is usually for secretaries or translators. Any girl who can type, take shorthand and who is completely fluent in a second language stands a chance of finding a job on the Continent. Any man who is fluent in a second language and who is a qualified professional worker stands a chance.

It's a good idea, when coming to Europe, to bring any documents you have proving your qualifications and experience in your field.

Many hitchers find their way into the movies as extras. Pay may be as much as £8 ($16.00) a day (considerably more if you can con someone into giving you a line to speak) and you might get work in a crowd scene for five to six days.

The main centres for film work at the moment are Madrid, Rome and London (London being well tied up by the unions).

You never know when this type of work is coming up. If you're interested, keep your ears open – there's usually someone in the hostels who knows what's happening.

Of course it's possible to find odd jobs in just about any European country if you're in the right place at the right time and if the employer takes a liking to you. For instance, in the summer there is limited (repeat *limited*) bar work available for pretty girls in most of the tourist resort areas – the Costa del Sol and Costa Brava in Spain, the Algarve and Costa do Sol area in Portugal, the French and Italian rivieras, etc. Also there is grape harvesting in southern France (Herault) and southern Germany (Mosel valley) in September and October. Most of this work is of a very temporary nature and badly paid. You'll make enough to live on but not enough to build up your roll. You and your employer may be breaking the law, but you'll probably get away with it. (Don't write to me if you don't.)

There are other ways of picking up money. Plenty of hitchers make a living with their guitars either playing in the street or in clubs or restaurants where they receive food, a percentage of the take on drinks and/or tips.

Another way, particularly in Paris where the cops seem to be fairly easy-going towards down-and-outs, is to join up with pavement artists. Get yourself a packet of chalks and make a huge abstract on the pavement and wait hopefully for the pennies to fall. Of course if you're a trained artist who is capable of making really good chalk drawings, your chances of making some bread are tripled.

Some people carry silver wire and pliers in their pack and make simple jewellery to sell on sidewalks or in outdoor markets. Plenty of hitchers pick up objects in one country (e.g. beads in Morocco) to sell in the next. One hitcher makes $1 a time by cutting paper silhouettes of people or animals. Another makes simple puppets out of scrap found on the side of the road which he sells for as much as $5. I've seen a hitcher who stages a quick magic show with handkerchiefs and lengths of rope while his wife passes a hat and keeps an eye out for the police.

Straight-out begging is another way but the cops from any country are hard down on that. But if you're really broke you might be forced to do it. If so, be persistent and expect plenty of abuse. You might get enough for a feed which will fortify you enough so that you can think of another idea.

Luck.

Hitchers' tips and comments

If you're down in Greece and Italy and in need of money or food make for a big port and approach one of the charter boats. They're always after crew, and even if you don't know about boats you can usually bluff your way to a job. You get free food, a lot of nautical miles, a few quid a week and a handful of blisters. Appearance isn't very important, but too much hair can lose you the better jobs.

It's nearly always possible to get a very temporary job as a kitchen porter (glorified pot washer) in both France and the UK without a permit. In small French cafés you usually get just food. In big hotels, a lot more work, but food *and* pay. In UK seaside towns in peak summer season cafés and hotels aren't too particular who works for them. You get money, food and sometimes a bed, which is good for a week's recuperation. Also in the UK fruit and potato picking jobs are available. Badly paid but good for a laugh and a kip.

Cheers and good hitching.

Clive Gill, Birchington, England

Since I've taken to tramping these last few years I can give a couple of hints on how to keep going financially. Winter – December until April or May – is no time for travelling. But in Switzerland you can work these months in hotels or for ski-lifts. You get good sleeping quarters, time enough for a bit of skiing and you can save enough to tramp the other months of the year. The Swiss newspaper *Hotel-Revue* lists all open hotel jobs in the country . . . jobs like porter, chauffeur, etc. It's room and board and about 950 francs a month. For ski-lift work it's a good idea to ask at ski-lift offices in each resort town. It's best to locate your job and sign a contract around October. (Then you can move down to Greece and lap up some sun before winter sets in and you have to start work.) Hotels and ski-lifts will arrange work permits – but step one is to find the job.

Aside from tramping it's fun and exciting to crew along on sailboats (if you've got a good stomach). It's possible to go to ports on the south coast

of England (Ramsgate, Gosport, Cowes, Plymouth, Lymington) on weekends and bum rides. Or for the more adventurous, boats often leave Gosport for France, Spain and other Mediterranean ports. Often this leads to a job as a paid hand. A few summers ago I bummed lifts on boats for four months and ended up fifty quid ahead!
Steve Blume, Chicago, USA

I've found if you're really broke a travelling circus is usually happy to pick you up. You get great food, a little money (lots of hard work!) and the chance to mix with truly fantastic people. I've done it twice and both times I just hated to leave.
James Daly, Dublin, Ireland

13 Photography

Whether you're a serious amateur with a £200 SLR or a happy-snapper with a £5 second-hand Instamatic, you'll probably be putting up with the extra weight of a camera in your pack to record your European hitch-trip.

For better pictures – especially if you've taken very few before – there are some simple hints you can follow:

1 Make sure you remove the lens cap before shooting. (If you don't you don't get any pictures!)

2 Keep your picture edges straight. Do this by lining up some vertical in the scene with the side of your view-finder.

3 Don't jerk your camera when you shoot a picture or the snap will be blurred. You can avoid camera-shake by keeping one foot forward of the other and by holding the weight of the camera in the left hand so that the right is free to carefully squeeze the shutter. Practise squeezing the shutter when your camera is empty.

4 If you own a camera with a built-in light-meter and you know nothing about the operation of cameras and light meters, here are some very basic rules. (*a*) If you are snapping a general view with the sky in it, point your camera slightly down towards the ground so that you eliminate *most* of the sky from the meter eye. *Now* set your camera according to the maker's instructions. You do this because there is more light reflected from the sky than there is from the ground and, presumably, you want a correct exposure for the landscape. (*b*) If you want to photograph the sky (a sunset or cloud formation) or make a silhouette, then you disregard rule (*a*) and take your reading from the sky. (*c*) If you are taking pictures in the white-washed villages of Spain, Italy, Greece, etc, then remember that the white walls reflect more light than the rest of the scene. If you aim your camera at an old lady sitting by a white wall, your meter will read the brightness of the wall and your old lady will come out too dark. What you must do is always take a reading from the subject you wish to photograph. If you can't go close enough to someone to measure the light on them, place your hand between six and nine inches in front of the camera meter eye so that the same light falls on your hand as on your subject, and take a reading from your own skin-tone.

5 If you're photographing sports, like skiing, car-racing, etc, remember that unless you have a sophisticated camera with very high speeds (1/500th of a second or better), you cannot stop action going directly across your view-finder – it will be blurred. Try and position yourself so that the car or skier is travelling at an angle towards you. If you can't, pan your camera with the action as you take the picture.

6 If you're photographing people, don't be afraid to approach them for a close-up. Most people don't mind, or if they do they'll simply say no. (But Muslim Arabs have a habit of getting very angry about cameras. They believe that the camera is capturing their spirit as well as their image.)

7 Don't keep film in your pocket for any length of time. Your body warmth can affect its colour balance. Keep the film in its container and keep the container in a side-pocket of your pack where there is some air circulation. Keep colour film away from the sun.

8 Always load and unload your camera in the shade. If there is none, turn your back to the sun and unload in your own shadow. This is to minimize the chance of light getting to the film and fogging it.

9 If you carry your camera in your pack, wrap it in a dry towel or shirt to protect it as much as possible from knocks and from car vibration which can loosen screws.

★Film Colour film prices in some countries are exorbitant. In Spain and France, for instance, it'll break your budget. Switzerland, Andorra and England are good places to buy film. In England make sure you go to a discount place. Boots (the chemist shops) seem to offer a good deal.

14 Weights and measures

Miles/Kilometres

A kilometre is roughly 6/10ths of a mile, so for a quick estimate multiply the number of kilometres by 6 and move the decimal point one place to the left (212 kilometres $\times 6 = 1272$. Insert decimal point one place to left $= 127 \cdot 2$ miles).

km	miles/km	miles
1·609	1	0·621
16·093	10	6·214
160·930	100	62·136
804·650	500	310·680
1609·300	1000	621·360

Pounds/Kilograms

There are roughly 2·2 pounds to a kilogram.

kg	lb/kg	lb
0·453	1	2·205
0·907	2	4·409
1·360	3	6·614
1·814	4	8·818
2·268	5	11·023

Litres/Gallons

For a rough calculation figure $4\frac{1}{2}$ litres to the British Imperial gallon. The American gallon is slightly less than 4 litres.

litres	gallons/ litres	gallons
4·55	1	0·22
22·73	5	1·10
45·46	10	2·20

Pounds per square inch/Kilograms per square centimetre

lb per sq in	kg per sq cm
18	1·266
20	1·406
22	1·547
25	1·758
29	2·039
32	2·250
35	2·461
36	2·531
39	2·742
40	2·812
42	2·953
43	3·023
45	3·164
46	3·234
50	3·515
60	4·218

Equivalent sizes

Women's clothing sizes

British	36	38	40	42	44	46
American	34	36	38	40	42	44
Continental	42	44	46	48	50	52

Men's Suits and Overcoats

British and American	36	38	40	42	44	46
Continental	46	48	50	52	54	56

Shirts

British and American	14	14½	15	15½	16	16½	17
Continental	36	37	38	39	41	42	43

Stockings

British and American	8	8½	9	9½	10	10½
Continental	0	1	2	3	4	5

Socks

British and American	9½	10	10½	11	11½
Continental	38/39	39/40	40/41	41/42	42/43

Shoes

British and American	3	4	5	6	7	8	9	10
Continental	36	37	38	39	41	42	43	44

Continental glove sizes are the same as in Britain and America.

Fahrenheit/Centigrade

The general rule for the conversion of Centigrade into Fahrenheit is to multiply by 9/5ths and add 32. To translate Fahrenheit into Centigrade, subtract 32 and multiply by 5/9ths.

15 Language

The vocabulary in this language section has been kept as concise as possible
for a very simple reason. When you can't speak a language and have no
intention of learning it, the fewer words you have to play with the better.
All you need are the basic words of survival and politeness. ('Thank you'
is undoubtedly the first word you should memorize in any language.)

Even this ultra-simple list could cause you problems. Example?
You're in Toledo and you want to go to Madrid, so you walk up to a
fellow and say, '*Por favor, donde esta la carreterra de Madrid?*' You say it
so nicely that the fellow thinks you can speak Spanish, so he rattles off his
answer: '*Pues, tiene que andar por la carreterra principal durante dos
kilometros y medio mas o menos, entonces tome Usted la calle a la derecha
en el primer cruce . . . mire! si quiere le llevo en mi coche, es mas sencillo!*'
From there on in you'd better think awful fast because if this guy is in a
hurry, odds are you're going to miss out on the ride up to the Madrid
road which he just offered you!

French

English	French	Pronounced
Thank you	Merci	Mair-see
Please	S'il vous plaît	sil voo play
Good morning	Bonjour	bon-joor
Goodbye	Au revoir	oh re-vwar
Yes	Oui	wee
No	Non	noh
I am . . .	Je suis . . .	jer swee
Do you go to . . . ?	Allez-vous vers . . . ?	allay voo ver
Where is . . . ?	Où est . . . ?	oo eh
the road to . . .	la route pour . . .	la root poor
the toilet	le lavabo	lu la-va-bow
the youth hostel	l'auberge de jeunesse	ohberge de-jerness
the station	la gare	la gar
I would like . . .	Je voudrais . . .	jer voo-dray
to eat	manger	mon-zhay

English	French	Pronounced
a room	une chambre	oon shombre
How much?	Combien?	kohm biyen
When?	Quand?	kon
Left	Gauche	gohshe
Right	Droit	dwar
Straight ahead	Tout droit	too dwar
Yesterday	Hier	ee yeh
Today	Aujourd-hui	oh-joor-dwee
Tomorrow	Demain	derman
1	un	urn
2	deux	der
3	trois	twah
4	quatre	catre
5	cinq	sank
6	six	sees
7	sept	set
8	huit	weet
9	neuf	nerf
10	dix	dees
11	onze	onz
12	douze	dooz
13	treize	traiz
14	quatorze	ka-torz
15	quinze	kanze
16	seize	seyz
17	dix-sept	dees-set
18	dix-huit	dees-weet
19	dix-neuf	dees-nerf
20	vingt	van
30	trente	trarnt
40	quarante	kar-rarnt
50	cinquante	san-karnt
60	soixante	swah-sant
70	soixante-dix	swah-sant dees
80	quatre-vingts	catre van
90	quatre-vingt-dix	catre van dees
100	cent	sonn
1,000	mille	meel

Shopping for food
Beer – *bière*. Biscuits – *biscuits*. Bread – *pain*. Chocolate – *chocolat*.
Coffee – *café*. Egg – *oeuf*. Fish – *poisson*. Fruit – *fruit*. Meat – *viande*.
Milk – *lait*. Mineral water – *eau minérale*. Salt – *sel*. Sandwich – *sandwich*.
Sausage – *saucisse*. Soup – *potage*. Sugar – *sucre*. Tea – *thé*.
Vegetables – *légumes*. Water – *eau*. Wine – *vin*.

German

English	German	Pronounced
Thank you	Danke schön	dan-ker-shern
Please	Bitte	bit-teh
Good morning	Guten Tag	goo-ten-targ
Goodbye	Auf Wiedersehen	owf-vee-dayr-sain
Yes	Ja	yah
No	Nein	nine
I am ...	Ich bin	ik bin
Do you go to ... ?	Gehen Sie nach ... ?	gay-en-see nark
Where is ... ?	Wo ist ... ?	vo eest
the road to ...	der Weg nach ...	der veg nark
the toilet	die Toilette	de twarlet-tuh
the youth hostel	der Jugendherberge	der you-gend-er-berga
the station	der Bahnhof	der barn-hof
I would like ...	Ich möchte ...	ik mersh-ta
to eat	essen	ess-en
a room	ein Zimmer	ein tzimmer
How much?	Wie viel?	vee-feel
When?	Wann?	varn
Left	Links	leenks
Right	Rechts	reshts
Straight ahead	Geradeaus	gay-ray-day-ous
Yesterday	Gestern	gay-stern
Today	Heute	hoy-tuh
Tomorrow	Morgen	mor-gen
1	eins	eintz
2	zwei	tzvai
3	drei	dry
4	vier	feer
5	funf	fewnf
6	sechs	zex

English	German	Pronounced
7	sieben	zee-ben
8	acht	arkt
9	neun	noyn
10	zehn	tzain
11	elf	elf
12	zwölf	tzuhlf
13	dreizehn	drytzain
14	vierzehn	feertzain
15	fünfzehn	fewnftzain
16	sechzehn	zextzain
17	siebzehn	zeebtzain
18	achtzehn	arktzain
19	neunzehn	noyntzain
20	zwanzig	tzvahntzig
30	dreissig	dry-tzig
40	vierzig	feer-tzig
50	fünfzig	fewnf-tzig
60	sechzig	zex-tzig
70	siebzig	zeeb-tzig
80	achtzig	ark-tzig
90	neunzig	noyn-tzig
100	hundert	hoon-dert
1,000	tausend	tow-sent

Shopping for food

Beer – *Bier*. Biscuits – *Plätzchen*. Bread – *Brot*. Chocolate – *Schokolade*. Coffee – *Kaffee*. Egg – *Ei*. Fish – *Fische*. Fruit – *Obst*. Meat – *Fleish*. Milk – *Milch*. Mineral water – *Mineralwasser*. Salt – *Salz*. Sandwich – *belegtes Bröt*. Sausage – *Wurst*. Soup – *Suppe*. Suger – *Zucker*. Tea – *Tee*. Vegetables – *Gemüse*. Water – *Wasser*. Wine – *Wein*.

Spanish

English	Spanish	Pronounced
Thank you	Gracias	grar-thee-ahs
Please	Por favor	por fav-or
Hello	Hola	ol-ah
Goodbye	Adios	ah-dee-os
Yes	Si	see
No	No	noh
I am ...	Yo soy ...	yo-soy
Do you go to ... ?	Va usted a ... ?	vah-oosted a
Where is ... ?	Donde esta ... ?	donday estah
the road to ...	la carreterra de ...	lar car-ray-terra day
the toilet	el retrete	el raytraytay
the youth hostel	el albergue des juveniles	el al-ber-goh days hoovay-neelays
the station	la estacion	la ay-star-thee-on
I would like ...	Quiero ...	kee-ayro
to eat	comer	com-mayr
a room	una habitacion	cona ahbee-tah-thee-on
How much?	Cuanto?	kwon-toe
When?	Cuando?	kwon-doe
Left	Izquierda	eeth-key-air-dah
Right	Derecha	day-ray-cha
Straight ahead	Todo derecho	toh-doh day-ray-choh
Yesterday	Ayer	a-yer
Today	Hoy	oy
Tomorrow	Mañana	marn-yar-nar
1	uno	oo-no
2	dos	dos
3	tres	treys
4	cuatro	kwat-ro
5	cinco	thin-ko
6	seis	sais
7	siete	see-ay-tay
8	ocho	o-choh
9	nueve	noo-ay-vay
10	diez	dee-eth
11	once	on-thay
12	doce	do-thay
13	trece	tray-thay

English	Spanish	Pronounced
14	catorce	ca-tor-thay
15	quince	keen-thay
16	dieciseis	dee-eth-ee-sais
17	diecisiete	dee-eth-ee-see-ay-tay
18	dieciocho	dee-eth-ee-o-choh
19	diecinueve	dee-eth-ee-noo-ay-vay
20	veinte	vain-tay
30	treinta	train-ta
40	cuarenta	kaw-renta
50	cincuenta	thin-kwenta
60	sesenta	say-senta
70	setenta	say-tenta
80	ochenta	o-chenta
90	noventa	no-venta
100	cien	thee-en
500	quinientas	keen-nee-entas
1,000	mil	meel

Shopping for food

Beer – *cerveza*. Biscuit – *ga'leta*. Bread – *pan*. Chocolate – *chocolate*.
Coffee – *café*. Egg – *huevo*. Fish – *pescado*. Fruit – *fruta*. Meat – *carne*.
Milk – *leche*. Mineral water – *água mineral*. Salt – *sal*. Sandwich – *bocadillo*.
Sausage – *salchichón*. Soup – *sopa*. Sugar – *azucar*. Tea – *té*.
Vegetables – *legumbres*. Water – *água*. Wine – *vino*.

Italian

English	Italian	Pronounced
Thank you	Grazie	grah-tzyeh
Please	Piacere	pee-ah-chay-ary
Good morning	Buon giorno	bwon-djor-no
Goodbye	Arrivederci	ar-reev-e-derch-ee
Yes	Si	see
No	No	noh
I am ...	Io sone ...	yo sohno
Do you go to ... ?	Dov'e vay ... ?	doh-vay var-ee
Where is ... ?	Dov'e ... ?	doh-vay
the road to ...	l'autostrada ...	l'otoh-stra-dah
the toilet	il gabinetto	eel-ga-bee-naytoh
the youth hostel	l'albergo per giovani	al bairgo per joh-vah-nee
the station	la stazione	la stah-tzyohnay
I would like ...	Volgio ...	vohl-yoh
to eat	mangiare	mahn-djah-ray
a room	una camera	oona kay-may-rah
How much?	Quanto?	kwan-toh
When?	Quando?	kwan-doh
Left	Sinistra	see-nee-strah
Right	Destra	dess-trah
Straight ahead	Tutto diretto	too-toh dee-ret-toh
Yesterday	Ieri	ee-yay-ree
Today	Oggi	oh-djee
Tomorrow	Domani	don-mar-nee
1	uno	oo-no
2	due	doo-au
3	tre	tray
4	quattro	kwar-tro
5	cinque	cheen-kway
6	sei	say
7	sette	set-tay
8	otto	aw-toh
9	nove	noh-vay
10	dieci	dee-ay-chee
11	undici	oon-dee-chee
12	dodici	doh-dee-chee
13	tredici	tray-dee-chee

English	Italian	Pronounced
14	quattordici	kwar-tor-dee-chee
15	quindici	kween-dee-chee
16	sedici	say-dee-chee
17	dicesette	dee-chay-se-tay
18	diciotto	dee-chiot-toh
19	dicenove	dee-chay-novay
20	venti	vayn-tee
30	trenta	trayn-ta
40	quaranta	kwah-rahn-ta
50	cinquanta	cheen-kwahn-ta
60	sessanta	sais-sarn-ta
70	settanta	set-tan-ta
80	ottanta	ot-tan-ta
90	novanta	no-van-ta
100	cento	chayn-to
1,000	mille	mee-lay

Shopping for food

Beer – *birra*. Biscuits – *biscotto*. Bread – *pane*. Chocolate – *cioccolata*.
Coffee – *caffe*. Egg – *uovo*. Fish – *pesce*. Fruit – *frutta*. Meat – *carne*.
Milk – *latta*. Mineral water – *acqua minerale*. Salt – *sale*. Sandwich – *panino*.
Sausage – *salsiccia*. Soup – *zuppa*. Sugar – *zucchero*. Tea – *té*.
Vegetables – *legumi*. Water – *acqua*. Wine – *vino*.

Dutch

English	Dutch	Pronounced
Thank you	Dank U	dahnk yu
Please	Alstublieft	als-too bleeft
Hello	Hallo	hah-loh
Goodbye	Dag	dahk
Yes	Ja	yah
No	Nee	nay
I am	Ik ben	ick ben
Do you go to . . . ?	Gaat U naar . . . ?	haht yu nahr
Where is . . . ?	Waar is . . . ?	vahr iss
the road to . . .	de weg naar . . .	der veg nahr
the toilet	het toilet	het twa-let
the youth hostel	de jeugdherberg	der yugd-hair-berk
the station	het station	het sta-si-on
I would like . . .	Ik wil . . .	ick vil
to eat	eten	ay-ten
a room	een kamer	ayn ka-mer
How much?	Hoe veel?	hu vehl
When?	Wanneer?	vah-nair
Left	Links	links
Right	Rechts	rekts
Straight ahead	Rechtdoor	rekts-door
Yesterday	gisteren	hist-erun
Today	Vandaag	fan-dak
Tomorrow	Morgen	morghen
1	één	ayn
2	twee	tvay
3	drie	dree
4	vier	feer
5	vijf	fife
6	zes	zess
7	zeven	zeh-ven
8	acht	ahkht
9	negen	neh-khen
10	tien	teen
11	elf	aylf
12	twaalf	tvahlf
13	dertien	dehr-teen
14	veertien	feer-teen

English	Dutch	Pronounced
15	vijftien	fife-teen
16	zestien	zess-teen
17	zeventien	zeh-ven-teen
18	achttien	ahkht-teen
19	negentien	neh-khen-teen
20	twintig	tventahk
30	dertig	dare-thak
40	veertig	fare-tahk
50	vijftig	fife-tahk
60	zestig	zess-tahk
70	zeventig	zeh-ven-tahk
80	tachtig	tahk-tahk
90	negentig	neh-khen-tahk
100	honderd	hohn-dert
1,000	duizend	doy-zent

Shopping for food

Beer – *bier*. Biscuits – *koekjes*. Bread – *brood*. Chocolate – *chocolade*.
Coffee – *koffee*. Egg – *ei*. Fish – *vis*. Fruit – *fruit*. Meat – *vlees*. Milk – *melk*.
Mineral water – *mineraal water*. Salt – *zout*. Sandwich – *sandwich*.
Sausage – *worst*. Soup – *soep*. Sugar – *suiker*. Tea – *thee*.
Vegetables – *groenten*. Water – *water*. Wine – *wijn*.

Swedish

English	Swedish	Pronounced
Thank you	Tack	tahck
Please	Var snäll och	vahr snel ok
Hello	Hallo	hal-loh
Goodbye	Adjö	ah-yuh
Yes	Ja	yaw
No	Nej	nay
I am	Jag är	yawg air
Do you go to ... ?	Reser ni ... ?	ray-sehr nee
Where is ... ?	Var är ... ?	vahr ehr
the road to ...	vägen ...	vay-gen
the toilet	toaletten	toh-ah-let-ten
the youth hostel	ynugdomshärbärge	yung-dums, hair-bahr-yeh
the station	järnvägsstationen	yehrn-vehgs-stah-shoh-nehn
I would like ...	Jag vill ha ...	yawg veel hah
to eat	att äta	aht-air-tah
a room	ett rum	eht room
How much?	Hur mycket?	huhr mew-keht
When?	När?	nehr
Left	Vänster	vehn-stehr
Right	Höger	huh-gehr
Straight ahead	rakt fram	rakt fram
Yesterday	I går	ee gohr
Today	I dag	ee dak
Tomorrow	I morgon	ee mohr-gohn
1	ett	et
2	två	tvoh
3	tre	treh
4	fyra	few-rah
5	fem	fem
6	sex	sex
7	sju	shew
8	åtta	oht-tah
9	nio	nee-yoh
10	tio	tee-yoh
11	elva	ehl-vah
12	tolv	tohlv
13	tretton	treht-ton

English	Swedish	Pronounced
14	fjorton	fyohr-ton
15	femton	fem-ton
16	sexton	sex-ton
17	sjutton	shew-ton
18	arton	air-ton
19	nitton	nit-ton
20	tjugo	tshu-goh
30	trettio	treht-tyee
40	fyrtio	fur-tyee
50	femtio	fem-tyee
60	sextio	sex-tyee
70	sjuttio	shew-tyee
80	åttio	oht-tyee
90	nittio	nit-tyee
100	ett hundra	et hun-dra
1,000	ett tusen	et too-sen

Shopping for food

Beer – *öl*. Biscuits – *kex*. Bread – *bröd*. Chocolate – *chokolad*. Coffee – *kaffe*. Egg – *ägg*. Fish – *fisk*. Fruit – *frukt*. Meat – *kött*. Milk – *mjölk*. Mineral water – *mineralvatter*. Salt – *salt*. Sandwich – *smörgas*. Sausage – *korv*. Soup – *soppa*. Sugar – *socker*. Tea – *té*. Vegetables – *grönsaker*. Water – *vatter*. Wine – *vin*.